U-Boots' escape to South America

Secret Of The Gray Wolves

D1640363

Dedicated to:
To our wives
Renata and Ala
and to our children
Kasia, Michał and Karolina

Mariusz Borowiak

Peter Wytykowski

U-Boots' escape to South America

Secret Of The Gray Wolves

The truth lies in the middle - maybe that's why it's in everybody's way?
Aristotle

To be righteous, it is not enough to omit certain truths.
One has to tell certain lies.
Victor Marie Hugo

Truth is stranger than fiction,
but it is because Fiction is obliged to stick to possibilities;
Truth isn't.
Mark Twain

KAGERO

FIRST EDITION
© by KAGERO Publishing, 2019

AUTHOR
Mariusz Borowiak
Peter Wytykowski

EDITORS
Mariusz Borowiak
Peter Wytykowski

TRANSLATION/PROOFREADING
Kazimierz Zygadło

COVER
Łukasz Maj

DTP
Kagero Studio, Jacek Sadowski

PHOTOGRAPHS AND ILLUSTRATIONS CREDITS
Photographs and drawings published in this book belong to the following collections: Mariusz Borowiak, Jarosław Dzierżawski, Łukasz Grześkowiak, Chris Kraska, Ryszard Leitner, Paul Manning, Grzegorz Nowak, Paweł Więcaszek, Derek Waller, Igor Witkowski, Peter Wytykowski, Ángela Alcázar de Velasco, The National Archives in Kew (England), National Archives and Records Administration (NARA) at College Park, Maryland (USA), Naval History and Heritage Command in Washington (USA), Archivo General de la Nación in Argentynie, Archivo General de la Administración (Cultura), Sjöhistoriska Museet in Stockholm, Mariners Museum at Newport News, US Submarine Museum at Groton (USA).

LUBLIN 2019

ISBN 978-83-66148-23-9

DISTRIBUTION
Kagero Publishing
ul. Akacjowa 100, os. Borek, Turka, 20-258 Lublin 62, Poland
phone +48 601-602-056, phone/fax +48 81 501-21-05
e-mail: marketing@kagero.pl
www.kagero.pl

Table of Contents

INTRODUCTION

"When the legend becomes fact... print the legend". This quote from *The Man Who Shot Liberty Valance*, one of the great American westerns directed by John Ford in 1962, can be translated to contemporary language: if a rumor is better than facts, you print rumor. It is still valid today with a difference that nowadays the less honorable and more discrediting the rumor is the better it sells.[1]

It turns out these words fit perfectly the climate of the entire book about U-Boots' escape to South America in 1945. After the World War II ended numerous studies appeared concerning German Nazis who fled to South America. The most effective means of transportation that helped war criminals escape justice were U-Boots - at least that is what some advocates of this theory claim. That should not come as a surprise - a legend is governed by its own rules. Over the last decades so many rumors appeared describing life of Nazi butchers in Argentina and other South American countries which make it difficult to decide where truth ends and legend begins.

Did 56-year-old Adolf Hitler, his newly-wed 33-year-old Eva Braun[2] and the Nazis' eminence grise Martin Bormann who allegedly survived the spring of 1945 in Berlin - as many conspiracy theorists claim - manage to flee to South America aboard a submarine?

Why were Argentina, Brazil[3], Paraguay, Chile or Uruguay the places where the Nazis sought refuge from justice?

Is it possible that a high-ranking SS officer, Lieutenant-general of the police Heinrich Müller, long-term chief of Department 4 in the Reich Main Security Office, who on May 1, 1945 was still in the Führer's Berlin bunker, escaped justice aboard a submarine to Argentina?[4]

Is it true that several months before the war ended Hitler's submarines had delivered huge amounts of currency and precious items to South America? Is it true that a day before the Third Reich's unconditional surrender and even a few months later, U-Boots called the „ghost convoy" dispatched from harbors in Germany, Norway and Spain carrying „little Führers", as one of historians called them, valuable

---

[1] http://kinetoskop.pl/publicystyka/recenzje/pewnego-razu-na-dzikim-zachodzie-czyli-najlepsze-westerny/.

[2] Hitler's lover who married him on April 29, 1945 r.

[3] In the Brazilian national archives (Arquivo Histórico), in Rio de Janeiro, documents concerning 20,000 German citizens who arrived at this country between 1945 and 1959 were found. According to Kurt Schrimm, German prosecutor in Ludwigsburg and one of the Nazi hunters, many of them came to South America under false names and with unclear past.

[4] I. Witkowski, *Gestapo. Anatomia systemu*, Warszawa 2005, p. 121.

documents, plans of the German Reich's secret weapons which were to change the course of the war, large quantities of stolen treasures mainly the Nazi's gold? Who of the high-ranking German dignitaries managed to flee the Allies unpunished aboard safe means of transportation - the U-Boot? Do we know the submarines that participated in the successful evacuation from Europe to South America?

To ask and answer so many key questions the authors spent the past four years conducting detailed archive research on two continents: in Europe and in North America. On the basis of declassified documents and witness testimonies the authors managed to decipher - according to current knowledge - at least some of the intriguing versions of the puzzle. It is not possible to reveal all the mysteries as some documents are still classified and withheld despite the fact that over 70 years have passed since the events in question. It is certain that many secrets concerning escapes of German submarines to South America (which is the main topic of the book) are still kept in archives in Germany, Great Britain, United States and Argentina. Without solid evidence, due to lack of authorization for access to documents that were out of reach or still classified, the authors were sometimes forced to present their own version of events. They had to ascertain what the historical truth was or to completely reject eye witnesses' reports as they purposely confabulated.

Heated discussions and disputes are still being conducted on the subject of localization of the legendary German U-Boot bases in Patagonia, a region in the southern part of South America in Argentina and Chile, where Hitler's "gray wolves" allegedly found refuge. There are researchers of the German World War II submarine fleet who pinpoint exact locations of the steel predators' haven.

Access to documents concerning activities of spies who worked for the German military intelligence in the pre-war era and between 1939 and 1945 which are kept in the National Archives and Records Administration in College Park, Maryland is still limited - they are still under security classification. The only entity authorized to declassify the entirety or at least part of the required documents is the United States Department of Justice and to be exact the Federal Bureau of Investigation - the national agency that deals with crime outside of a given state. It is one of special agencies protecting the United States security. That is why it is difficult or impossible to gain access to military intelligence files. History researchers have to be extremely patient and they have no guarantee that their efforts to reach required document will be successful. Those were the obstacles the authors of the book had to face.

It is known that a majority of Nazi criminals never stood trial and many high-ranking murderers escaped justice under new identity. In the south-west Argentina, in Bariloche, a paradise at the foot of the Andes, surrounded by lakes and mountains, with the quiet consent of the authorities, criminals from Auschwitz and other concentration camps lived happily till old age[5].

---

[5] Bariloche was initially inhabited in 1895 by immigrants from Austria and Germany.

For several decades there has been a dispute among historians, journalists and people opposing official versions of facts, concerning a role played by the mysterious organization ODESSA in helping wanted criminals escape to Argentina and other countries of the continent. At the beginning of the 1970s public attention turned to a novel *The Odessa File* by the British writer Frederick Forsyth who wrote:

Many [criminals -M.B., P.W.] *never left Germany at all, preferring to remain under cover with false names and papers while the Allies ruled; others came back, suitably protected by a new identity. The few very top men remained abroad to manipulate the organization from the safety of a comfortable exile*[6].

The plot of Forsyth's novel revolves around a secret organization of former members of the SS which was tasked with assisting war criminals in their escape from law enforcing authorities and providing them with safety and comfort of their new lives in Argentina and other places of the globe. Although there are no credible documents that confirm the creation of an organized SS members group called ODESSA[7], the existence of such secret organizations is unquestionable. Their members arranged new identities for their comrades serving under the Totenkopf (dead's head) sign, facilitated their departure and provided them with financial means necessary to lead a peaceful life. And where did the funds come from? They were valuables, huge amounts of gold and money owned by the elite Nazi formation, the SS (Schutzstaffel), stolen during the war and later deposited on encoded, secret bank accounts in Europe and South America.

Those covert organizations helped war criminals like Adolf Eichmann, Josef Mengele, Klaus Barbie, Erich Priebke and many others.

It was during the war that the Nazis had already began preparing their safe havens. They were to provide shelter in case of a defeat. The main destination were countries in South America. The predictions turned out to be prophetic. After the fall of the Third Reich, evacuation routes, which were called rat lines, went via Bremen, Frankfurt, Stuttgart and Munich to Memmingen in Bavaria. Then the transfer route led to Lindau at Lake Constance where it branched (to Austria or to Switzerland), the other route led to Innsbruck and through the Brenner Pass to Italy. After a stop in Rome the fugitives would arrive at one of the Italian harbors (e.g. Genoa) where they received new identities and passports and boarded liners that carried them to Argentina, Chile and Brazil. As far as possible from Germany and people called the Nazi hunters.

The Nazis would most often use Argentinean consulates in Denmark, Switzerland, Italy and Spain where they were given entry visas to the country. The visas

---

[6] F. Forsyth, *The Odessa File*, New York 1972, p. 2.

[7] G. Steinacher, *Zbiegli naziści. Jak hitlerowscy zbrodniarze uciekli przed sprawiedliwością*, Wołowiec 2015, p. 20-21.

were issued on the basis of lists prepared by civilian officers in Buenos Aires, approved by so called Peralty Committee - people working with president Juan Domingo Perón who was in favor of that cause and gave criminals a guarantee of stabilization in Argentina.

Vatican City also played a huge role in protecting the Nazis and their escape from Europe which is a disgraceful period in its history. A significant role was played by the Austrian bishop Alois Hudal provost of Santa Maria dell'Anima and... a member of the National Socialist German Workers' Party (proudly wearing his NSDAP badge) and Hitler's supporter. Vatican would commission the International Red Cross to issue passports with a name or nickname given by a criminal in an application form[8]. We know that in 1948 bishop Hudal personally wrote a letter to the Argentinean president general Juan Perón asking for 5,000 visas for Germans and Austrians who „fought with courage" against communism. He did not recognize the definition of „war criminal" and believed that those he helped had a clear conscience as they only followed orders of their superiors! We need to add that the Pope Pius XII never officially confirmed Vatican's participation in organization of an assistance network but one cannot exclude the possibility that he had full knowledge of the operation as the Church was the anti-communism bastion[9].

Argentina was not the only Nazi safe haven as it was purported for dozens of years. Nazi criminals also found refuge in Syria, Egypt, Canada and Spain.

It is commonly known that the United States also helped war criminals as the US government recruited and employed thousands of German scientists and technicians (with not very clear conscience) in weapon research projects in the army, navy, air force, Central Intelligence Agency (starting in 1947) and other organizations within „Operation Paperclip"[10]. Everything was authorized by president Harry Truman. The U.S. Department of State provided the Nazi scientists not only with safety but also employment in the USA. When the fact that Washington harbored and financially supported war criminals came into light, an international scandal broke out. However, it did not matter as long-time, dedicated members of the Nazi party lived in safety and wealth provided by their new fatherland. They were given immunity. They were able to walk freely through Manhattan and streets of American cities without fear of being indicted for crimes committed during World War II. They never stood trial before the International Court of Justice. Their new employers made sure they were not harassed for their disgraceful past. It was during the time when the Soviet leaders - as Annie Jacobsen, famous American journalist and writer, wrote - entered the "path to world dominance". The Soviets were working on nuclear weapons, guided missiles and strategic air forces. They were also in progress of developing biological and chemical warfare programs[11].

---

[8] M. Aarons, J. Loftus, *Akcja ocalenie. Watykańska przystań nazistów*, Warszawa 1994.

[9] N. Bascomb, *Wytropić Eichmanna. Pościg za największym zbrodniarzem w historii*, Kraków 2015, p. 116-117.

[10] A. Jacobsen, *Operacja „Paperclip"*, Warszawa 2015. See also: G. Steinacher, *Zbiegli naziści...*, p. 227-228.

[11] A. Jacobsen, *Operacja „Paperclip"...*, p. 252.

Mark Felton in his book about the last Nazis wrote: "Some fugitives remained free for decades. Those recognized by the hunters not always stood trial before German court as they resided in countries that did not have extradition agreements with Germany. Israel took other measures like kidnapping or murder to administer justice to those responsible for mass killings, who were so well-off in exile. [...] After settling down in South America the wanted war criminals tried to remain out of sight. They were quite safe in dictator-ran countries, most of them were still using false names and documents, changed their whereabouts every few years to mislead a possible pursuit"[12].

It turns out many rumors and incredible theories concerning German U-Boot crews' escapes to Argentina have appeared. At the beginning of the second half of the 1940s, foreign press published sensational news about seaborne transport routes for the Nazis. Are we able to, putting the evidence together, separate reality from fabrication? Many unconfirmed stories have appeared concerning the ships that managed to reach Argentina. It is certain that such voyages of the last Kriegsmarine submarines took place - it was one of the ways to safely deliver German war criminals to South America. But did U-Boots carry German Nazi executioners?

Huge confusion and doubts concerning Nazi murderers were first created by Argentinean journalists who, chasing attractive stories, published sensations which later turned out to be literary fiction. Newspapers gained popularity with readers using different methods including publishing fabricated information which are still being treated by amateur historians, studying war criminals transfer to South America, as credible historical source. That, in turn, allowed publicists and organized intelligence agencies in Europe and the United States in the 1940s and 1950s formulate the most fantastic hypotheses which were supposedly shrouded in a deep fog of mystery. However, sensationalists, government agents and collaborators of foreign military intelligence were not always able to prove their information with evidence like documents or witness reports. After all evidence was exhausted or in the face of lack of thereof, what was left were unexplained facts necessary to determine the case, which was conducive for creation of new conspiracy theories.

Publications describing the Nazis' escape to South America have been very popular in America. They include books by authors who, without any criticism or necessary commentary, quote memoires of spies and the Third Reich criminals. Those books are less than reliable and they blur the line between fact and fiction. We are talking mainly about the U-Bootwaffe submarines which, after the Second World War, were allegedly seen off the coast of Argentina. According to those people the U-Boots brought secret cargo of money, high valuables and special passengers who, after disembarking, disappeared in German enclaves and farms across South America well protected against uninvited guests.

---

[12] M. Felton, *Polowanie na ostatnich nazistów*, Warszawa 2013, p. 51-52.

Several voyages (or planned trips) of submarine transport ships of the Kriegsmarine to the continent of South America are indisputable historical facts proven by credible documents and records of U-Boots' crews interviews. However, there are many people who swear to know exact positions of U-Boots sunk at the Argentine coast. These places were later explored by professional divers who... found no trace of any submarine. This encourages mystery researchers to formulate new hypotheses and to present even more unrealistic views.

Critical readers certainly asked themselves questions if a transatlantic U-Boot trip of Hitler or other high-ranking dignitaries of the Third Reich had been made up by media for cheap sensation.

It is hard to believe that Hitler (had he survived and managed to flee from Berlin under siege), highly susceptible to seasickness, would have decided to evacuate aboard a submarine. He was made fun of as he was supposed to get sick after boarding an anchored battleship. At the end of the war he was a wreck of a man. He would have suffered incredibly had he been locked for a few weeks in a several-dozen-meters-long and a few-meter diameter steel tube, in claustrophobic tightness. Moreover, there were problems with ventilation and omnipresent cold and humidity. Sailors suffered from dermatological problems. Conditions of living and working were very hard to cope with even for a young and healthy individual and we know how rough the Atlantic can be.

There are also skeptics, which is understandable, who think that all information about Nazis aboard submarines is a product of imagination of irresponsible journalists seeking sensation and popularity. Only a person without imagination and unaware of hardships of U-Boot service could create such and intrigue. Had this story been well documented, it would have been worth millions of dollars in the journalist world.

Nowadays, many conspiracy theorists believe in such incredible stories as the one talking about German criminals being evacuated to... an arctic stronghold. Did U-Boots participate in operations to carry Nazis or other high-ranking SS officers to the Antarctic, to the alleged "New Swabia" or, as other sensationalists prefer, to new " Berchtesgaden" - a place they could command from and deal a great blow to the Allies? [13] There are many supporters of surprising theories pointing to Queen Maud Land, the glacier covered part of the East Antarctic. Will we live to see a breakthrough in historical research? What is the probability of such events taking place?

What was the fate of the Kriegsmarine U-Boots which after reaching Argentina became spoils of war for the Allies? What happened to officers and crews of those submarines? The authors answer these and other questions and discuss other events that could be salvaged from the abyss of mystery. The truth does not favor anything. It is harsh.

---

[13] Berchtesgaden, Bavaria, between 1934 and 1945, was the place of the Führer of the Third Reich, Adolf Hitler's residence – Berghof.

Secret of The Gray Wolves. U-Boots' escape to South America is a detective documentary style book as events that took place at the end of World War II are both interesting and enlightening. The authors separated sparse facts from numerous myths. They based their work mainly on declassified documents and credible eye witnesses' reports , accompanied by their commentary. It unveiled the mysteries of U-Boots voyages to Argentina in 1945. The authors' main goal was purely to reach the truth no matter who is right.

CHAPTER I

LAST YEAR OF THE WAR. U-BOOTS' DEFEAT

There are lies disguised as the truth,
it would be a mistake not to be deceived by them.
François de La Rochefoucauld

In January 1944 the Germans had over 436 submarines including 168 combat ready; 87 served in training flotillas and 181 were under construction. They were mostly outdated, middle size, sea-going Type VII U-Boots and large Type IX ocean-going vessels not able to defeat Allied escort ships or to effectively protect themselves against air force. Although German shipyards, production facilities and harbors were regularly bombed by the large Allied air force fleet (carpet raids), more steel predators - in spite of logic and the helpless situation of the German military in Europe and other theaters of operation - entered naval service. The Germans managed to retain high tempo of submarine construction.

Submarines, after returning from exhausting combat patrols that lasted several weeks or months, and after necessary refits, returned to the north and mid Atlantic, shores of North America, Africa and the far Indian Ocean.

German submarines prowled all seas where they relentlessly torpedoed transport ships belonging to the Allies and to neutral countries. As the Luftwaffe had no sufficient number of long range aircraft to observe convoys, U-Boots would remain submerged most of the time thus having no possibility to attack large groups of Allied ships supplying Great Britain. This translated to tonnage of ships sunk by them - in the first quarter of 1944 the U-Bootwaffe submarines sunk only 39 ships including 10 in the Atlantic and 15 warships. At the same time the Kriegsmarine lost 60 vessels. 2,165 German seamen lost their lives. It is worth noting that in the second half of 1943 the hunters became the prey.

For U-Boots' crews survival was more important than engaging in suicide attacks. Seamen were blindly obedient. Until 1944 there had been no examples of mutiny. Due to heavy losses, submarines went on patrol missions manned by crews with no combat experience. Twenty-year-old lieutenants were give command after a submarine school, a few moths training and seamanship as a watch officer. It was their first and last submarine. Manning newly built submarines presented a tough logistic task for the Germans. The most famous submariners, credited with the highest numbers of kills and the largest GRT (merchantman's total internal volume) sunk, had been lost in action or taken prisoner. The times of U-Boots' aces' spectacular combat successes were over.

It is commonly known that in 1944 U-Boots during combat missions would patrol areas where possibility of encountering the enemy was the lowest. It was a way to consciously avoid combat. One could possibly think that the commanders' main concern was to stay away from Allied airplanes and escort ships. U-Boots' crews used many tricks like dumping oil or previously prepared pieces of supposedly destroyed equipment which was to create impression that a submarine was sunk. In other circumstances "the gray wolves", as the U-Bootwaffe crews were called, stood little chance against their pursuers.

Majority of Allied transport ships torpedoed by submarines, were unescorted. The Germans were sometimes able to sink one or two ships moving in convoys. Consequences of their actions were cruel as escort ships or support elements dealt with submarines, commanded by inexperienced officers, without mercy.

The Commander-in-chief of the Kriegsmarine Grossadmiral (Grand Admiral) Karl Dönitz and Adolf Hitler did not take note of the fact that Germany had already lost the submarine war. The Allies had managed to eliminate one of the most important U-Boots' assets - the ability to operate on surface during nighttime. Since the Coastal Command had sufficient numbers of aircraft, trained aircrews and strong anti-submarine surface forces, U-Boots' in the Atlantic found themselves in dire straits. The Allies developed their anti-submarine capabilities thanks to the latest radar equipment. The first operational air-to-surface radar entered service in August, 1940. Earlier, detecting a lone submarine operating at high seas was virtually impossible. The new device was able to detect a U-Boot or a surface unit with radio waves which allowed aircraft to attack targets with depth charges and onboard armament.

High efficiency of the U-Bootwaffe was significantly limited to the second half of 1943. It was estimated that the average life expectancy of a German U-Boot crew member was no longer than 6-7 months. From mid 1944 life expectancy of a seaman aboard a U-Boot was about four months. Later the situation got even worse - in 1945 U-Boot crews on patrol were expected to survive no more than 40 days. The unfavorable balance of naval warfare was never to be changed, not even with revolutionary technical solutions of German constructors. Some older U-Boot types and their modern counterparts that entered combat service were equipped with snorkels (Schnorchel) that allowed diesel engines to be used while submerged. Submarines' hulls were strengthened to be able to operate at greater depths. All these improvements only slowed down the inevitable defeat of the German Reich.

In winter of 1944 the command HQ of the U-Boot arm (Befehlshaber der Unterseeboote) decided to abort the system of "wolf packs"; a large group of submarines, when detected, was easy to be hunted down by aircraft or escort ships. The method of group attack which had been employed by the Kriegsmarine in October, 1939, was no longer effective. However, 53-year-old Karl Dönitz did not stop sending U-Boots against North Atlantic convoys. U-Boots no longer posed a deadly threat to merchant fleets and they frightened crews of freighters and tankers cruising the Atlantic in Allied convoys. The peak of the U-Bootwaffe activity was over. During the first days of the war in Europe U-Boots sank, on average, one ship a day - German submariners destroyed 69% of all merchant ships lost by the Allies. U-Boot crews fought everywhere their orders sent them - from the Bear Island in the Arctic Ocean to Bermuda, from Greenland to Gibraltar and in the Mediterranean Sea.

New generation attack ships, operating alone, had greater chances of survival. They would attack convoy ships in intervals of 30 nmi between U-Boots, 250 nmi (463 km) off the Great Britain coast where convoys were disbanded and the escort vigilance was low. Dönitz could only count on single successes. Despite defeats and heavy losses among submarines during the first quarter of 1944, he encouraged his subordinates to be more aggressive and to continue combat operations in the Atlantic. He stood by his decision to make U-Boots conduct night attacks despite the fact that effective observation was very difficult in these conditions. An attempt to inspire submariners to greater sacrifice had no effect. In the first half of 1944, eighty nine convoys (a total of 4,656 ships) crossed the northern Atlantic. U-Boots managed to sink 76 merchant ships.

What was U-Boots' situation like on other convoy routes? In winter 1944 up to 18 submarines operated near the Murmansk convoy routes with little success - in January they sank three ships including the British destroyer HMS *Hardy*.

When the Kriegsmarine battleships had been eliminated from the fight, the British Admiralty stopped dividing the Murmansk convoys into two parts (A and B). From then on single large groups, protected by strong escort, were formed. The escort took over tasks of a close cover. According to new orders, the main escort included escort aircraft carriers and light cruisers. It was difficult for the Germans to wage submarine war as limited U-Boots' successes came with a heavy price.

In April the U-Bootwaffe's suffered very substantial losses. Twenty two U-Boots were sunk and 799 men perished. Meanwhile, the Allies lost only six ships on the Atlantic. It was Dönitz's another defeat.

On April 10, U-Boots attacked the RA.58 convoy (37 ships) from Russia to Great Britain and failed. On April 30, during the attack against the RA.59 convoy (45 ships), *U 711* commanded by Kapitänleutnant (lieutenant) Hans-Günther Lange sank the American freighter *William S. Thayer*. The attackers lost three U-Boots. Another failure. In April and at the beginning of May the Germans lost a total number of 304 men in the Arctic waters. In June and July the Allies did not send any convoys on the Arctic routes due to landings in Normandy.

In August, U-Boots returned to the Arctic seaways. They attacked the JW.59 convoy (40 ships) was attacked. On August 21, Oberleutnant zur See (lieutenant junior grade) Friedrich-Georg Herrle, commander of *U 307*, sank the escort ship, sloop HMS *Kite* (1,350 t). On the following day *U 354* (Capt. Hans-Jürgen Sthamer) seriously mauled the Canadian escort aircraft carrier *Nabob* (she did not sink but her damage was so severe the ship never went to sea again) and damaged the British frigate *Bickerton*.

On August 22, as a sort of retaliation, *U 344* (Capt. Ulrich Pietsch) was sunk north north east of the North Cape. The entire crew (50 seamen) was killed after being depth charged by the Swordfish X aircraft of the 825. Naval Air Squadron of the Royal Navy Fleet Air Arm from the escort aircraft carrier HMS *Vindex*. Two days later *U 354* (commanded by Capt. Hans-Jürgen Sthamer) met the same fate north east of the Bear Island. The submarine was attacked with depth charges by the British warships: sloops HMS *Mermaid* and HMS *Peacock*, frigate Loch *Dunvegan* and destroyer *Keppel*.

In the following months of 1944, U-Boots unsuccessfully attacked the Arctic convoys. An attempt to torpedo a small convoy code-named RA.59A (nine ships) failed. The operation went so bad that, on September 2, *U 394* (commanded by Lieutenant Ernst-Günther Unterhorst) was destroyed. The submarine sank south east of Jan Mayen after being hit with bombs dropped by the Swordfish V aircraft from the 825. FAA Squadron of the escort aircraft carrier HMC *Vindex* and depth charges from destroyers HMS *Keppel*, HMS *Whitehall* and sloops *Mermaid* and *Peacock*.

At the end of September the RA.60 return convoy (32 ships) lost two cargo ships sunk by 24-year-old Lieutenant Wolfgang Ley (*U 310*). The JW.60 convoy (30 ships) with no difficulties and no losses reached its destination after nine days of steaming, on September 23. At that time, after September 24, contact was lost with *U 921* (Lieutenant Alfred Werner) north west of Narvik. The last report was sent from a position 74°45'N and 13°50'E; the submarine's commander informed the U-Boot-waffe headquarters of a completed patrol and his return to the Narvik base. This information is very important as *U 921*, at the end of the first week of September, set off for her third patrol with orders to operate against the JW.60 convoy.

On October 26-27, *U 956*, *U 365*, *U 995* and *U 295* carried out an unsuccessful attack against the JW.61 convoy (34 ships). On November 2, the latter of the aforementioned U-Boots managed to torpedo and damage the destroyer escort *Mounsey*. Another U-Boot was lost on the Norwegian Sea on October 27. The Type VII F submarine transport ship *U 1060*, commanded by Lieutenant Herbert Brammer, one day into her voyage, was bombed and strafed west of Velfjord by crews of the Firefly aircraft of the 1771. FAA Squadron of the aircraft carrier HMS *Implacable*, two British Halifax aircraft D and T of the 502. RAF Squadron and two Czechoslovak Liberators H and Y from the 311. RAF Squadron/Czechoslovak. The *U 1060* wreckage was finished off on November 4.

On December 10 and 11, the RA.62 convoy (30 ships) was attacked by *U 365* (Lt. Diether Todenhagen). The young lieutenant fired two acoustic torpedoes one of which damaged the British destroyer *Cassandra* (1,710 t). The destroyer was towed back to Murmansk. The culprit was destroyed, east of the Jan Mayen Island, on the next day by depth charges from two Swordfish aircraft L and Q of the 813. FAA Squadron from the escort aircraft carrier HMS *Campania*.

In 1944, two hundred forty three ships with military and other supplies reached the Soviet Union. The convoy protection was very successful. In January only three U-Boots managed to torpedo three ships of the JW.56A convoy. The price the U-Bootwaffe paid was horrendous. In 1944, on the Arctic waters, 24 submarines were sunk, most of them with entire crews. Despite the fact that U-Boots actions in the region were inefficient, the BdU would still send them on patrols. The situation did not change until the end of the war. From January to April 1945, U-Boots operating in the Arctic waters lacked spectacular successes that would help maintain high morale of German crews. The U-Bootwaffe's effectiveness was poor. Two ships and six warships were sunk.

The JW.64 convoy did not lose a single of the 31 ships similarly to three other groups sent to Russia - JW.65, JW.66 and JW.67 (a total of 82 transport ships). Convoys codenamed RA.64, RA.65, RA.66 and RA.67 (112 ships) also safely reached their destination.

And how did the Kriegsmarine submarine fleet fare in other regions? In the Mediterranean Sea, where the Germans had 13 submarines, which is a large number given the small area of operations, between January and May 1944, ten ships were sunk including several Arab merchant sailing ships of small tonnage. The British lost five warships (cruiser *Penelope*, destroyer *Laforey* and three landing craft) and the Americans lost the destroyer escort *Fetchteler* in the GUS.38 convoy and the submarine chaser *PC 558*.

Life was not easy for Hitler's submarines. Due to a difficult situation the Germans were only able to use bases in French Toulon and La Spezia in Italy. In the first quarter of 1944 only nine U-Boots were sent to attack Allied shipping. All U-Boots lost were of the VII C type - the most extensively used submarines.

On May 19, *U 453* (Lt. Dierk Lührs) sank the British freighter *Fort Missanabie* which was part of the HA.43 convoy (20 ships were escorted by four warships). It was the U-Bootwaffe's last success in the Mediterranean Sea. In March 1944 convoys on the Mediterranean routes were mostly attacked by the Luftwaffe aircraft.

In July, after a dozen or so months break, U-Boots returned to the Baltic. During the following six months they sank only five ships and 11 small warships the largest of which was the Finnish destroyer *Rigel* sunk by *U 242* (Lt. Heinrich Riedel) on October 28, 1944.

On the Black Sea U-Boots operated until September of 1944. Within eight months, combat operations of coastal submarines - small Type II U-Boots called "kayaks" (*U 9*, *U 18*, *U 19*, *U 20*, *U 23* and *U 24*) - were only symbolic in nature. Two ships and three small warships were sunk.

The farthest area of operations for U-Boots was the Indian Ocean. In the first quarter of 1944, 17 ships were torpedoed and sunk. Majority of them belonged to British and American ship owners but they were also cargo ships sailing under Greek, Chinese and Norwegian flags. The most energetic submariners were Lt.Cdr. Alfred Eick (*U 510*) and Korvettenkapitän (lieutenant commander) Siegfried Lüdden (*U 188*). The former sank five ships and damaged one, the latter added six transport ships destroyed into his account.

From June 1944 to February 1945 U-Boots prowled the Indian Ocean with limited success. Meanwhile, submarines not equipped with snorkels returned to Europe. Within eight months 20 ships were destroyed. They were mostly British and American cargo ships. Allied ships also fell victim to Japanese submarines.

What happened next in the Atlantic? In May the Germans sank three ships sailing unaccompanied in the South Atlantic. Furthermore, *U 473* (Lt.Cdr. Heinz Sternberg) managed to damage the American destroyer escort *Donnell*, *U 548* (Lt. Eberhard Zimmermann) torpedoed the Canadian frigate *Valleyfield* sailing as part of the ONM.234 convoy escort, *U 549* (Lt.Cdr. Detlav Krankenhagen) sank the American escort aircraft carrier *Black Island* (the most precious German prize of the time) and damaged the destroyer escort USS *Barr*. Only three U-Boots operated in the North Atlantic.

The Allied response to the sustained losses was sinking six German submarines in the Atlantic. A total of 22 U-Boots were destroyed in that time period.

U-Boots sent by the Kriegsmarine command from the Baltic to the Atlantic and to northern Norway did not use the Norwegian route as they used to but headed for the open waters of the North Sea. That was supposed to create a chance to attack aircraft carriers of the Home Fleet operating against the German shipping in the Norwegian waters. However, short arctic nights were not submariners' allies as they did not have enough time to charge their batteries. Furthermore, U-Boots remaining on surface at dawn or dusk were vulnerable to attacks by aircraft from escort aircraft carriers and by Coastal Command. After the number of patrols had been increased, even more U-Boots were destroyed.

From March to May 1944 U-Boots had local successes far from the North Atlantic and the British coast. None of subsequent operations in the area fulfilled the expectations. Admiral Dönitz was in despair and had to accept the increasing losses. The Germans were not able to fight the much stronger and better organized opponent. Losses in the Atlantic were still very high. It was one of the reasons to move U-Boots to other areas - to arctic waters and to the Indian Ocean.

From June 1, all U-Boots without snorkels were forbidden from conducting combat operations in the Atlantic. During the same month fate struck Dönitz again. At the end of the first week of June, a huge armada of 6,100 watercrafts carrying an army of 150,000 Allied soldiers left harbors in the southern coast of Great Britain and headed for the Seine estuary in Normandy. The Operation Overlord began. It lasted from June 6 to August 31, 1944 and its operations covered the area of the north west France. The largest landing operation in the history of warfare was to be beginning of the demise of the Third Reich. It opened the second front in Europe.

The Kriegsmarine commander-in-chief was completely surprised by the Allied landings in France. In May the U-Bootwaffe command, preparing for the anticipated landing, but at a different location (the Germans expected the invasion through the English Channel and thousands of soldiers were to land 20-50 miles from Great Britain), brought U-Boots to the Bay of Biscay. Almost 70 warships were amassed in French Atlantic ports. The German naval forces were too weak to oppose the Allies. Two strike groups were created. 36 U-Boots of the "Landwirt" group were to operate in the area of the Bay of Biscay and at the southern coast of Britain. The "Mitte" group comprised 22 submarines, 5-6 of them were sent to the eastern part of the English Channel and the remaining majority were to operate in the Norwegian Sea and the North Sea. In the area patrolled by U-Boots of the "Mitte" group the sea was empty.

Hitler's headquarters ordered U-Boots to attack and sink the invasion fleet and if necessary ram the enemy ships.

None of the U-Bootwaffe commanders decided to conduct the desperate suicide attack. The Führer was no longer able to inspire submarine crews to make a greater sacrifice. At that time people strived to survive, they wanted to live...

The "Landwirt" group lost six U-Boots and another five were forced to return to their bases. The only submarines able to operate in the northern France, in the English Channel were the ones equipped with snorkels. Commanders of U-Boots not fitted with that device not only had no chance to survive but also could not dream of successful attacks. These were suicide patrol missions.

To counter U-Boot operations the Allies deployed almost 500 warships of various types. Facing this kind of opposition the U-Bootwaffe stood no chance of victory.

Shortly before the invasion, on June 4, the Task Force 22.3 ("Hunter-Killer" Group), commanded by Captain Daniel V. Gallery, comprised of the aircraft carrier *Guadalcanal* (famous for sinking of *U 544*, *U 68* and *U 515*) and five destroyer escorts (*Pillsbury*, *Chatelain*, *Flaherty*, *Jenks* i *Pope*) began pursuit of the German submarine *U 505* (Lt. Harald Lange) in the mid Atlantic. North of Dakar, after being depth charged, fired upon by artillery from the American escort ship *Pillsbury* and after attack by two Wildcat carrier-borne aircraft, the Type IX C U-Boot was captured. It was the first ship captured by boarding by the US Navy in the 20th century. *U 505* was towed to the Royal Bay harbor on the Bermuda Islands. The submarine was later sent to the United States where she was thoroughly tested; she survived the war and from 1955 can be seen as an exhibit in the Chicago Science and Industry Museum.

The Americans found many valuable documents aboard *U 505* including a code book for U-Boots in the Atlantic and Indian Ocean, several information about a new radio dispatch sending protocol called "Courier" and five fully operational electric, self-guided, Type T-V torpedoes. The most important was the fact that the Americans were able to keep the U-Boot's capture in secret from the Kriegsmarine until January 1945.

The German U-Bootwaffe had some successes at the approaches to Normandy. On June 15, *U 621* (Lt. Hermann Stuckmann) sank the American landing craft *LST*

280, *U 767* (Lt. Waler Dankleff) destroyed the British frigate *Mourne* and *U 764* sank the destroyer escort HMS *Blackwood*.

On June 25, *U 984* commanded by Lt. Heinz Sieder damaged the British destroyer escort HMS *Goodson*, and *U 988* (Lt. Erich Dobberstein) damaged the British corvette HMS *Pink* and seriously battered four American Liberty class ships (*Henry G. Blasdel, Edward H. House, John A. Treutlen, James A. Farrell*) that were part of the EMC.17 convoy partaking in the invasion of Normandy.

In June the Germans lost 24 U-Boots including the captured *U 505*. Due to redeploying U-Boots against the invasion forces, dynamics of operations in the Atlantic were reduced significantly.

In July the U-Bootwaffe lost a total of 24 submarines, in August - 47, in September - 21. Most of the U-Boots were lost with entire crews. At that time the Germans commissioned only 49 new submarines. From July to September the Germans sank 20 ships in the Atlantic.

After the French Atlantic bases had been lost and evacuated and U-Boots transferred to Norway, the Allies were forced to alter convoy routes. The previous routes in the North Atlantic running north of Ireland or near Iceland were within range of U-Boots operating from bases in Norway. I these circumstances, at the end of summer, convoys were sent along a new route near the Portuguese coast.

Implementation of those measures was crucial as the Germans, having established the Norwegian bases, deployed more U-Boots to the Atlantic.

On September 9, the last U-Boot left the Lorient harbor and reached Norway after a month. From that moment submarines were able to use only their Norwegian bases and the German bases in the North Sea and the Baltic.

At the beginning of September, the largest convoy, code named HX.306, comprising 115 ships, came from Canada to Great Britain. Without any losses the convoy transported over one million tons of cargo.

October 1944 was the first period of the World War II when the Allies did not lose any cargo ships in the Atlantic and the surrounding seas. At that time there were 141 submarines of different types, flying the Third Reich colors, patrolling the Atlantic, Arctic Sea, Baltic and the Indian Ocean. The Germans lost 15 ships. In November and December the situation did not change much. The allies lost 11 transport ships. Twenty five U-Boots were sunk.

Although the Germans introduced new submarines, equipped with snorkels and the latest technical novelties, with devotion and determination, they were not able to alter the course of events. Defeat of Hitler's submarine fleet was inevitable. The German loss in the Battle of the Atlantic can be illustrated by the fact that in 1944 the Allies ran 266 convoys that comprised 12,907 ships but U-Boots under the command of Admiral of the Fleet Karl Dönitz managed to sink only... 55 cargo ships and 25 warships!

The last period of the war was the time of intensive but not very effective operational activity of midget submarines and "human torpedoes". Forty three submarines operated in January 1945, 39 in the European waters, including the first Type

XXIII U-Boot. During the last months of the war, the Germans main target were merchant ships sailing in convoys through the Irish Sea. The British Admiralty was ready to meet the enemy. Apart from the convoys' main escort, six groups on search and destroy missions were deployed into the high threat area. The RAF aircraft conducted patrol operations. Detecting a submarine equipped with the snorkel was not an easy task but the Allies were extensively experienced in chasing down enemy submarines. Usually the underwater intruder was sunk right after being detected. That is why U-Boots, despite incredible dedication and sacrifice of their crews, had not many opportunities to fulfill the command's orders. Losses increased. In April, five weeks before the general ceasefire, at least 44 U-Boots left their bases to hunt the enemy. Moreover, 35 submarines left the Kiel base and headed for Norway in order to enter the Atlantic in later time. They did not manage to complete all tasks assigned by Dönitz.

In January 1945 the war reached Germany. Due to the progress of the Red Army offensive, the U-Bootwaffe headquarters had to be transferred to Wilhelmshaven. Admiral Dönitz, still residing in Berlin, was finally forced to resign from commanding the submarine warfare. However, U-Boot commanders did not want to abort the hunt for enemy ships and warships. Between January and May 1945 the Germans sank 60 ships in the Atlantic. Until Germany's capitulation the U-Bootwaffe lost a total of 136 submarines. They were being slaughtered.

Before the end of the war, only one high-tech submarine was sent to combat operations. The Type XXI (U 2511) was a revolutionary and innovative design. The ship's commander, 31-year-old Lieutenant Commander Adalbert Schnee, had experience of 12 combat patrols when he was transferred to Admiral Dönitz's headquarters where he would assist in supervising the project.

The German propaganda, regularly, until the very end, informed of the U-Bootwaffe wonderful weapon - the Elektroboote (electrical submarines) which was supposed to alter the course of the Battle of the Atlantic. The Allies were apprehensive of the state-of-the-art, ocean-going, electric U-Boots that could resume the Kriegsmarine's operations on a huge scale that would resemble that of 1942. It was suspected that had only 50 Type XXI submarines become operational, the American supply operations through the North Atlantic would have been disrupted. The Type XXI had powerful batteries which gave a submerged submarine huge range and speed of 17 knots. The electric underwater predators were able to become silent and hard to detect when moving at low speeds. Another feature of the Type XXI submarines was their ability to crash dive extremely fast. However, luckily for the Allies, assembly, sea trials and crew harmonization lasted too long. Anxiety of the British and the Allies was groundless. It was another program that the Germans did not manage to complete according to plans. Shipyards in Bremen, Hamburg and Gdansk (Danzig) were seriously damaged during carpet bombings and supplies of basic devices, subcomponents and equipment (most electric motors of the new type were produced in Berlin and Mannheim) were irregular or non-existent.

In 1944-1955, a total of 140 Type XXI submarines (120 entered service) were launched. Only the most experienced and talented commanders the U-Bootwaffe could be assigned to the new electric U-Boots. Due to catastrophic delays the Germans had no opportunity to use the "wonder weapon"[14]. Upon close inspection of the captured Type XXI U-Boots the Allies quickly appreciated their revolutionary technological solutions.

In April and May there were five Type XXIII coastal submarines conducting patrol operations but they were too scarce to change the course of the already lost war.

Did the „The Lion" Dönitz believe in regaining the initiative? If so, his faith was not substantiated. Although the Type XXI U-Boots with new electric motors and batteries were the best submarines constructed during World War II, Germany had already lost the war. Had the modern electric boats been produced earlier. But all this was just unfulfilled dream.

In the last year of the war, a single U-Boot attack against an escorted convoy was a suicide. Despite that, some commanders attempted such attacks but they were unsuccessful. One of them was the commander of *U 1232* (Type IX C) Lt. Götz Roth who attacked ships of convoys SH.194 and BX.141.

During the war Dönitz suffered a personal loss - his two sons, both serving in the Kriegsmarine, were killed in action. At the end, after Hitler's suicide[15], the commander-in-chief of the German fleet was, according to the last will and private testament of the previous leader of the Third Reich, assigned to be the new Führer - President of the Reich and Supreme Commander of the Armed Forces. Dönitz appointed his new government in the Kriegsmarine barracks in Eutin, one of very few places not yet captured by the Allies.

The new German government settled aboard the liner *Patria* which was anchored in the Flensburg harbor. Dönitz was joined by Reichsführer-SS Heinrich Himmler - chief of the Ministry of Internal Affairs, previous Foreign Minister Joachim von Ribbentrop (both of them unsuccessfully applied for whatever position in Dönitz's government), Minister of Armaments and War Production Albert Speer, field marshals Wilhelm Keitel and Robert Ritter von Greim, the new commander in chief of the Luftwaffe (shortly before Hitler's death Reichsmarschall Hermann Göring, commander of the air force who was preparing coup d'etat to take over the power in Germany, was deprived of all his positions), General Alfred Jodl - chief of the headquarters in the Oberkommando der Wehrmacht (OKW) and others.

---

[14] E. Bagnasco, *Uboote im 2. Weltkrieg*, Stuttgart 1997; E. Gröner, *Die deutschen Kriegsschiffe 1815-1945*, vol. 3, Koblenz 1985; B. Herzog, *Deutsche U-Boote 1906-1966*, Bonn 1993; E. Möller, W. Brack, *The Encyclopedia of U-boats. From 1904 to the Present Day*, London 2004; E. Rössler, *U-Boottyp XXI*, Bonn 2002; idem, *The U-Boat. The evolution and technical history of German submarines*, London 2001; M. Westphal, *Walka o panowanie w głębinach. Historia powstania U-Boota typu XXI*, Gdańsk 2014.

[15] A. Beevor, *Berlin 1945. Upadek*, Kraków 2009; I. Kershaw, *Hitler 1936-1945. Nemezis*, vol. 2, Poznań 2002; J. Mayo, E. Craigie, *Ostatni dzień Hitlera*, Warszawa 2016; J. Toland, *Hitler. Reportaż biograficzny*, Warszawa 2014; H. Trevor-Roper, *Ostatnie dni Hitlera*, Poznań 1966.

The main goal of the new leader and commander in chief of the three military branches (for his previous position Dönitz appointed Generaladmiral Hans-Georg von Friedeburg, his closest associate in the submarine warfare) was to save Germany from annihilation. The admiral wanted the highest number of German soldiers possible to surrender to the British and American forces not to the Red Army which inspired the Germans with a feeling of utter horror.

When Dönitz took over the power of the leadership over the crumbling Third Reich, he had several hundred submarines which, at least on paper, posed a deadly threat to Allied warships and cargo ships operating in the North Atlantic, British coastal waters and other areas of operation. Germany was still a formidable enemy as the number of submarines was concerned.

On May 4, 1945, the headquarters of the Kriegsmarine, during the last days of the Third Reich, was in the Marineschule (Naval Academy) in Mürwik near Flensburg. The Admiral of the Fleet ordered all U-Boot crews still operating at sea to cease all hostilities and return to bases either friendly or the enemy's. The crews were to prepare to surrender. Other ships capitulated in bases in Germany and Norway. Over 200 commanders sank their steel predators executing the "Regenbogen" protocol[16].

German forces suffered an overwhelming defeat on the ground. in the air and at sea. The war was coming to the end in all corners of Europe. Partially, German forces capitulated in the Netherlands, in north-west Germany including the Frisian Islands and Heligoland, in Schleswik-Holstein and Denmark.

The Kriegsmarine command took advantage of the time given to them. Having destroyers, torpedo boats, large cargo ships and other smaller vessels at their disposal, additional evacuation was initiated for soldiers and civilians from the Ventspils harbor in the west Courland and from the Hel harbor at the Baltic Sea towards the west. That way several tens of thousands of people were evacuated. Thousands were also evacuated from Liepāja (Libau) in Latvia. Until the last moments, attempts were made to evacuate as many soldiers and refugees from enclaves at the east Baltic as possible. The task was feasible thanks to the favorable position of the British command that allowed the Kriegsmarine warships, stationed in bases in the areas captured or the ones to be taken over by the British according to the capitulation treaty, to participate in the evacuation operation despite the partial capitulation signed in sir Marshall Bernard Law Montgomery's headquarters near Hamburg[17]. During the

---

[16] According to the Allied records, made in fall of 1945, which were later corrected several times, at night from May 4 to 5 German crews sank 222 U-Boots (their vast majority was in harbors of North Germany) in the Jade Bight, in the mouths of the Weser and Elbe, in the Bay of Lübeck and Eckernförde and in Norway (Bergen) - which happened against the terms of the capitulation signed on May 4 Montgomery's headquarters. 174 submarines surrendered to the Allied forces.

[17] The arrangement was signed with agreement of the American General Dwight Eisenhower, commander of the Allied forces in North-West Europe who also prepared the Normandy landings in June 1944 and commanded the Allied march though Europe. After the victory in Europe he was appointed commander in chief of the American occupational forces in Germany. On January 20, 1953, he was sworn in as the 34th President of the United States of America.

talks concerning the conditions of capitulation Germany was represented by: Generaladmiral Hans-Georg von Friedeburg, Admiral Gerhard Wagner, commander of the Army Group „North West", General Alfred Jodl, Chief of the Operation Staff of the OKW and other higher officers.

On May 7, at nighttime, in one of the school buildings - in General Dwight Eisenhower's Headquarters of the Allied Expeditionary Forces in Reims, France - Germany capitulated in the western front to representatives of the armies of the United States and the British Commonwealth. General Jodl, authorized by Dönitz signed the act of complete, unconditional surrender of all German forces[18]. On the same day in the North Sea, *U 2336* (LCdr. Emil Klusmeier), a 35 m long, modern, Type XXIII submarine sank two last cargo ships of the World War II - Norwegian *Sneland* and British *Avondale Park*. Also on the same day, *U 320* (Lt. Heinz Emmrich) was damaged in the Norwegian Sea by depth charges dropped by the Catalina flying boat of the 210. RAF Squadron. At night, on May 8, after the Germany's surrender, the crew scuttled the U-Boot north west of Bergen. *U 249* (LCdr. Uwe Kock), the first German submarine that, according to the capitulation treaty, surrendered to the British (operation "Pledge"), entered the Portland-Weymouth harbor on May 10. The detachment assigned to the guard duty aboard the U-Boot was a unit of the Polish Navy from the torpedo boat flotilla.

⋆ ⋆ ⋆

Of 1,169 U-Boots that entered service, 863 participated in combat operations but 550 of them did not sink any ships. The U-Bootwaffe lost 794 submarines (the US Air Force and Navy destroyed 188); 25,870 officers and men lost their lives during patrols and combat operations - according to the Wehrmacht bureau of information in Berlin. The RAF aircraft sank more German submarines than the Royal Navy ships. Karl Dönitz, the long time commander in chief of the U-Bootwaffe and the Kriegsmarine was sentenced, during the Nuremberg trials, to 10 years in prison.

On all theaters of operations German submariners sank 2,603 Allied and neutral ships. They sank and damaged : 2 battleships (60,250 t), 3 aircraft carriers (67,700 t), 3 escort aircraft carriers (34,148 t) and 2 damaged beyond repair (22,820 t), 5 battle cruisers (26,240 t), 44 destroyers and destroyer escorts (62,512 t) and 1 damaged beyond repair (1,540 t), 9 frigates (11,802 t) and 9 damaged beyond repair (11,545

---

[18] On May 8 1945 the capitulation ceremony was repeated in Berlin. Upon categorical demands of the Supreme Commander, Generalissimus of the Soviet Union Josef V. Stalin, in the officer school at Zwiselerstrasse 2 in the district of Karlshorst in Berlin the unconditional surrender, this time of entire Germany, ceremony was repeated before representatives of the four powers - the Soviet Union, United States, Great Britain and France. The capitulation of the German ground forces was signed by Field Marshall Wilhelm Keitel, Gen. Stumpff and Generaladmiral Friedeburg. The capitulation was signed in presence of Marshall Georgy K. Zhukov, Marshall Arthur Tedder, Gen. Carl Andrew Spaatz and Gen. Jean de Lattre de Tassigny. The Germans were to surrender on all fronts until midnight of May 9, 1945.

t), 12 gunboats and sloops (18,201 t) and 1 damaged beyond repair (1,350 t), 24 mine-sweepers (12,244 t), 9 submarines (5,520 t) and one friendly Vichy (1,379 t), 21 corvettes (18,951 t) and 3 damaged beyond repair (2,910 t), 3 minelayers (4,021 t), 1 mine hunter (840 t), 1 destroyer depot ship (10,850 t), 2 torpedo boats (108 t), 9 submarine chasers (1,463 t), 2 patrol boats (262 t), 21 landing craft (18,122 t), landing boats (27 t), landing barges (20 t) and 1 mine-sweeping boat (35 t).

The total tonnage sunk is 177 (353,376 t) and one friendly Vichy submarine (1,379 t) sunk by mistake. 16 ships were damaged beyond repair (40,165 t), 36 warships were damaged (149,085 t). The total number of ships sunk is 194 (394,920 t).

U-Boots damaged: 3 battleships (68,150 t), 6 light battle cruisers (54,350 t), 14 destroyers (19,405 t), 1 sloop (1,190 t), 1 frigate (1,150 t), 1 minelayer (2,650 t), 1 submarine (412 t), 2 landing craft (505 t), 2 mine-sweepers (1,061 t), 3 submarine chasers (185 t) and 2 torpedo boats (64 t).

Between 1939 and 1945 German submarines also sank auxiliary ships: 9 auxiliary cruisers (145,857 GRT), 2 ocean boarding vessels (OBVs) (10,411 GRT), 5 armed troop carriers (45,502 GRT), 1 Q-ship (3,209 GRT), 2 submarines' tenders (25,432 GRT) 1 armed tender ((1,330 t), 2 auxiliary patrol boats (1,090 GRT), 1 auxiliary unit (411 t), armed trawlers (18,295 t), 1 auxiliary minesweeper (534 t), 1 auxiliary mine hunter (209 t), 4 armed yachts (3,302 t), 1 armed rescue ship (1,440 t). 63 ships were sunk (224,249 GRT + 25,521 t; total volume and displacement).

U-Boots damaged : 5 auxiliary cruisers (71,172 GRT), 3 armed troop carriers (22,101 GRT) and 4 tankers (34,916 GRT). A total of 12 auxiliary vessels (127,189 GRT) were damaged.

The opinion stating that German submariners' operations were criminal in nature is false. The statement above has as many supporters as opponents. For many years naval historians have fought a battle over the issue - did the U-Bootwaffe, in comparison to other countries using submarines operating on the seas and oceans between 1939 and 1945, fight honorably?

At the end of the war one disgraceful event took place on March 13, 1944, when a 28-year-old LCdr. Heinz-Wilhelm Eck, commander of U 852, used his machine guns to execute survivors from the torpedoed Greek freighter *Peleus*. He was sentenced to death by the Allied court and, along with two officers of U 852, executed by firing squad on November 30, 1945. Most of U-Boot crews fought with bravery and honor. Their morale and discipline were remarkable even in the face of inevitable defeat.

We need to add that Allied submariners' conscience was not clear either. On January 26, 1943, the American submarine USS *Wahoo* torpedoed the Japanese transport ship *Buyo Maru* south east of the Palau Islands. *Buyo Maru* carried 1,126 soldiers and officers of the Imperial Japanese Army and prisoners of war of the 2. Battalion from the16 Punjab Regiment. Commander Dudley Morton gave orders to use small arms and machine guns to fire upon life boats carrying survivors from the sunk ship. As a result of the attack 195 Indian prisoners and 87 Japanese soldiers died.

CHAPTER II

WHY ARGENTINA?

The man who fears no truths
has nothing to fear from lies.
Thomas Jefferson

In October 1946, a dozen or so months after the end of one of the most atrocious wars in the history of mankind, the International Military Tribunal managed to sentence only 22 war criminals during the Nuremberg trials (12 were sentenced to death including one in absentia[19], three - to life imprisonment, four - to long term imprisonment, three were acquitted)[20]. For many months the trials were followed by 300 press and radio correspondents.

---

[19] On October 1, 1946, after almost 220 working days, having listened to testimonies of 240 witnesses, presenting over 5 thousand documents and writing a 16 000 page protocol, sentences in the Nuremberg trials were pronounced. The following people were sentenced to death: Hermann Göring - the Reich Marshal, commander of the Luftwaffe, creator of the Gestapo (committed suicide right before his execution), Joachim von Ribbentrop - Foreign Minister, Wilhelm Keitel - Field Marshal of the Reich, Cief of the Wehrmacht High Command, Ernst Kaltenbrunner - Chief of the Reich Main Security Office, Alfred Rosenberg - the NSDAP ideologist, Reich Minister for the Occupied Eastern Territories, Alfred Jodl - Chief of the Operations Staff of the Wehrmacht High Command, Hans Frank - chief of the occupied Poland "General Government" territory, Wilhelm Frick - SS and SA general, governor of the Protectorate of Bohemia and Moravia, Julius Streicher - publisher of „Der Stürmer", one of the masterminds behind the extermination of Jews, Fritz Sauckel - SS and SA general, organizer of the labor deployment and Arthur Seyess-Inquart - Commissioner of the Reich in the Netherlands. The man sentenced in absentia was Martin Bormann - head of Hitler's chancellery and chief of the NSDAP. Robert Ley - head of the German Labor front, hanged himself in his cell just before the trials. The war criminals were hanged on October 16, 1946, by a professional executioner of the American Army, Master Sergeant John C. Wood. Life imprisonment sentence was given to: Erich Raeder – commander of the German fleet (Kriegsmarine) between 1935 and 1943, Rudolf Hess - Hitler's deputy and Walter Funk - Reich Minister for Financial and Economic Affairs. Long term sentences were pronounced on: Albert Speer - Minister of Armaments, Baldur von Schirach - commander of the Hitlerjugend, Constantin von Neurath - governor of the Protectorate of Bohemia and Moravia, Karl Dönitz – creator and commander of the submarine fleet (U-Bootwaffe), commander in chief of the Kriegsmarine between 1943 and 1945 and the last Führer. The following were acquitted: Franz von Papen - former Reich Chancellor (before Hitler), Hans Fritzsche - Reich's main censor and chief of the radio, Hjalmar Schacht - president of the Reischbank.

[20] See: J.J. Heydecker, J. Leeb, *Proces Norymberski. Trzecia Rzesza przed sądem*, Warszawa 2016; D. Irving, *Norymberga. Ostatnia bitwa*, Warszawa 1999, A. Zwiagincew, *Proces Norymberski. Nieznane fakty*, Warszawa 2014.

However, many war criminals avoided punishment. They found refuge in many parts of the globe, mainly in South America. How many of them boarded a passenger ship or a submarine and ran away to the world's end? Long before the German defeat, preparations had been made to provide the German leaders with safety and secure their financial resources, archives and other valuables. We know that false passport had been prepared and entries in files of Registry Offices forged. The German secret service had created „stage points" for fugitives transported to other countries. Vatican also played an important role in the operation. „We know that in many countries, including Switzerland, secret bank accounts were opened and companies of different kinds were created" - wrote Lew Bezymienski, journalist and the Soviet intelligence agent (living in Bonn) who had access to numerous classified documents[21].

Since the end of the World War II the issue of organized evacuation of the known war criminals closest to Adolf Hitler, Heinrich Himmler, Herman Göring and other German leaders, later chased, with determination and dedication, by the Nazi hunters[22], has become the topic of countless articles, books, documentaries and films. Thanks to extensive work of historians and other naval researchers, we are familiar with evacuation routes, means of transportation and names of people who helped German criminals reach South America. Of course, the knowledge is not final. Every year, archives around the world declassify files containing hundreds of documents that shed new light into the matter.

It turns out, we still know very little about the main representatives of the Third Reich who escaped justice crossing the Atlantic aboard U-Boots. Foreign authors who, in the last decades, have dedicated their work to hunting Nazi fugitives, have devoted little or none of their research to the Kriegsmarine submarines which were safe means of transport.

The U-Bootwaffe submarine crews that, in 1945, escaped to Argentina (or tried to reach Japan) - which is discussed further in the book - were interrogated by the Argentine and United States intelligence. Their cases were also thoroughly investigated by the British. Most of the Kriegsmarine officers and men were uncooperative. Prisoners avoided answering questions about their service in the navy, their participation in combat patrols and their last combat missions. While being questioned, some of them were uptight which was not unnoticed by the investigators,

---

[21] U. Bahnsen, J. O'Donnel, *Katakumba. Ostatnie dni w bunkrze Hitlera*, Warszawa 1995, p. 319. In April 1945 L. Bezymienski as a young officer served in the headquarters of Marshal Georgy Zhukov, commander of the 1. Belarussian Front, in Strausberg, east of Berlin. Marshal Zhukov orchestrated the Berlin operation. See also: L. Bezymienski, *Śladami Martina Bormanna*, Warszawa 1967, p. 139-140. The topic is further discussed by: M. Aarons, N. Bascomb, U. Goñi, A. Jacobsen, J. Loftus, G. Steinacher and others. See: Bibliography.

[22] The most famous hunter of German war criminals was Jewish activist Simon Wiesenthal (1908-2005). After the war he set his life goal to hunt Nazi criminals. In 1947 he was the co-creator of the Jewish Historical Documentation Center in Linz (Austria), the organization whose role was to gather documents concerning war criminals and their atrocities. He helped hunt down and sentence many people close to Adolf Hitler. Thanks to the Jewish Historical Documentation Center (closed in 1954) it was possible to make over one thousand Nazi criminals stand trial.

they would refuse to answer detailed questions, hiding behind military secrets. They also did not want to sign their confessions. Documents prepared by the American investigators state that higher and lower ranking non-commissioned officers of the German fleet were strongly influenced by their superiors. Life of sailors who were „more talkative and cooperative" and were not separated from their comrades could be in danger - that is what the US Navy investigators LtCdr. W.W. Webb and Lt. A.W. Green Ret. wrote in their report from July 24, 1945.

According to extensive documents (reports) of the American intelligence authorities in Argentina, that had been declassified and can be found in the National Archives w College Park in Maryland and in the Library of Congress in Washington, an experienced investigator was able to lead an interrogation so that higher ranking NCOs would say more about events that took place during the last days of the war and during the U-Boots' evacuation cruise to Argentina. The most cooperative sailors (their names are documented) claimed that the U-Boots did not carry fugitive German politicians (criminals), high ranking military officials nor prisoners of war. They would also insist that nobody left the deck during the several thousand miles of the submarines' voyage from Europe to South America. Did they tell the truth or maybe they wanted to mislead the investigators? Were the submariners part of the conspiracy of silence? That was the case of at least one U-Boot which is discussed in another chapter of the book.

Uki Goñi, an Argentine writer, journalist and an experienced Reuter's correspondent wrote in the 1960s:

In Argentina, where I live, there are many reports concerning uptight men in Nazi uniforms disembarking rubber dinghies on the shores of Patagonia right after the end of the war. At night, large boxes allegedly laden with gold (stolen by the Nazis) and Hitler's secret documents were taken from the windy beaches and transported inland to isolated hideouts in the Andes. According to these (mostly made up) stories, Hitler lived until his dying day in South Argentina where he was buried and his successor, Martin Bormann, settled nearby as a wealthy land owner, first in Chile than in Bolivia and finally in Argentina. [...]

In 1992, accompanied by camera flashes, the Peronist government, led by the President Carlos Menem, agreed to make the files concerning the Nazis available to Argentine researchers. Journalists from all over the world came to Buenos Aires hoping to find the truth hiding behind rumors about a mysterious pact between Perón and Hitler. However, no discoveries were made.

Reporters and researchers found only a pile of old "intelligence" documents containing faded press clippings that included almost no new information. Documents concerning Bormann [...] contained a newspaper article talking about his alleged arrival to Argentina aboard a submarine. [...] The journalists were disappointed with the declassified documents but the researchers quietly (but with content) admitted that the lack of documents seemed to confirm the theory, widespread among scientists, about non-existence of Odessa[23] *and about the Nazis' individual attempts to evacuate who, in their search of escape routes, did not have any organized assistance*[24].

When in May 1945, the war in Europe ended, not all submarine crews operating on different oceans and seas under the Grossadmiral Karl Dönitz command, followed the Führer's last order calling for them to stop all hostilities and abort all combat operations. U-Boots were to immediately return to one of the Norwegian harbors. According to the Allied instructions, submarines were to raise a black flag atop their periscope mast and turn on navigation lights at night as a sign of capitulation. There is no doubt that two German commanders, who were in their twenties at the time, having consulted the issue with their crews, intended neither to surrender to the Americans nor to the British, not to mention surrendering their submarines and themselves to the Soviets. They decided to flee to Argentina.

Did countries in South America, mainly Argentina and Uruguay, give them refuge? Was their decision not to surrender to the Allies forced by the fact that their U-Boots carried the Nazi criminals who would find safe haven in the new distant land? Why did the butchers seek safety from justice there?[25] What, following 1945, made Argentina the favorite place among the Nazi criminals?

Financial cooperation between the Third Reich and Argentina began during the war. We are talking about German companies, banks and private assets. Already in 1942, Joseph Goebbels, the Reich Minister of Propaganda, deposited over 12.8 million dollars in one of the banks in Buenos Aires. As far as placement of funds is concerned, for the Nazis, Argentina was the number two country right after Switzerland. The Kriegsmarine submarines would allegedly arrive at the Rio de la Plata area on numerous occasions. According to local witnesses, the steel predators were filled with gold, silver and diamonds which were guarded by German agents. The size of the wealth is unknown.

In January 1845, Stanley Ross, the Overseas News Agency[26] correspondent in Buenos Aires reported that U-Boots' activity increased significantly. They carried millions of dollars of the German spoils of war that were to help the Nazis. Ross wrote:

A German submarine surfaced off the Argentine coast near Mar del Plata. A tugboat belonging to the Delfino shipping line from Buenos Aires was seen carrying about

---

[23] ODESSA (Organisation der ehemaligen SS-Angehörigen), organization of former SS members that was allegedly formed at the end of the war with the initiative of Heinrich Himmler and former members of the Reich Security Service, whose task was to help war criminals escape from the pursuing Allies.

[24] U. Goñi, *Prawdziwa Odessa. Jak Peron sprowadził hitlerowskich zbrodniarzy do Argentyny*, Zakrzewo 2016, p. 19-21.

[25] The Nazi and semi-Nazi organizations existed not only in Argentina and Brazil but also in Peru, Chile, Paraguay, Uruguay and Colombia - almost all countries of the continent.

[26] The Overseas News Agency was a secret British propaganda operation conducted as part of the British - American cooperation.

German Type VII medium size submarine during the a combat patrol
in the Atlantic Ocean in 1940.

Grand Admiral Karl Dönitz, responsible
for both the rise and fall of the German
submarine fleet during World War II.

U 664, under command of Lt. Adolf Graef,
was sunk in the North Atlantic by depth
charges and strafing of two Avengers and
one Wildcat aircraft (VC-1 USN) of the
escort aircraft carrier USS Card.

British escort aircraft carrier HMS *Vindex*, commissioned in 1944.

US destroyer escort USS *John C. Butler* (1,350 t), commissioned in 1944.

US destroyer USS *Hopkins* (1,190 t). Following a conversion, during World War II, she served as high-speed minesweeper.

In 1944, the most spectacular patrols of U-Boot aces were nothing more than history.

British escort aircraft carrier HMS *Ruler* (11,200 t), ex. USS *St. Joseph*, in a 1944 photograph.

Sloop HMS *Starling* (Black Swan class, after modifications), commissioned in April 1943. Famous for taking part in the battle of the Atlantic.

U 534 in a 1945 photograph.

Type II B U-Boot – *U 24*, scuttled near the coast of Turkey, in vicinity of Zonguldak in August 1944. Eighteen of her crewmen were interned in Turkey. The photo shows her in the 1930s.

German Type II submarine *U 9* in a photograph taken in the late 1930s.

US submarine chaser *PC 461* (280 t), commissioned in 1942.

The 105 mm deck gun and conning tower of *U 177*.

Snorkel was invented to allow the submarines to make long, safe passages. The photo of *U 889* (Type IX C/40) shows the electro-pneumatic operated snorkel mast.

US escort aircraft carrier USS *Hollandia* (Casablanca class) of 8,700 tons.

US escort aircraft carrier USS *Block Island*.

The survivors from *U 515* (Type IX C) are being rescued. The German submarine was sunk in the North Atlantic in April 1944, by rockets from two Avenger and two Wildcat aircraft of the US escort aircraft carrier USS *Guadalcanal* and depth charges from US destroyer escorts *Chatelain*, *Flaherty*, *Pillsbury* and *Pope*.

U 505, the first warship in 20th century captured by boarding by the US Navy.

June 1944, US destroyer escort USS *Pillsbury* (in the background) with the German submarine *U 505*.

37 and 20 mm anti-aircraft guns of Type VII C submarine.

In October 1944, for the first time during World War II, the Allies did not loose any merchantmen in the Atlantic Ocean or in the adjacent seas. At that time, as many as 141 German submarines of various classes were operating in the Atlantic, the Arctic Sea, the Baltic and the Indian Ocean. The photograph shows the conning tower of Type IX submarine. A single 20 mm anti-aircraft gun is visible.

Final moments of one of the Hitler's workhorses. On May 24, 1944, *U 675* was sunk in the Norwegian Sea by depth charges from a British Short Sunderland flying boat of the No.4 Coastal Operational Training Unit RAF.

U-boots moored at Portsmouth, USA. The long-range cargo submarine *U 234* is the one the right with her mine shafts converted into cargo holds visible on deck and in the sides. The ocean-going Type IX D2 submarine *U 873* can be seen on the left. The photograph was taken in 1945.

From the right: U 3008 (Type XXI), surrendered at Kiel in May 1945.

German submarines *U 1234* and *U 1235*.

From the left: U 2513 (Type XXI), surrendered at Horton in May 1945. Later US prize.
The photograph was taken in 1944.

On May 14, 1945, *U 805*, under command of Commander Richard Bernardelli, surrendered by entering the base at Portsmouth, USA. The photo shows US Navy sailors after the takeover of the German submarine.

Allied freighter is sinking after being hit by a torpedo fired by a U-Boot.

Karl Dönitz, long-serving Commander in Chief of the U-Bootwaffe and Kriegsmarine, sentenced to ten years' imprisonment during the Nuremberg Trials.

German Type XXI (*U 2511*) and Type VII submarines at Bergen, Norway in May 1945.

Surrender of 42 U-Boots at Lisahally base in Norther Ireland, June 1945. The submarines are prepared to be scuttled as part of Operation Deadlight.

Adolf Hitler during a meeting with Grand Admiral Karl Dönitz, the architect of the U-Bootwaffe's might during World War II.

In February 1945, German submarines brought a valuable cargo consisting of currency and precious stones – rough and cut diamonds to the shores of San Matias Bay on the coast of Argentina. The photograph shows one of the U-Boots during a wartime cruise.

In October 1946, Martin Bormann was tried in absentia and sentenced to death by
the International Military Tribunal. The photo shows Adolf Hitler accompanied by his
personal secretary Bormann.

Type IX C/40 submarine *U 530* in a 1945 photograph.

Juan Domingo Perón (1895
-1974) - Argentinian general
and politician.

Swedish freighter *Milos*.

The Third Reich Naval Intelligence
Headquarters was established in Buenos
Aires. During the war, it transmitted detailed
information concerning the movements of
Allied merchant and naval vessels in the South
Atlantic to the Kriegsmarine command using
undercover radio stations. The photograph
shows U-Boots on the way to hunt…

Spanish journalist and diplomat
Ángel Alcázar de Velasco (1909-
2001) was a long-time German spy
and collaborator of the Japanese
military intelligence service.

Johann S. Becker, recognized
by the Americans as one of the
most dangerous spies in South
America.

The *U 530* (Type IX C/40) submarine can be seen
in the background. On July 10, 1945, the German
submarine surrendered by entering the Argentinian
submarine base at Mar del Plata. In the foreground,
the Argentinian depot ship *General Belgrano*.

M.N.L95–1939   J.H.A.

                                                                                H

ISSUED BY THE INTELLIGENCE DIVISION
OFFICE OF CHIEF OF NAVAL OPERATIONS
NAVY DEPARTMENT

RESTRICTED

INTELLIGENCE REPORT

Serial ___R-197-45___
(Start new series each year, i. e. 1–45, 2–45)

Monograph Index Guide No. ___915-400___
(To correspond with SUBJECT given below. See O. N. I. Index Guide.)
(Make separate report for each main title.)

From ___Naval Attaché___ at ___Buenos Aires___ Date ___18 July___ 45
(Ship, fleet, unit, district, office, station or person)

Reference (a) ___Alusna Baires Conf.Disp. 172323 of July 1945___
(b) N.A. Baires R-195-45 (Dispatch, file number, etc.) (Report, subject and serial, cover page, etc., if applicable)

Source ___Official press release - Official___ Evaluation ___A-1___
(Is official, personal observation, publication, press, conversation, etc.)
Identify when practicable, etc.)

Subject ___Argentina___ ___Navy___ ___Movements of Enemy Vessels___
(Nation reported on) (Main title as per Index guide) (Subtitles) (Make separate report for each title)

BRIEF—(Here enter careful summary of report, containing substance succinctly stated; include important facts, names, places, dates, etc.)

The Argentine Government has resolved to place the surrendered German submarine, U-530, her crew, the reports
and the findings of the Argentine naval authorities with
regard to her arrival and surrender at the disposal of
the United States and British Governments.

– –

Dr. Cesar Ameghino, the Argentine Minister of Foreign
Affairs, yesterday announced the Government's decision to place
the surrendered German submarine, U-530, her crew, and the reports and findings of the Argentine naval authorities with regard to her arrival and surrender at the disposal of the United
States and British Governments, adding that it had been arrived
at earlier in the day at a special Cabinet meeting convoked to
consider the question.

The Minister of Foreign Affairs stated that it had been
resolved to deliver the submarine to the United States and British
Governments in view of the fact that the Supreme Command of the
Allied Expeditionary Forces, to whom the submarine should have
surrendered, had been dissolved, and that the Supreme Command
depended from these two nations. A translation of the decree
reads as follows:

"Reviewing the surrender of the German submarine, U-530,
to the Argentine naval authorities at the submarine base
at Mar del Plata, and considering:

"That, according to the report made by the Ministry of
Foreign Affairs that following the unconditional surrender
of Germany, the forces of air, land and sea should have
been delivered in accordance with the terms established
by the Allies,

Distribution By Originator ___Comsolant; NA's Uruguay, Brazil___

Routing space below for use O. N. I.   RESTRICTED

A-3-e   CominCh
Mono   BAD
State   Op-20-G
NID   PA-4
IADB
Op-17
Op-13
FBI
B-7
IG-Z
IG-FT
USCG

A copy of the U.S. intelligence report stating that the *U 530* submarine, its crew, reports and
the results of the investigation carried out by the Argentinian Navy authorities would be at
the disposal of the U.S. and the British governments. The document from the collection of
the National Archives and Records Administration at College Park, Maryland (USA).

Captain Peter Gretton.

On April 5, 1943, *U 530* (Lt.Cdr. Kurt Lange) sank the American tanker *Sunoil* (9,005 GRT) with three torpedoes at the position 58°16'N and 34°14'W.

The crew of *U 530* in the German submarine base in Brest, a photograph taken in 1942.

On December 26, 1943, the *U 530* damaged the American tanker *Chapultepec* (10,195 GRT) about 100-150 miles north of Colon in Panama (10°30'N and 78°58'W).

In March 1945, seven more Type IX U-boots departed from Norway. These were: *U 518* (in the photo), *U 546*, *U 805*, *U 858*, *U 880*, *U 881* and *U 1235*. Following the order of the Kriegsmarine High Command, they formed the "Seewolf" wolfpack.

In February 1945, Lt. Otto Wermuth was appointed the new commander of *U 530*.

U 530 in Argentina, a photo taken in July 1945.

U.S. escort aircraft carrier USS *Bogue*.

From the left: the submarines *U 1234* and *U 1235* (which was assigned to the "Seewolf" wolfpack ordered to destroy Allied shipping off eastern coast of the United States, south of New York).

WERMUTH refused to state whether or not the U-530 was alone or a member of a flotilla, but did say that he operated directly from Berlin. He was ordered to proceed to his combat area to attack enemy shipping, but refused to state the location of that area.

He said that he left Christiansand on 3 March 1945 and proceeded to Horten (Oslo Fjord), Norway, where for some reason not stated he remained for ten days. At the end of that time he sailed for his combat area. He stated that he did not know the route chosen, but that it was to the north of England and that to reach it they traveled continuously submerged for approximately three weeks, charging their batteries at night by means of the Schnorkel device, with which the U-530 is equipped. This undersea travel was for the purpose of avoiding air attacks which he stated were terrible.

WERMUTH said that while in his combat area, as was the common procedure, he did not report attacks made or received. His only radio messages sent were daily weather reports. He said that the last contact that he had with his commanding officer in Berlin was on 26 April, which was a message concerning defensive measures to be taken.

He stated that he received a message over his regular wave length to cease hostilities on 8 May. Subsequently he changed this date to 10 May. These messages were received for several days, according to him. These messages instructed all submarines to cease attacks, to use navigation lights at night, to fly a blue flag, to travel only on the surface, and to proceed to the nearest United Nations port for surrender. Further, they ordered that detonators be removed from all torpedoes, that mines be immunized, and that all ammunition be dumped overboard.

WERMUTH stated that he did not believe these orders to be official but, rather, to be an enemy trick.

Whether he did or not, he attached sufficient weight to them to decide to quit his zone of action, according to his testimony, and intern his submarine and crew in some neutral country. He said that Portugal and Spain were discarded as being too close to the battle zone. He said that at that time, though they knew that Argentina had broken diplomatic relations with Germany, they did not know that they had declared war and that he decided to come here for internment because it was far from the fighting zone and because he thought they would get better treatment here. He said that he did not learn that this country had declared war until he arrived in Mar del Plata.

He stated that immediately upon receiving the surrender orders (which he considered false) they quit their attack zone and that at that time they were approximately 1000 miles east-northeast of Puerto Rico. They ran for some time underwater, for fear of aerial attack, and throughout the whole voyage ran underwater during the daylight hours. He stated that they passed between the Rocks of Saints Peter and Paul and the island of San Fernando Naronha and that on 17 June 1945 they crossed the Equator.

xHxxxxxd

Enclosure (A)
NA BAires R-201-45   -2-   CONFIDENTIAL

Copy (page 2) of Lt. Wermuth's testimony following the internment of *U 530* in Argentina in July 1945. The document is held by the National Archives and Records Administration at College Park, Maryland, USA.

On July 14, 1945, one of Argentinian newspapers published thrilling news that *U 530* brought Adolf Hitler from Europe.

Argentinian editors got the wind of a sensational subject and immediately reacted to the news of the appearance of *U 530* at Mar del Plata on July 10, 1945.

DECLASSIFIED
Authority NND 873041

… another page of the same article.

Another photo of the German submarine *U
530* at Mar del Plata in July 1945.

BASIC PERSONNEL RECORD
(Alien Enemy or Prisoner of War)

7G - 177 - NA
(Internment serial number)

F. P. C.* _____

WERMUTH, Otto Heinrich
(Name of internee)

Reference * _____

Male
(Sex)

Height **6** ft. _____ in.

Weight 63 kilograms

Eyes brown

Skin fair

Hair brown

Age 25

Distinguishing marks or characteristics:

birth mark (mole) on left hip

INVENTORY OF PERSONAL EFFECTS TAKEN FROM INTERNEE

1. _____
2. _____
3. _____
4. _____
5. _____
6. _____
7. _____
8. _____
9. _____
10. _____

The above is correct;

(Signature of internee)

7G-177-NA   7G-177-NA

1 Aug. 1945, DIO-7ND, Miami, Florida
(Date and place where processed (Army enclosure, naval station, or other place))

Right Hand

1. Thumb	2. Index finger	3. Middle finger	4. Ring finger	5. Little finger

Left Hand

6. Thumb	7. Index finger	8. Middle finger	9. Ring finger	10. Little finger

W. D., P. M. G. Form No. 2
December 9, 1941   16—25525-1

Note amputations in proper space

* Do not fill in.

A unique document – POW's ID card with Lt. Otto Wermuth's fingerprints...

A unique photograph of *U 350* taken in Argentina in August 1945.

1. Oberleutnant z. See
   (Grade and arm or service)
2. U-530
   (Hostile unit or vessel)
3. ___
   (Hostile serial number)
4. 28 July 1920 at **Aalen, Wuerttemberg, Germ.**
   (Date and country of birth)
5. Ludwigstrasse No. 1, Aalen, Wuertt., Germ.
   (Place of permanent residence)
6. Father: Otto Wermuth
   (Name, relationship of nearest relative [1])
7. Ludwigstrasse No. 1, Aaalen, Wuertt., Germ.
   (Address of above)
8. None
   (Number of dependents and relationship)
9. ___
   (Address of above)

10. **10 July 1945**
    (Date of capture or arrest)
11. **Mar del Plata, Argentine**
    (Place of capture or arrest)
12. ___
    (Unit or vessel making capture or arresting agency)
13. Graduate of "Oberrealschule"
    (Occupation)
14. Oberrealschule; Flottenoffiziersschule
    (Education)
15. German; French, English
    (Knowledge of languages)
16. good
    (Physical condition at time of capture or arrest)
17. single
    (Married or single)
18. cath.
    (Religious preference)

ADDITIONAL DATA:

Transferred from	Date depart	Transferred to	Date received	Official signature of receiving officer	Personal effects not transferred [2]
Santa Cruz	30 July	Miami, Fla.	1 Aug.	*W.M.Rehrstens*	
DIO-7ND USN	1 Aug.	PM U.S.Army	1 Aug.	*Robert J Pope*	

REMARKS:

[1] If no relative, name person to be notified in case of emergency.
[2] If personal effects taken from individual are not transferred, note exceptions and place of storage or depot.

GPO 16—25525—1

...second part of the same document. Photograph taken at National Archives and Records Administration at College Park, Maryland, USA.

Thanks to declassification of the files by the FBI, we know that the first reports concerning.... Hitler's presence in Argentina date back to the end of May 1945. One of such notes, dated August 14, 1945, was prepared by the FBI field office in Los Angeles.

CONFIDENTIAL

CONFIDENTIAL

7. (B-2) At 4 pm on 7 June 1945, an individual unknown to any of the habitués of the port area arrived at the port of Mar del Plata aboard the shark fishing boat "Juncal" and left immediately for Buenos Aires. This man appeared to be from 40 to 45 years of age, 6'6" tall, thin, blond, partly bald, and with a large nose. The "Juncal" is a 17-meter ocean-going fishing boat with a speed of 13 knots and can and does stay at sea from three to four days at a time. She has sleeping space for five and is at sea a great deal, but brings in very few sharks.

(B-2) At 6 pm on 5 July 1945, the ocean-going yacht "San Lorenzo" put in at the port of Mar del Plata with persons aboard who were entirely unknown to the fishermen of the port area.

8. (B-3) A Nazi agent, known to have been in the employ of Pedro ILVESTO, who was considered one of Juan Sigfrido BECKER's right-hand men, was seen in Miramar, south of Mar del Plata, the first week in July. It is unusual for anyone to go to this resort town during the winter unless they have some unusual business in mind.

9. (B-2) At about 3 pm on 17 July 1945, two submarines were sighted some three kilometers off General Lavalle, halfway between Buenos Aires and Mar del Plata. Visibility was such that they could not be identified but at 4 pm they were reported to be heading for Mar del Plata escorted by Argentine navy planes. On the morning of 18 July, the Argentine Navy denied that there were any German submarines, other than the U-530, in Argentine waters.

10. The above rumors are being investigated and further reports will be submitted. A careful interrogation of the crew (four of whom have Polish names) by experts will probably furnish the best evidence as to whether or not the sub actually landed passengers.

0106 D. F. GIBBONS
Major, Cavalry
Asst. Military Attaché

Approved and forwarded

A. R. HARRIS
Brig Gen, USA
Military Attaché

DFG/sa

In the first days of June 1945, the FBI office in Buenos Aires was informed by a secret collaborator that on the seventh day of the month, at 4 p.m., two unknown men were seen – one of them was a tall, balding man, over forty years old. They had got off the seventeen-meter-long fishing boat *Juncal*.

Lt. Wermuth's Argentinian ID card from the collection of the National Archives and Records Administration at College Park, Maryland, USA.

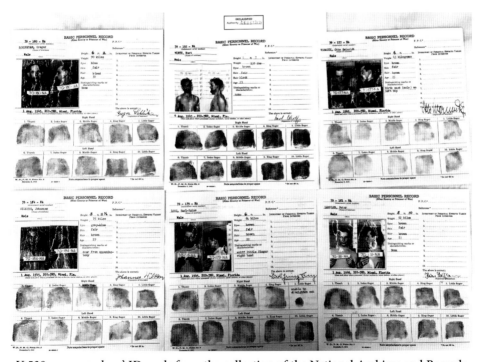

U 530 crew members' ID cards from the collection of the National Archives and Records Administration at College Park, Maryland, USA.

F.B.I. RADIOGRAM

DECODED COPY

Mr. E. A. Tamm___
Mr. Clegg_____
Mr. Coffey_____
Mr. Glavin_____
Mr. Ladd_____
Mr. Nichols_____
Mr. Rosen_____
Mr. Tracy_____
Mr. Carson_____
Mr. Egan_____
Mr. Hendon_____
Mr. Pennington___
Mr. Quinn Tamm___
Mr. Nease_____
Miss Gandy_____

FROM BUENOS AIRES ▮▮▮▮▮ NR 134 ▮▮▮▮▮

REPORT HITLER IN ARGENTINA. DATA AVAILABLE THIS OFFICE CONTAINED
IN REPORT OF SPECIAL AGENT ▮▮▮▮▮ JULY 18 ENTITLED SURRENDER
OF GERMAN SUB U 530, MAR DEL PLATA. CONCERNING RUMOR RE LANDING
SAN JULIAN, ARGENTINA, ▮▮▮▮▮ THERE NOW REPORTS HE
DISCOVERED TWO SETS FOOT PRINTS LEADING IN ONE DIRECTION ONLY
FROM HIGH WATER MARK THEN ACROSS MUD FLATS TO SHORE PROPER NEAR
SAN JULIAN. AT POINT WHERE FOOT PRINTS ENDED TIRE MARKS FOUND
INDICATING CAR HAD BEEN TURNED AT RIGHT ANGLE TO SHORE. FOOT
PRINTS MUST HAVE BEEN MADE ABOUT JUNE 25 WHILE FLATS COVERED WITH
FLOOD WATERS AS AREA FROZEN THIS TIME OF YEAR. EFFORTS BEING
MADE TO TRACE CAR. INQUIRIES CONTINUING AT VERONICA.

RECEIVED ▮▮▮▮▮ ▮▮▮▮▮

RECORDED 65-53615-7X

FEDERAL BUREAU OF INVESTIGATION
AUG 1 1945
U. S. DEPARTMENT OF JUSTICE

EX. 22

ORIGINAL COPY FILED IN

If the intelligence contained in the above message is to be disseminated
outside the Bureau, it is suggested that it be suitably paraphrased in
order to protect the Bureau's cryptographic systems.

Declassified document, which was prepared by an FBI agent No. 134 in Buenos Aires
in August 1945.

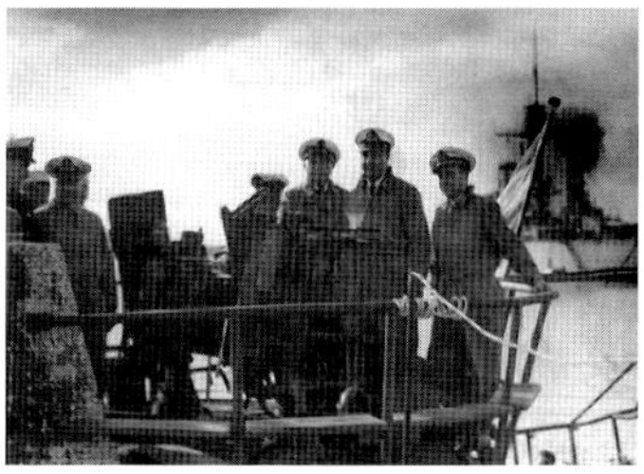

Argentinian officers inspecting *U 530*
at Mar del Plata, July 1945.

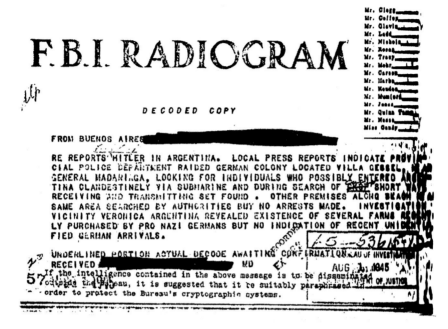

FBI radiogram from the Buenos Aires office (without decryption date) - additional information concerning reports of the presence of German fugitives in the town of Veronica.

Personal belongings of the *U 530* crew members and an excerpt from an article about the escape of the U-boot from Europe to South America.

F. 561

Sigismund Kolasinski

Neg. fotog. N.º .075

N.º Secc. .086

Pront. ...

Fotografía tomada el mes de 12 de Julio *de 194*5

.... N⁰ ----

Domicilio.. N⁰ ....   *Labios* medianos

Estatura 1, 69 *ctms.*

Cuerpo normal   *Orejas* medianas

Color {
del cutis blanco
del cabello castaño
de la barba afeitada
}

Individual dactiloscópica V-3333 - I-2222

Instrucción primaria

Aspecto social en la vida ordinaria humilde

SEÑAS PARTICULARES

....
....
....
....
....

ID card of Seaman Sigismund Kolasinski's of *U 530*.

40 boxes and Willi Koehn, the German chief of the Latin America department in the Foreign Ministry. He met the leader of the Nazi party in Chile and other high ranking agents and collaborators in Buenos Aires[27].

In winter 1945, six German submarines[28], as part of the „Aktion Feuerland" („Operation Fireland"), brought to the shores of the San Matias Bay in Argentina a secret cargo of huge value, designated with number 17-44. It comprised: 187,692,400 German marks, 17,576,386 US dollars, 4,682,500 Italian liras, 24,976,442 Swiss francs, 8,370,000 Dutch florins, 17,281,000 pounds sterling, 54,968,000 French francs, 87 (100?) kg of platinum, 2.7 (16?) t of gold, 4,683 carats of diamonds and rough diamonds and hundreds of works of art[29]. Apart from the precious cargo the submarines carried the Third Reich's top ranking officials who were transported to an undisclosed enclave or estancia (kind of agricultural homestead in North Argentina) called Monte Riera[30]. In the 1960s the Argentine Committee for Anti-Argentine Activity, using information gathered by the country's intelligence services, proved that the abovementioned Third Reich treasure had been delivered to Ludwig Freude[31], an Argentine banker of German descent, closely connected with the Nazis, collaborating with the Abwehr in Buenos Aires. The millionaire was one of four trustees of the treasure which was deposited in the treasuries of the German Transatlantic Bank, Tornquist Bank and Strupp Bank. All deposits were placed under the name of Juan Domingo Perón and his future wife Maria Eva Duarte de Perón. After the money had been deposited, Feude was accused of numerous criminal offences[32]. In September 1946, the investigation was suddenly aborted. According to the official statement, it happened upon the Argentine president's order.

Although the size of the precious cargo does not raise any doubts, it could not have been brought by *U 530* (Type IX C/40). On October 4, 1944, the U-Boot commanded by LtCdr. Kurt Lange, after returning from her sixth combat patrol, was

---

[27] S. Dunstan, G. Williams, *Grey Wolf. The Escapade of Adolf Hitler*, New York 2011, p. 229.

[28] H. Thomas, *Sobowtór. Tajemnice berlińskiego bunkra*, Warszawa 1997, p. 198. In his book, I. Witkowski, *Supertajne bronie Hitlera. Tropem złota i ostatnich broni*, vol. 4, Warszawa 2000, p. 77 and 160 writes that it was only *U 530*. The same author, in *Hitler w Argentynie i Czwarta Rzesza*, Warszawa 2009, p. 46 and 100-101, is not certain whether it is that particular German submarine.

[29] S. Dunstan, G. Williams, *Grey Wolf. The Escapade of Adolf Hitler…*, p. 264; H. Thomas, *Sobowtór. Tajemnice berlińskiego bunkra…*, p. 198.

[30] A. Omilianowicz, *Dolina wilków*, Przekrój", from April 17 and 24, 1985.

[31] L. Freude was a close friend of Perón's, responsible for coordinating the fund raising operations for his presidential campaign in 1946. The money came from different companies connected with the Nazis.

[32] In 1952 Freude was found dead at a set table; for breakfast he had drunk poisoned coffee. The second of the trustees was Ricardo Staudt, a known businessman, the second man on the American list of the top Nazis residing in South America – died hit by an unidentified driver. The third trustee died in dramatic circumstances – body of murdered Ricardo von Leute, employee of the Banco Alemán Transatlántico, was found in Buenos Aires 1950. The fourth trustee – Dr Heinrich Dorge, advisor to the Nazi financier, Hjalmar Schacht, met similar fate as his comrades. He was murdered in 1949 and his body was dumped on a street in Buenos Aires.

assigned to the 33. U-Flottille in Flensburg[33]. During the next months, according to documents and western historians, the submarine's line duty is not mentioned. For over four months the U-Boot was not sent to combat patrols. We know that the ship was sent for overhaul. Officially, it was not until February 19, 1945, when the submarine, commanded by Lt. Otto Wermuth, left the Kiel harbor and headed for Norway. Then, at the beginning of March she went for her seventh and last combat mission which ended in mid July in Argentina.

There are many indications that U-Boots conducted further transport missions taking huge amounts of valuables from Germany to South America or trying to deliver them to Japan. The author of the book *Hitler in Argentina, the Fourth Reich* writes:

This information comes from a testimony of a single witness, inhabitant of a former German enclave, isolated from the world in Chile [...] and it is hard to recognize it as a proof. However, the witness demanded anonymity which speaks in his favor. The information coming from him is directly confirmed by materials of the Chilean secret service that talk about a very similar transport. That is why this information is worthy of mention.

It says that in 1945, a submarine entered one of the Patagonian bays (the southern coast of Chile is also Patagonia) carrying a cargo of: 250,000 gold coins, mainly golden pounds sterling, 20 gold bars weighing 12 kg each, 2,000,000 US dollars in banknotes, 2,000,000 Swiss francs in banknotes, jewel boxes containing diamonds from Namibia (former German South-West Africa), paintings, collections of rare postage stamps and technical documentation of secret weapons[34].

It turns out that not only Argentina's remote location but also its political climate was conducive to German scientists and war criminals. They ran away to a safe stronghold from the punishing hand of justice:

After the Axis defeat, the Argentineans were very eager to recruit specialists from Germany. It was a solid financial investment. Argentina covered just the travel costs while Germany invested millions in training of scientists and technicians[35].

It is worth mentioning that between 1946 and 1955, the president of Argentina was Juan Domingo Perón who introduced dictatorship. This general and politician had a quiet agreement with the fascists dating back to 1939-1941 when he was the Argentine military attaché in Italy and Germany. It is not a secret that during his stay in Europe he became fascinated with the Italian leader of the fascist movement,

---

[33] R. Busch, H-J. Röll, *Der U-Boot-Krieg 1939-1945. Der U-Boat-Bau auf Deutschen Werften*, vol. 2, Hamburg-Berlin-Bonn 1997, p. 369; K. Wynn, *U-Boat Operations of the Second World War*, vol. 2, London 2003, p. 17.

[34] I. Witkowski, *Hitler w Argentynie...*, p. 105-106. See also: A. Basti, *Dicen que El oro nazi ingreso en submarinos*, Manana del Sur, from December 6, 1996.

[35] G. Steinacher, *Zbiegli naziści...*, p. 273.

Benito Mussolini and the idea of leadership which he later put into practice. Upon his return to the country, Perón took part in a military coup d'etat organized in June 1943 by pro-fascist officers. As the Minister of War and later vice president of Argentina, from July 1944 Perón was in good relations with the most influential people in the Third Reich. His close contacts with the elite were facilitated by his knowledge of the German language and the fact that he had graduated from the Military Academy in Berlin. His collaboration with the Security Service SS (Sicherheitsdienst)[36] agents resulted in gaining access to secret information concerning countries of South America. In return, he guaranteed an asylum and peaceful life after the war for the Nazis in Argentina.

At the end of the war, Argentina became the country of very high hopes for the leaders of the falling Third Reich. It was the country with very liberal attitude towards economic relationships with the Axis countries (Germany, Italy and Japan). For a long time the country had had strong economic ties with Germany which enabled creation of secret channels for trade exchange that later turned into evacuation channels. This situation was a result of multiple overlapping factors. First of all, it was made possible by personal contacts between high ranking German politicians with members of the Argentine establishment, mainly connected with the military and people around the president Edelmiro Farrell (he was in the office from February 1944 to June 1946) who introduced military junta rule.

There were many more reasons Argentina was so popular among the Nazis. Lew Bezymienski writes about them:

Among the Germans living there, there were about 50 thousand former citizens of the Third Reich. [...] 11 thousand of them were earlier directly controlled by the "foreign organization" NSDAP, led by Gauleiter Wilhelm Bohle. [...] During the war, the intelligence [German - M.B., P.W.] was based there. And finally - for a long time, the place had been the home for Argentine fascist organizations.

As early as at the end of 1944, officers of the Nazi regime began arriving at Argentina to seek refuge especially when fat accounts had been opened in numerous banks of Buenos Aires. Other measures had also been taken, particularly those concerning the intelligence and the SS. A very important role was played by the Ibero-American Institute in Berlin which was the center of the Nazi movement in Latin America[37].

A strong and very influential German emigration had always existed in Argentina. It was connected with powerful land owners and industry, including arms industry, traditionally associated with military circles. A huge role was played by traditional anti-USA sympathies and a need to find possibilities to create a counterbalance, an

---

[36] K. Grünberg, *SS Gwardia Hitlera*, Warszawa 1994; H. Höhne, *Zakon trupiej czaszki*, Warszawa 2006; A. Ramme, *Służba Bezpieczeństwa SS*, Warszawa 1975.

[37] L. Bezymienski, *Śladami Martina Bormanna...*, p. 126-127.

alternative potential in face of the growing US influence on the continent and the expected US expansionism in Latin America. With the war coming to an end, the influence was growing which paradoxically increased the pro-German sentiment in certain circles of the Argentine authorities.

At the end of the war, Argentina was wealthy economically and had no debt (for the first time in its history). Argentina became one of the leading food producers and its coal industry placed it among the top mining countries in the world. Meanwhile, nations actively engaged in the war favored mainly the armaments industry. In the first years of the war, 70% of the Argentine export went to Great Britain and the trade in food products and raw materials with the USA was booming. Argentina tried to remain neutral almost until the end of the war in Europe.

At the end of the mid 1940s, Argentina was on the path of fast development and intensive modernization. Its subsequent leaders intended to introduce their homeland to the group of developed and industrialized countries. Perón dreamed of a strong, militarized country. The chance to develop Argentina's industry and to make its arms production self sufficient was increased by inviting superb German engineers, doctors, jet aircraft constructors, nuclear technology experts and mid-level technical staff to South American continent. For recruitment, Perón's diplomats liked to employ Argentineans of German origin. Cooperating with the SS members and Italian smugglers of people, they organized an efficient system of official and also illegal recruitment in Italy. It is not a mystery that the SS members with their extensive contacts wanted to realize their own goals and they were far less interested in recruiting specialists for Perón than helping their old comrades (war criminals and the SS officers with tarnished past) cross borders.

It was Perón who intended to change the traditional Argentinean society into an industrial one after introducing economy based on mechanization of production governed according to plan with use of certain management methods. When Perón came to power, his dream for Argentina was to achieve self sufficiency in the armament industry but the country faced problems recruiting suitable specialists.

Perón did not care about the fact that after the war hundreds of Nazis escaped from Europe through the "back door" and found refuge in Argentina. Importing war criminals was not the official policy for the Argentine leader but an acceptable practice. "Contrary to the occupying powers, the Argentineans could not employ specialists from Germany and Austria officially so a plan was conceived to take advantage of the refugee chaos in Europe" said Gerald Steinacher from the University of Nebraska-Lincoln[38]. The American professor of History and Judaism continues:

Because many emigrants wanted to leave Europe via Italian harbors, the Argentineans concentrated their efforts in Italy. The Argentine consular representatives in

---

[38] G. Steinacher, *Zbiegli naziści...*, p. 265.

Genoa and Rome were tasked with recruitment and a special committee was sent to Italy. Recruiters talked to refugees in Italy or smuggled them there though the border. Between 1946 and 1955, Argentina and other countries conducted active operations in northern Italy making the region a kind of "Germany's kitchen courtyard"[39].

It is easy to conclude that pragmatism suppressed ideology unless it was the case of communism which, for Perón, was the most serious threat. Fascism was for the 50-year-old Argentine politician an unsuccessful attempt to defeat communism. Contrary to other representatives of the "free world" he viewed the USA more like a menace than a savior of mankind.

It was not until long after the war when president Perón confessed to the true nature of the mechanism of contacts with the Third Reich and talked about the Nazis' evacuation to Argentina in 1945 and the following years. The main goal was the country's modernization:

Long before the end of the war we had been ready for the post-war period. Germany was defeated, we knew that, and the victors wanted to take advantage of huge technological progress that country had made during the previous decade. Industrial plants could not be used as they had been destroyed. The only thing to be used were people and it was them we were interested in[40].

Later Perón remembers:

We informed the Germans that we were going to declare war on them to save thousands of people's lives [German lives - M.B., P.W.]. We exchanged messages via Sweden and Spain. Franco immediately understood our intentions and helped us. The Germans also agreed. When the war ended the same Germans helped us build new factories and improve those we had. In time, we helped them[41].

Fighter pilot and close friend of Perón's, Colonel Adolf Galland[42], one of the most colorful characters in the Luftwaffe, wrote:

In this situation, inactivity of many German scientists, technicians and other specialists after 1945 was in favor of Argentina. It also secured what Argentina invested in them. German specialists who came to Argentina did it on their own will and had a

---

[39] Ibidem, p. 265.

[40] H. Meding, *Flucht vor Nürnberg? Deutsche und österreichische Einwanderung in Argentinien 1945-1955*, Köln 1992, p. 87.

[41] Quoted from: I. Witkowski, *Hitler w Argentynie...*, p. 16. See also: A. Basti, *Bariloche nazi*, Argentina 2004 (self published).

[42] Invited by Perón he participated in pilot training and creation of aviation schools for the Argentine Air Force between 1948 and 1955.

feeling that not only were they treated fairly but they also served the country that had accepted them kindly and without bias, simultaneously serving their fatherland[43].

When the war broke out, Argentina did not take any sides. Like during World War I, it proclaimed neutrality. that policy allowed the country to drive huge financial profits from different fractions. In February 1945, the vice-president and minister of war Perón met leaders of the influential German minority in Buenos Aires who were very enthusiastic about the Third Reich and announced that Argentina was going to abandon its neutrality and declare war on Germany. It was just a formality. During the meeting Perón made it clear that he did not intend to leave the German minority behind[44]. Moreover, Perón considered his friendship for Germany and citizens of other Axis countries his duty and that is why he helped all those who wanted to start a new life in Argentina regardless of what they did during the war.

It was an open secret that it was Argentina that gave refuge to the Nazi intelligence and that it was the base for secret military operations conducted in the Western Hemisphere. Buenos Aires was also the center of the Third Reich's naval intelligence that conveyed information to the Kriegsmarine command via a network of secret radio stations. The information concerning movement of Allied ships and warships in the South Atlantic helped coordinate U-Boot operations in the area.

At the end of March 1945, under tremendous pressure of the United States, Argentina joined the anti-Nazi coalition, which was a well thought out decision, and... became the refuge for war criminals escaping from the old continent. Since Argentina joined the Allies (as the last to declare war on Germany), they no longer kept their watchful eye on the country. All operations were conducted in secrecy and only very few people closest to president Farrell and his successor Perón were informed about specific actions. All undertakings became classified. The police was not initiated into the subject of "transfer routes" and further life of German war criminals and other SS members (with new identity). Among fugitives there were specialists and educated people who could increase the development tempo of military research which was advantageous for further development of science, industry and economy in Argentina.

Perón considered the trials of Nazi Germany and Italian leaders in Nuremberg to be the "insult that history would never forgive" and assured that he would do everything in his power to help others to avoid the fate of the accused leaders. "He was less favorable to those who wanted to join the large Argentinean Jewish community" wrote Neal Bascomb[45].

The system of transporting Germans to South America was known only to the Argentine military intelligence which worked without cooperation with other insti-

---

[43] A. Galland, *Die Ersten Und die Letzten. Die Jagdflieger im Zweiten Weltkrieg*, München 1953, p. 9.

[44] N. Bascomb, *Wytropić Eichmanna...*, p. 114.

[45] N. Bascomb, *Wytropić Eichmanna...*, p. 115.

tutions of the state nor was it controlled by them. The key operations of smuggling Nazis to Argentina were supervised by the chief of the military intelligence cell, at the president's office, known as the „Division Informaciones" - Rodolfo Freude aka „Rudi", son of the abovementioned Ludwig Freude, rich Argentine business-man with extensive contacts with the Nazis. In 1946, Freude was appointed chief of Perón's Information Bureau and participated in financing the general's presidential campaign. Actions of the Argentine military intelligence and the Reich Main Se-curity Office (SD) concerning evacuation of German technology and people were coordinated by the long-term commander of the Navy, Vice-Admiral Mario Fincati (1865-1962).

The network also included Carlos Fuldner, a German with Argentinean roots, former captain of the SS, closely connected with Himmler, member of Perón's gov-ernment who was responsible for transferring Nazis to Argentina. In 1945, the for-mer SS agent was sent on a special mission to Madrid where he departed from to his native Buenos Aires. Three years later, he returned to Europe, as a special agent working for Perón, with a task of organizing assistance centers for Nazis in Genoa and Bern.

The abovementioned network also included members of the Waffen-SS, Abwehr and a Spanish journalist Ángel Alcázar de Velasco who had been actively working on the Iberian Peninsula for the German intelligence almost since the beginning of the war, recruiting agents. He closely cooperated with SS-Standartenführer (colo-nel) Karle-Eriche Kühlenthale[46] who, in the Kriegsorganisation (War Organization, the Abwehr representation), was responsible for recruitment and supervision of the most important liaisons (foreign spies) in England, USA, Canada, Portugal, North Africa, Gibraltar and France.

The Argentine intelligence also employed war criminals from Belgium, France, Czechoslovakia, Netherlands and Germany who repaid their debt of freedom by saving others. Agents would receive orders directly from Freude, from the Casa Ro-sada presidential palace in the very heart of Buenos Aires. As N. Bascomb writes:

Their task was to facilitate financial operations, bribing local officials, organizing hideouts and transport, obtaining residence permits and other documents from the immigrations office and Argentine consulates and coordinating operations with repre-sentatives of Vatican[47].

The closeness of the relations between Germany and Argentina before the begin-ning of the war can be proven by the existence of a permanent delegation of five Reichswehr officers in the Argentine General Headquarters (the Wehrmacht was

---

[46] See: D. Kahn, *Szpiedzy Hitlera. Niemiecki wywiad wojskowy w czasie II wojny światowej*, Warszawa 2004, p. 88 and others; https://pl.scribd.com/document/212550269/209029872-the-Factual-List-of-Nazis-Protected-by--Spain-Doc.

[47] N. Bascomb, *Wytropić Eichmanna...*, p. 116.

created in 1935 as the entirety of the Third Reich military forces) who acted as military advisers. Due to the Treaty of Versailles limitations, German officers advised unofficially as private individuals. It was an ideal way to gain influence by the Third Reich in South America.

However, the Germans did not play fair. They broke their relations with Argentina by sending a group of secret agents to that country. The most famous case was that of Carlos Leitner. The spy and the SD (organization that combined political and intelligence functions with a widespread internal and external information network) officer sent by the Berlin headquarters was one of top employees of the German intelligence in Argentina. In December 1944, agents of the Argentine counter-intelligence (Coordinacion Federal - a special cell working against the Nazi secret service) arrested Leitner. Similar situations took place very often until the end of the war - the Argentineans successfully uncovered the SD network. Soon after the scandal had broken out, the United States intelligence found out about the state of affairs. Soon after that, a foreign FBI branch was organized in Buenos Aires with a task to expose the SD residents. In spring of 1945, many SD agents were arrested in Argentina and Paraguay.

The extended network of German agents operating in Argentina was led by Cpt. Siegfried Becker who probably was one of the most cunning and effective Himmler's agents on the Western Hemisphere. Since 1943, he had been using false documents with a name of Juan Rodolfo and he was an Argentinean with British roots. During the war, he conspired along with Perón to overthrow the Allies-backed Bolivian government. Later he probably assisted the Nazis in bringing money to Argentina[48]. The declassified American and Argentine documents mention a Hans Harnish - the Abwehr and SD collaborator working mainly with economy intelligence. Other sources name the SS officer Wolf Franczok as responsible for communications network. The Americans discovered that the most active German spy in Argentina was Pablo Klemme who was thought to be the Gestapo officer. The secret Nazi police had its intelligence cells in neutral countries and in the USA.

At the end of the war, substantial amounts of money began to flow from Germany to Argentina. Witkowski writes about this:

On December 16 [1944 – M.B., P.W.] an information surprised the Americans stating that Heinrich Dorge, a representative of the German Industry Bank, drew a salary as an official advisor to the Argentine minister of finance. He was suspected, not without grounds, to be the chief executer of the Reich's investments which in fact were financial evacuations. In that case the Americans were helpless. Dorge was one of many "high ranking" advisors who later, at the turn of the 1940's and 1950's, disappeared in mysterious circumstances. However, it was not the Mossad [Israeli intelligence – M.B.,

---

[48] U. Goñi, *Prawdziwa Odessa...*, p. 23.

P.W.] *but the Argentineans themselves who cut the ties that could lead to solve certain cases from 1945 and sources of certain funds[49].*

Large sums of money were deposited on secret accounts in banks of Buenos Aires - Argentine pesos, American dollars and pounds sterling, bonds, valuables (gemstones) and gold. The gathered fortune came from Germany (stolen in occupied countries), from German institutions and companies in Argentina and from people who supported the national socialism and willingly shared their riches to achieve certain goals. The "capital" enabled opening a special fund whose financial means were sufficient to transfer wanted war criminals from Europe to South America. The largest groups of Nazis and the Wehrmacht officers were sent to mansions far from large Argentine cities.

The International Red Cross also played an infamous role helping the Nazis. Witkowski writes:

It was established beyond all doubts that a G. Pasch, chief of the International Red Cross [IRC] headquarters in Geneva was a German agent. The same can be said about a German representative of the Red Cross in Geneva, von Engelbrechten, who, at that time, was also the press attaché for the German consulate and a resident of the German intelligence in that city. His duties as the employee of the Red Cross included issuing documents that allowed for releasing prisoners of war from camps. Von Engelbrechten and Pasch were exposed mainly as a result of an arrest of another agent and the IRC employee in Algiers on October 14, 1943. Through these people, the Reich special services effectively managed the IRC in Europe according to their own needs. Many other names appeared on a dozen or so American documents' pages [...] A lot of space was devoted to infiltration of North Africa. The documents also described the case of Hans Bon, the Swiss army colonel and representative of the IRC to the Near East, working for Germany. Two of his brothers were also German agents... One of the agents was the chairman of the so called Mixed Committee of the IRC in Geneva, Dr Paul Burkhard, the Swiss... Jew. He was the principal of the IRC hospital in Naples and after the fall of the southern Italy he was responsible for camps for Italian and German prisoners of war in that area. Information about him was found in notes of a German spy named Heidschuch, operating in Italy. Burkhard maintained his contacts via a "connection" - George Kuhne. His correspondence included information concerning using the IRC ship sailing on the Mediterranean Sea, s/s Canada[50].

An infamous role in espionage and organizing transports for the Third Reich was also played by other ships sailing as humanitarian transports under flags of neutral countries, mainly Portugal.

---

[49] I. Witkowski, *Hitler w Argentynie...*, p. 17, on the basis of: Washington Office items previously withheld, Entry 196, Box 74, NARA, sign. RG-226 (OSS).

[50] I. Witkowski, *Hitler w Argentynie...*, p. 20.

CHAPTER III

U 530 - WARTIME STORY OF THE FIRST (?)

GERMAN SUBMARINE IN ARGENTINA

> *The man is created to search for the truth,*
> *not to own it.*
> Blaise Pascal

On July 10, 1945, *U 530*, commanded by the 25-year-old Lt. Otto Wermuth, was the first German submarine to officially reach the shores of Argentina. The Argentine Navy (AN) decided to keep the U-Boot and raise the blue, white and blue ensign on the ship. Meanwhile the American government demanded the submarine along with 54 crew members to be transferred to the USA. On June 17, during a special cabinet meeting, the Argentine government, not willing to get into conflict with the mighty ally over such an "insignificant matter" decided that the large, ocean-going, Type IX C/40 U-Boot that had surrendered at Mar del Plata would be at the USA and Great Britain governments' disposal along with her crew, their testimonies and all interrogation reports[51]. Instructions were issued by the Argentine Foreign Minister Dr Cesar Ameghino.

After considering the case, the Ministry of Foreign Affairs announced that:

Fulfilling the orders of the unconditional surrender of all German air, land forces and the navy, the submarine should be transferred according to the requirements put forth by the Allies[52].

Did the U-Boot bring (in the opinion of the British and American intelligence) key personnel of the Third Reich to South America?

---

[51] Inteligence Report, serial R-197-45, Nor. 915-400; From Naval Attaché at Buenos Aires, 18 July 1945, NARA, sign. ADM 199, p. 1, typed.

[52] Ibidem, s. 1, typed.

* * *

What do we know about combat records of *U 530*[53] in the World War II? On October 14, 1942, the almost 80-meter-long submarine with 6.9 m beam, entered service with the Kriegsmarine. The U-Boot was one of eighty seven ocean-going, Type IX C/40 submarines[54]. During several months of standard and weapons training (torpedoes, anti aircraft and deck guns) on the Baltic Sea, the crew was assigned to the 4. U-Flotille training unit in Stettin. The first commanding officer of the U-Boot was 39-year-old Lt.Cdr. Kurt Lange. The CO was responsible for the seamen training before departing for the first combat patrol. Lt.Cdr. Kurt Lange demanded his subordinates to fulfill all tasks perfectly. The training program was realized according to the U-Bootwaffe high command's orders for trials and training.

U 530 departed for her maiden voyage from Kiel to the North Atlantic on February 20, 1943. The U-Boot joined the other warships of the "Neuland" group (on March 4-6) that were operating at the shores of western Ireland. On March 7, *U 530* and other units were sent north west where (March 6-11), along with the "Ostmark" group, they were to take part in a hunt for merchantmen. During her first, several-weeks-long voyage, U 530 achieved a big success that strengthened the morale of the submarine's inexperienced crew.

On February 23, an armada of 59 cargo ships of the SC.121 convoy departed from New York and headed for the Atlantic. The ships were carrying supplies for the Allied invasion forces. On the fourth day of the voyage, near Newfoundland, the convoy met the Escort Group A3 (commanded by Cpt. Heineman) that was to provide cover along the convoy's route to Great Britain. The close escort comprised the American Coast Guard gunboat *Spencer*, Canadian corvettes *Trillium*, *Rosthern* and *Dauphin* and the British corvette *Dianthus*. The task force was also joined by the America destroyer *Greer*.

Due to bad weather conditions, the German submarines became separated. The U-Boots of the temporary "Westmark" wolfpack were not able to maintain visual contact. The Kriegsmarine commander[55] who had planned the U-Boots' attack near Newfoundland was not aware of the fact that the British intelligence had intercepted his signals sent to the „gray wolves". The ships, having received the orders, made a sharp turn to the north and, on March 5, despite the fact that the convoy was forced to reroute, were not detected by the U-Boots. Only by chance, a lone U-Boot, *U*

---

[53] Construction of *U 530* was contracted to the Deutsche A.G. Werft shipyard in Hamburg. The agreement was signed on August 15, 1940, the ship was laid down on December 8, 1941 and launched on July 28, 1942.

[54] A total of 194 type IX submarines entered combat service. They were built in three shipyards in Germany – 8 type IX A, 14 – type IX B, 54 – type IX C, 87 – type IX C/40, 2 – type IX D1, 28 – type IX D2 and 1 – type IX D2/42.

[55] On January 31, 1943 the commander in chief of the Kriegsmarine – by the decision of Adolf Hitler – was the former commander of the German submarine fleet, 51-year-old Karl Dönitz, promoted to the rank of Grossadmiral. In February 1943, Generaladmiral Hans-Georg von Friedeburg became commander of the U-Bootwaffe, however he lacked the charisma and intuition of his predecessor. Although Dönitz retained his title of the flag officer of the German submarine fleet, his new position meant that the direct operational command was transferred to the Chief of the Operational Staff, Rear-Admiral Eberhard Godt.

405 commanded by Cdr. Rolf-Heinrich Hopman, patrolling her sector outside the wolfpack, spotted the SC.121 about 90 nmi (about 170 km) north east of two U-Boot groups waiting passively for the convoy. Commander Hopman notified the U-Bootwaffe headquarters of the convoy SC.121 position and positioned his submarine behind the last ships. Soon he successfully entered the fight.

GENERAL CHARACTERISTICS OF THE TYPE IX C/40 SUBMARINE	
Length	76.8 m
Beam	6.9 m
Draught	4.7 m
Height	9.5 m
Pressure hull length	58.7 m
Pressure hull beam	4.4 m
Pressure hull thickness	18.5 mm
Displacement surfaced	1,144 t
Displacement submerged	1,257 t
Combat displacement submerged (max)	1,545 t
Propulsion Surfaced	2 x 2,200 hp, Type M9V 40/46 MAN supercharged, nine-cylinder, four stroke diesel engines, producing 470-490 rev./min.
Propulsion submerged (without the snorkel)	2 x 500 hp, Type 2GU 345/34 electric motors by the SSW company, producing 275 rev./min.
Batteries	2 accumulator batteries, 62 cells each (in containers with protective rubber layer), Type AFA 33 MAL 740 W with 11,300 Ah capacity, total weight 74.9 t
Fuel capacity	214.2 t (maximum 245 t)
Speed surfaced	18.3 knots
Speed submerged	7.3 knots
Range surfaced	13,850 nmi at 10 knots 11,400 nmi at 12 knots
Range submerged	63 nmi at 4 knots 128 nmi at 2 knots
Maximum depth	100 m
Collapse depth	200 m
Propellers	2
Crash dive time	35 s
Periscopes	2 – combat and search
Armament	1 - 105 mm gun (between 1941 and 1942; removed between 1943 and 1944)*, 1 - 37 mm AA gun, 4 - 20 mm AA guns (2 X II). 22 to 24 - 533 mm torpedoes or 66 Type TMB mines or 44 Type TMA mines
Complement (since 1943)	4 officers, 56 non-commissioned officers and enlisted men (complement in 1945 - 54)

* *U 530* was not armed with 105 mm gun.

The U-Boots began their hunt. Dönitz believed that his "boys" would defeat the escort and take care of the convoy. Due to the awful weather (strong storm, fog, squall with snow and hail) the convoy loosened its formation and was spread along a large area. The American escort got confused. At night from March 6 to 7, *U 230* (commanded by Lt.Cdr. Paul Siegmann) and *U 591* (Lt.Cdr. Hans-Jürgen Zetzsche) each torpedoed one British freighter. The wind force was 10 in the Beaufort scale and neither the commanders of the aforementioned submarines nor those from the others decided to launch an attack in the next dozen or so hours. The U-Boots, however, did not lose contact with SC. 121. Another attack came in the evening of March 8. One hit was scored by each of the crews of *U 591*, *U 190* (Lt.Cdr. Max Wintermeyer) and *U 642* (Lt.Cdr. Herbert Brünning), *U 527* (Lt.Cdr. Herbert Uhlig) sank two ships including a landing craft.

On March 9, the group got reorganized, some U-Boots went to France, several submarines, including *U 530,* arrived. In the evening, the new wolfpack codenamed "Ostmark" began picking off more ships. The escort crews were not able to hunt down the enemy. The convoy was spread thin and the escort ships with damaged radars and active sonar devices, with crews unfamiliar with difficult weather conditions did not launch a single attack against the German submarines. More marauders were in danger. The U-Boots sank five more ships including a tanker and a landing craft. The torpedoes were fired by *U 409* (commanded by Lt. Hanns-Ferdinand Massmann), *U 405* and *U 229* (Lt. Robert Schetelig). The crew of *U 530* were also lucky. On March 9, at 21.36, Lt.Cdr. Lange attacked and sank the Swedish freighter *Milos* (3,058 GRT) at coordinates 58°00'N and 24°00'W. The freighter go separated from the convoy due to heavy storms[56]. Two days later the submarine became part of the wolfpack "Stürmer" and from March 21 to 30, 1943, the submarine operated with the "Seewolf" group.

The fight for the convoy SC.121 ended on March 10, before noon. Reinforcements from Iceland (American escort ships *Bibb, Ingham* and the destroyer *Babbitt* and the British destroyed HMS *Harvester*) and strong air cover (British and American long range aircraft) prevented the U-Boots from launching further attacks.

The SC.121 convoy lost 12 ships, 2 LCTs (landing craft, tank) and one ship damaged. Almost 100,000 tons of military equipment went to the bottom, several hundred sailors perished. The two wolfpacks, after the fight, received orders from Berlin to search for convoys SC.123 and HX.230 in better weather conditions.

The only answer to the losses suffered by SC.121 was ramming *U 633* (Lt. Bernhard Müller) by the British freighter *Scorton*, west-north-west of Rockall. The twen-

---

[56] C. Blair, *Hitlera wojna U-Bootów*, vol. 2, Warszawa 1998, p. 285; M. Borowiak, *Zabójcy U-Bootów. Bitwa o Atlantyk 1939-1945*, Warszawa 2013, p. 248-249; R. Busch, H.-J. Röll, *Der U-Boot-Krieg 1939-1945. Deutsche U-Boot-Erflogfe von September 1939 bis Mai 1945*, vol. 3, Hamburg-Berlin-Bonn 2001, p. 228; A. Perepeczko, *Burza nad Atlantykiem*, vol. 3, Warszawa 2002, p. 432; J. Rohwer, *The Critical Convoy Battles of March 1943*, London 1977, p. 55; V.E. Tarrant, *Kurs West. Die deutschen U-Boot-Offensiven 1914-1945*, Stuttgart 1998, p. 157; Wynn K., *U-Boat Operations of the Second World War*, vol. 2..., p. 16.

ty-eight-year-old commander of the Type VII C submarine died along his entire 43-men crew during their first patrol, three weeks after leaving Kiel. The SC.121 convoy was the last one in the North Atlantic with escort comprising mainly the US Navy ships, which ended in disaster.

The crew of *U 530* waited for their next success until next month. On April 4, Lt.Cdr. Lange detected the HX.231 convoy with 61 ships including 22 tankers[57]. Escorted by the destroyer *Vidette*, frigate *Tay* and four corvettes (Cpt. Peter Gretton's Task Force B-7). The U-Boot's reports brought submarines of the "Löwenherz" pack to the area. On April 5, at 22.00 - in a surprise attack - Lange fired a salvo of three torpedoes and sank the American tanker *Sunoil* (9,005 GRT) at coordinates 58°16'N and 34°14'W, the ship had been previously damaged by a medium size U-Boot, *U563* commanded by Lt.Cdr. Götz von Hartmann[58]. The U-Boot attacked an easier target that was outside visual range of the convoy's escort. The Royal Navy ships were called to the rescue. The U-Boot was detected by one of the British Flower class corvettes, which were part of the additional escort of the HX.231 convoy, and attacked with 30 depth charges. *U 503* had little chance to escape unscathed. However, despite many attacks the submarine survived. The exploding depth charges damaged her bow torpedo tubes[59] and the top deck of the „grey wolf". The battered U-Boot managed to escape. During the patrol, Lange sank two ships of 12,063 GRT. *U 530* reached Lorient on April 22 after 62 days at the sea.

Lt.Cdr. Lange's U-Boot was assigned to the 10. U-Flotille (combat unit) in Lorient which had been formed on January 15, 1942, under the command of Lt.Cdr. Günther Kuhnke. The flotilla comprised 80 long range submarines Type IX C (26), Type IX C/40 (41), Type IX D1 (2), Type IX D2 (4), Type X B (1) and 6 supply submarines Type XIV, so called milk cows. Some of the U-Boots participated in patrols on exotic waters of south-east Asia, however most of them operated on the Atlantic from Greenland, through the middle of the ocean and the Caribbean Sea to the shores of South America and southern Africa.

During her month long stay at Lorient, *U 530* was sent to the dry dock for repairs and to have her hull painted grey. On May 29, the U-Boot departed for her second patrol to the Mid Atlantic. The submarine operated north west of the Canary Islands where she acted as a temporary tanker. In the third week of the patrol, the U-Boot supplied fuel to *U 172*, *U 572*, *U 759* and *U 180* transport submarine returning to base with a cargo of two tons of gold and a deadly weapon - the Japanese Long Lance torpedoes[60]. The Japanese torpedoes were faster and had greater range than any other torpedo in the world. During her mission, *U 530* did not perform any

---

[57] More in: P. Gretton, *Convoy Escort Commander*, London 1971, p. 120-136.

[58] The HX.231 convoy lost 6 ships (41,600 GRT). The Germans lost type VII submarines - *U 632* and *U 635*, several others were heavily damaged.

[59] *U 530* had four bow and two stern torpedo tubes.

[60] The precious cargo was supplied by the Japanese submarine *I-29*. On April 26, 1943, *U 180* met the Japanese sub on the south African waters.

torpedo attacks. While returning to Europe, the U-Boot was ineffectively attacked in the Bay of Biscay by a Sunderland aircraft of the 10. Royal Australian Air Force Squadron that dropped three bombs but did not damage the submarine. On July 3, the U-Boot entered Bordeaux after 36 days at the sea[61].

The crew spent over two months in the German U-Boot base on the west coast of France. Meanwhile, the submarine was overhauled. Due to the constant threat of the Allied air raids, the ship was moved to one of the huge concrete shelters that could house large, long range supply submarines Type IX D2, Type XIV and even larger, almost 90-meter long, Type X B minelayers[62].

On September 21, U 530 left Bordeaux and in the evening arrived at another base on the west coast of France - La Pallice, where she moored in a shelter about 6 km west from the old harbor. The short journey was classified as patrol number three. Patrol number four lasted from September 27 to 29 and the submarine returned to La Pallice. U 530 spent exactly the same amount of time at sea during her fifth patrol which started on October 3 and lasted until October 5. The U-Boot was overhauled in La Pallice and was soon to depart for a few-months-long mission in the Caribbean Sea, north of South America.

On October 17, the U-Boot left La Pallice. On November 12, U 530 arrived at the patrol area between the Caribbean and the Panama Canal where she met a "milk cow" - U 488 (Lt. Erwin Bartke); took about 40 t of fuel and replenished her food supplies for next two weeks of the patrol. The submarine resumed the patrol and headed south operating between the Caribbean and the Panama Canal. For two weeks, the U-Boot hunted large cargo ships sailing the Caribbean Sea alone with their precious cargo. The transport ships travelling without the US Navy escort were an easy prey for Hitler's underwater predator. However, this time U 530 was not so lucky. On December 26, at 12.24, in the area of the Panamanian Colon (10°30'N and 78°58'W) the submarine scored two torpedo hits on the large American tanker *Chapultepec* (10,195 GRT) but did not sink the ship[63]. Three days later, she attacked another American tanker - *Esso Buffalo*. Not only did Lange miss three torpedo shots but the maneuvering ship hit the U-Boot, completely unaware of that fact. The U-Boot descended to 240 m with damaged bow displacement container and ballast tank number eight. The damage was repaired and Lange continued the patrol. The submarine sailed between the Caribbean islands of Martinique and Dominica, north of South America and returned to Lorient on February 22, 1944. Near the Azores, the submarine was often attacked with aerial bombs and depth charges.

---

[61] Special Activities Branch sign. Op-16-Z (A): *U 530* [Interrogation reports – final and rough copies; story and detailed characteristics of submarines that surrendered to the American, Canadian and Argentine authorities– M.B., P.W.], NARA, p. 2, typed. See also: J.F. White, „*Mleczne Krowy". Podwodne zaopatrzeniowce atlantyckich wilczych stad 1941-1945*, Warszawa 2001, p. 207; K. Wynn, *U-Boat Operations of the Second World War*, vol. 2..., p. 16.

[62] J.P. Mallmann-Showell, *Hitler's U-Boat Bases*, Gloucestershire 2002, p. 123.

[63] J. Rohwer, *Axis Submarine Successes of World War Two...*, p. 176.

Fortunately she did not sustain further damage. The patrol lasted 129 days without a single confirmed kill.

Due to sustained damage and the need to install the snorkel[64] on the submarine (three containers for spare torpedoes were removed from the front deck), Lt.Cdr. Lange, recipient of the Iron Cross 1st and 2nd class, was not ready for his sixth combat patrol until three months later.

On May 22, 1944, the submarine left Lorient and headed for the Caribbean Sea. Due to vigilant Allied aerial patrols, it took almost two weeks for the U-Boot to pass the Azores, the archipelago of nine Portuguese volcanic islands (about 1,500 km from the coast of the Iberian Peninsula). It turns out, *U 530* was not a front line submarine "by chance". After two weeks time, on June 23, at night, between Freetown and Trinidad - according to plan - she met the Japanese submarine cruiser *I 52* which was heading to Europe carrying a precious cargo. The allied submarine's mission began in March in the Kure harbor. A short stop was scheduled in Singapore. One of the three powerful, Type C 3 submarines[65] (over 108 m in length with surface displacement of 2,564 t and submerged - 3,644 t) [66], with crew of 95 (full-time crew of 101 men) and fourteen passengers - engineers from the Mitsubishi company, sent to the Third Reich to observe construction of anti-aircraft guns, jet engines and destroyers, carried a cargo of 2 tons of gold in 146 bars[67]. Additionally, the submarine was laden with 654 tons of raw rubber, 228 t of tin, 11 t of wolfram, 3 t of quinine, over 2 t of opium, 54 kg of caffeine and molybdenum. The meeting was short. *I 52* was boarded by the navigation officer Lt.Cdr. Schäfer and two radio operators - according to documents kept in the College Park, Maryland[68]. A radar device „Naxos" was loaded onto the ship. The Japanese submarine cruiser was also supplied with fuel.

---

[64] The device allowed for operation of Diesel engines when submerged; it comprised two pipes in one cowling (height – 8.5 m from the deck, diameter - 318 mm), one of them was used as exhaust and one as air intake. The device not only supported the engines but also provided oxygen to the crew. Simultaneously it pumped out exhaust fumes from the engines. The bottom part of the air mast was mounted by articulated joints to the base on the weather deck of a submarine. In the first versions the mast was raised and lowered with a winch hand cranked from inside the submarine. Soon, a hydraulic hoist was introduced, powered by periscope lift installations. Thanks to this device the submerged operating time of a U-Boot was limited only by fuel supplies. For more information on the snorkel device see: D. Botting, *Die deutsche Unterseeboote im 1. Und 2. Weltkrieg. Date – Fakte – kommentare*, Bindlach 2001, p. 159-161, 164; P. Kemp, *Submarine Action*, London 2000, p. 15, 33-39; E. Möller, W. Brack, *The Encyclopedia of U-boats. From 1904 to the Present Day*, London 2004, p. 160-161; P. Padfield, *War Beneath the Sea. Submarine conflict 1939-1945*, London 1998, p. 374, 427 and subsequent; E. Rössler, *The U-Boat. The evolution and technical history of German submarines*, London 2001, p. 198-204; R.C. Stern, *U-Boats in action*, Carrollton (Texas) 1977, p. 33; G. Williamson, *Wolf Pack. The Story of the U-Boat in World War II*, Oxford 2006; p. 79-80.

[65] The other two were *I 53* and *I 55*.

[66] E. Bagnasco, *Uboote im 2. Weltkrieg...*, p. 214-215; D. Miller, *Submarines oft he World*, London 2002, p. 196-197.

[67] The gold was a payment for the latest optical technology made available for Japan. Other sources state that the precious metal was to be exchanged to German currency as the Japanese yen was no longer accepted as payment medium.

[68] Special Activities Branch, sign. Op-16-Z (A): *U 530...*, NARA, p. 3, typed. C. Blair, *Hitlera wojna U-Bootów*, t. 2..., p. 594 says that a German officer and a radar operator entered the submarine with a radar device.

Allied cryptanalysts deciphering German and Japanese radio messages - which is mentioned by Clay Blair - tracked both vessels. The American historian writes:

On June 2, anti-submarine task force of the escort aircraft carrier USS "Bogue" left Casablanca under command of freshly-appointed Aurelius B. Vosseller, with a task to thwart the planned randez-vous. [...]

The "Bogue" task force intercepted radio message exchange between "U 530" and "I 52". On June 23, Vosseller sent his Avengers to search for the two submarines. Two of the aircraft, piloted by A.L. Hirsbrunner and Jesse D. Taylor, independently got radar contact and dropped hydro-acoustic buoys. When they registered sounds of a working submarine propeller, Taylor attacked the target with depth charges and [American aerial, self-guiding, acoustic torpedo - M.B., P.W.] the Fido. After three minutes Taylor and his crew heard a sound of a crushed can or a twig being broken.

When he reported: " I got the son of a bitch", Vosseller launched another Avenger with a task to sink "the other" submarine. Piloted by Williama D. "Flash" Gordon and guided to the estimated position by Hirsbrunner, the aircraft dropped sonar buoys, made contact and attacked the target with the Fido. Gordon reported a miss, however, eighteen minutes later, he heard a "long and thundering explosion" that lasted almost a minute.

Vosseller was convinced that his planes sank both submarines but he was wrong. It is possible that Taylor's Fido damaged "I 52" and Gordon's Fido hit the remains of the sub [June 24 – M.B., P.W]. Anyway, on the following day, a destroyer of USS "Bogue" escort found one hundred fifteen blocks of raw rubber and numerous fragments of mahogany wood floating in the sea which seemed to be the proof of sinking the Japanese "I 52". However, the success was called into question by one of deciphered Japanese messages. On July 31, the Japanese naval attachè in Berlin reported to Tokyo that he had made radio contact with "I 52" that informed him that she would be entering Lorient on August 4. He also reported that the Japanese "welcoming committee" had already left Berlin. German escort ships arrived at the meeting place on August 1, and remained there until August 4, however, they did not find any trace of "I 52". On August 6, the Japanese naval attachè informed that the German escort had returned to base and demanded to be given an estimated time of the submarine cruiser arrival, however, he received no reply[69].

---

[69] C. Blair, *Hitlera wojna U-Bootów*, vol. 2..., p. 594-595. See also: D.B. Carpenter, N. Polmar, *Submarines of the Imperial Japanese Navy 1904–1945*, London 1986, p. 107; J. Hernández, *Zagadki i tajemnice drugiej wojny światowej*, Warszawa 2009, p. 180-186. In 1995 the American sea rescuer, Paul Tidwell, and a team of his experts, equipped with latest gear, found the wreckage of *I-52*, lying 850 NM (about 1,600 km) west of Cape Verde at 5,200 m. Thanks to a remotely operated underwater vehicle fitted with video cameras, they were able to see the "straight and untouched" submarine... with the exception of a "torpedo-torn gap" in the starboard side. In 1998, Tidwell returned to the wreck aboard the Russian research vessel *Akademik Mstislav Kieldysh* - used by the Oceanography Institute of the Russian Academy of Sciences in Moscow. It is the largest research ship in the world. She is the only vessel equipped with two deep sea vehicles *Mir 1* and *Mir 2*. In 1997, the ship "played" a role in Jamesa Cameron's *Titanic*. The wreck's hull thickness makes it impossible to make a hole large enough for the underwater robot to enter and explore the submarine. Due to lack of funds (10 million dollars are required) and problems of legal nature, it has been impossible to explore the wreck which still holds huge amounts of gold.

The U-Boot continued her voyage along the route Trinidad - Georgetown - Toba-go. However, the submarine was not able to attack the widely spread convoy. It was *U 503*'s last patrol in the Caribbean Sea. After several months at sea, she received orders to return to Norway. Due to faulty lubrication, the snorkel was not used during the U-Boot's trip to base. On October 1, U 530 entered Kristiansand and three days later Lange brought his submarine to Flensburg. Lt.Cdr. Lange's sixth patrol lasted 136 days - it was the last combat mission of the forty-year-old Kriegsmarine officer and the longest one in the history of *U 530*. Soon, Lange received new tasks on land.

∗ ∗ ∗

In January 1945, *U 530* received a new commanding officer. Lt.Cdr. Kurt Lange, after exhausting combat patrols, was assigned a position of department manager in a training facility for submariners. He also became commander of the Hel harbor[70]. The training facility on the Hel Peninsula in the Baltic Sea (operating since August 1941), familiarized U-Boots' crews with no combat experience with crisis situations in conditions similar to combat environment. After passing the course, U-Boots were given combat assignments. The training usually lasted 9 days, but it was longer for fresh crews. The practice included simulation of all possible damages that a submarine could sustain on the surface and in submergence. Crews were also trained in convoy attacks, air defense etc. All instructors were battle hardened commanders with experience of over a dozen combat patrols on the Atlantic. After passing all tests, a submarine was given an unofficial emblem „Frontreif" (ready for the front).

U 530's preparation for her next combat mission lasted until mid February 1945. The new commander of the "nine" became 25-year-old Otto Wermuth who had a short time experience serving on surface ships and submarines. The high command of the submarine fleet had not given him command of a U-Boot probably due to his young age and lack of required experience.

What do we know about Wermuth's service in the navy? He was born On July 28, 1920 in Aalen, Württemberg[71]. On September 16, 1939, almost two and a half weeks after Germany's attack against Poland, at the age of 19 - having graduated from high school - he joined the Kriegsmarine as a cadet. From November 1939 to April 1940, he served on the training battleship *Schleswig-Holstein*. Between April and September 1940, Wermuth was trained in the Marineschule in Mürwik-Flensburg. On July 1, 1940, he was promoted to the rank of Fähnrich zur See (Petty Officer First Class). He wanted to serve on submarines, however, he had to wait. From September to November 1940, he was trained in Emden (a town in Saxony) where he got familiar with submarines' diesel and electric engines. Between November 1940 and January

---

[70] K. Lange died on November 14, 1960 in Wedel, Germany at the age of 57.

[71] Otto Wermuth's father was a merchant.

1941, he attended a course in conducting attacks and torpedo deployment operations in Mürwik. From February 1941 to March 1941, he participated in training in the naval aviation base in Dievenow (Dziwnów). In March and April 1941, he had his seamanship on the destroyer *Z 23*. From April to September 1941, he was trained on submarines. On July 1, 1941, Wermuth was promoted to Oberfähnrich zur See (Senior Chief Petty Officer). As a watch officer he spent his seamanship on the Type IX A submarine - *U 37* (September 1941 - June 1942). On March 1, 1842, he was promoted to his first officer rank - Leutnant zur See (Ensign).

From July 1942 to February 1944, he participated in 4 combat patrols as a 1st and 2nd watch officer on the veteran Type IXB submarine - *U 103* (He spent over 150 days at sea) commanded by Lt.Cdr. Gustav-Adolf Janssen. During the U-Boot's last combat operation, before she was reclassified as a training submarine, she participated in a secret mission. On September 1943, when *U 103* departed from Brest, her crew was assigned a risky task. The U-Boot was sent to African coast to lay mines at the Takoradi harbor. Although *U 103* completed her objective and laid mines on October 23 (during the operation, the U-Boot hit a steel anti-submarine net but managed to get out), it brought no results - no Allied ship was damaged or destroyed[72].

On October 1, 1943, Wermuth was promoted to Lieutenant. From March 1944 to July 1944, he attended courses for submarine commanders in the 3. U-Lehrdivision, 23. U-Flottille in Danzig (Gdańsk) and 27. U-Flottille in Gotenhafen (Gdynia). From July 10, 1944 to August 31, 1944, he was commander of *U 853* (Type IX C/40)[73] but, due to prolonging overhaul of the submarine in Lorient, he did not take part in combat patrols. He was later sent to Hamburg where, from September 14, 1944 to January 1945, was a watch officer (supernumerary) on *U 530*.

It is highly improbable that the U-Boot commander with no successes in fighting Allied shipping[74] was given such an important mission, in February 1945, as carrying the Third Reich's treasure to Argentina. I. Witkowski, quoted in this book, tried to prove it in one of his *Supertajne bronie Hitlera. Tropem złota i ostatnich broni* [75].

There is one more reason why *U 530* could not have carried such a mission. The ship was battered after combat patrols and required long overhaul in docks of the Deutsche A.G. Werft shipyard in Hamburg. After a long break, the submarine was sent to several-days-long training before departing for the next combat mission.

Grossadmiral Karl Dönitz had new submarines at his disposal, larger than the Type IX C/40, like the Type X B[76] submarine minelayers, several new Type IX D2

---

[72] See: Interrogation Otto Wermuth 27 August 1945, Fully Transcribed; NARA, sign. NND 750122, part #2, p. 7, typed (Interrogation of Lt. Otto Wermuth by Cpt. Halle (observer Mr Duevell) in USA, August 27, 1945).

[73] Wermuth was assigned the position of a U-Boot commander by Generaladmiral Hans-Georg von Friedeburg.

[74] Lieutenant Wermuth receive four decorations: Iron Cross I and II class, service medal – Frontabzeichen and submarine service medal – Kriegsabzeichen für U-Boote.

[75] I. Witkowski, *Supertajne bronie Hitlera...*, p. 77 and 160.

[76] J. M. Scalia, *Germany's Last Mission to Japan. The Failed Voyage of U-234*, Annapolis, Maryland 2000.

submarine cruisers and the super modern Type XXI submarines. There were several commanders still alive, great personalities of the U-Bootwaffe, proudly bearing their Knight's Crosses of the Iron Cross with Oak Leaves and Swords (Captain-
Junior Grade Erich Topp, Captain-Junior Grade Reinhard Suhren, Captain-Junior
Grade Albrecht Brandi and Lieutenant Commander Wolfgang Lüth). They were the
Kriegsmarine officers worthy of Dönitz's trust to be assigned a mission to safely
evacuate the Nazi treasure in a submarine.

U 530 left Kiel on February 19, 1945, with 14-day supplies[77] that included fresh
fruit, and additional canned provisions for at least 18 weeks. Four days later, the
U-Boot, travelling submerged, using the snorkel for most of her voyage, reached
Horten. After a short stop, the submarine resumed her patrol heading south to Kristiansand. On March 3, U 530, along with her sister submarine U 548, commanded
by 24-year-old Lt. Erich Krempl (took command on February 9, 1945)[78], left the
Norwegian Kriegsmarine base. U 530's crew comprised the commander, two deck
officers, two engineer officers, 49 non-commissioned officers and seamen. The submarine carried 225 tons of fuel. However, for that patrol, she only took 14 electri-
cally powered torpedoes[79] (8 – G7e T-IIIa with Pi2 [fuse] and 6 – G7es T-V with
Pi4c)[80]. The U-Boot was able to reach the maximum speed of 18 knots on the surface
(officially) and 7 knots while submerged with the snorkel.

In March, nine more Type IX C, Type IX C/40 and Type IX D2 submarines left
Germany and Norway - U 518, U 546, U 805, U 858, U 873, U 880, U 1235, U 530 and
U 548 which, by decision of the Kriegsmarine high command, formed the "Seewolf"
pack tasked with attacking Allied shipping at the East Coast of the United States,
south of New York[81]. However, the last two of the aforementioned „see wolves" were
ordered to sail to the northern part of the East Coast of the United States and to
Canadian waters. They were to hunt freighters near Halifax (Canada).

Wermuth initially headed for the North Sea (sailing mostly submerged) and then
he took course for the North Atlantic. At night he would charge batteries using the
snorkel, which U 530 was fitted with. Finally, he headed for the west Atlantic - according to orders received from the U-Bootwaffe headquarters. From the moment

---

[77] Other sources claim that a week-worth of fresh supplies were taken. See: Resume of Interrogation of Lieut.
(j.g.) Otto Wermuth, Commanding Officer of the German submarine U 530, Special Activities Branch Op-16-Z,
NARA, p. 1, typed.

[78] From July 1943 to January 1945 he commanded U 71, U 28 and U 1162, but did not participate in combat
patrols. Other sources claim that U 548 left for her first patrol from Horten March 5, 1945.

[79] In 1990, Otto Wermuth during a conversation Harry Copppere said that he had taken 14-16 torpedoes. See:
H. Cooper, More to U 530 skipper Wermuth, KTB Nr 292 (The Official History Publication of the U-Bootwaffe),
www.sharkhunters.com, p. 11 (electronic version).

[80] Report on the Interrogation of Prisoners from U 530 surrendered at Mar del Plata, 10 July 1945 (NARA,
sign. Op-16-Z (A), p. 1, typed.

[81] For more information about the "Seewolf" pack see: C. Blair, Hitlera wojna U-Bootów..., vol. 2, p. 708 and
subsequent; S. Dunstan, G. Williams, Grey Wolf..., p. 174-192; V.E. Tarrant, Das letzte Jahr der deutsche Kriegsmarine. Mai 1944 – Mai 1945, Podzun-Pallas 1996, p. 250-252.

the U-Boot arrived at the assigned area of operations, she spent most of her time at periscope depth. At night the submarine would use the snorkel for four hours and then descend to 60 meters. The U-Boot was forced to run underwater due to the threat of aerial attacks which were lethal to a submarine.

After reaching coordinates 61°N and 19°W, *U 530* was to send regular weather reports. At the end of April, the task was later taken over by *U 548* near Halifax.

Wermuth found no opportunities to use his torpedoes so the U-Bootwaffe headquarters ordered him to move to an area of operations farther south, near New York. From mid April, strong German long wave radio station ("Goliath") stopped broadcasting[82]. A week later *U 530* resumed using the snorkel. Receiving reports was still possible on short waves until the end of April. The U-Boot's crew was unaware of the fact that Argentina had entered the war against Germany.

On April 27-28, *U 530* came near Long Island where she stayed for about two weeks. One time the submarine came as close as 2-3 miles (3.7-5.5 km) to the land. For the next several days, the crew saw different ships of two, scattered due to dense fog, convoys (probably they were HX.35 - 95 ships or the ON.298 – 67) which they attacked.

On May 4, Wermuth aimed three torpedoes at a convoy of about 10-20 freighters and tankers. Two torpedoes missed and the third "eel" got stuck in the tube due to battery explosion. Two days later the U-Boot spotted a large group of ships approaching. Again, two torpedoes missed their targets. A single torpedo passed close to a large tanker. An hour later, another torpedo missed the tanker. After an hour, during another attack, a single torpedo was aimed at a lone ship (a marauder) - without success. On May 7, Wermuth used two electric torpedoes with the G7es T-V passive self-guiding system - they both missed. The commander attacked Allied ships several times firing nine of his fourteen torpedoes[83]. The U-Boot's operations in the assigned area were unsuccessful. At that time the crew observed two airships and one aircraft through the periscope. Several aerial bombs and one depth charge fell near the U-Boot but the submarine was not seriously damaged. In those circumstances, after leaving the operation sector, Wermuth decided to contact the command in Germany. He was sailing at depths of 40 to 50 meters.

On May 8, the submarine was near Long Island when the radio operators received information about Germany's surrender. Initially, the crew treated the news as a provocation. They continued their march to the south east. *U 530*'s commanding officer did not believe the message was authentic as it had not been signed by

---

[82] Germans built a large transmitter named "Goliath" at the river Milde. The station, built by the Lorenz company, had a power of 6 x 300 kW, wave length of 12,000-20,000 m, it was equipped with three 100 m antennas and 15 antennas 60-80 m high connected by antenna wires. The transmitter allowed U-Boots to receive long waves when submerged, for example: in the Mediterranean Sea at depths of up to 28 m, in the Mid Atlantic to 30 m, in the Indian Ocean to 25 m. The "Goliath" transmitter was blown up before the end of World War II.

[83] Four months later Lt. Wermuth testified before American investigators that in May 1945 he fired 7 torpedoes with no effect. Information from the authors' collection.

Dönitz nor his deputy. He attempted to contact the Navy headquarters on May 15 or 16 - at least that is what the preserved documents claim. The German signal was received as a non encrypted message and it ordered the crew to surrender the U-Boot. The navigation lights were to be turned on at night time. After revealing themselves and giving their position, the crew was to proceed to coordinates at the given longitude and latitude.

I survived the war and I said to myself I was not going to get caught like that. [...] I will find a neutral place. Maybe, along the way, I will receive some news from the command. During the march a transmitting station went silent. That was when I had to ask myself a question. Where to? I told myself: maybe the war is still being waged in Germany. I thought it was possible. We do not surrender, we are fighting in Berlin, Budapest and Breslau[84] and we will fight to the last man. I was not aware of the fact that Hitler was dead. I said to myself - we are marching on - remembered Lt. Wermuth in August 1945. [85]

Having consulted the other four officers and the rest of the crew, Lieutenant Wermuth decided to escape to Portugal, Spain or Argentina which, according to him, were friendly to the Germans. He was not going to return to Germany. Wermuth's plan was approved by almost the entire crew with exception of several men who did not want to surrender. Their opinion had no influence on the decision. It was a bold escape plan. Finally they decided to head to South America. Internment in Argentina or even settling down in the country, convinced most of the men. The U-Boot took a new course - South America.

The commander ordered firing (along the way) 5 torpedoes into the sea. Then, the remaining ammunition for the anti-aircraft gun, all secret documents and the Enigma codes were put into bags, weighed down and thrown overboard. The crew also got rid of valuable passive and active hydro-acoustic and radar equipment. The submarine's log and navigation log were temporarily retained. Heading south, they passed the Bermudas from the east, about 100 miles (185 km) from the coast. The submarine crossed the equator on June 17. After reaching 20° south latitude, they were travelling with speed of 7.5 knots on the surface, while charging the batteries, and 2 knots submerged. After passing the latitude, they increased the speed to 9 knots on surface.

At night, on July 9, the crew spotted lights of Mar de Plata. The commander ordered full speed on the diesels for 15 minutes without proper lubrication. About litter and a half of acid was added to the engine lubricant. The caustic substance was also poured into the engine cylinders. It was an act of sabotage. On the following day, on July 10, at 6.30 local time, *U 530*, using her electric engines, with navigation

---

[84] The siege of Breslau (Wrocław in Poland) lasted from February 13 to May 6, 1945. Those were clashes between German and Soviet forces.

[85] Report in the authors' collection.

lights on, entered the submarine base at Mar del Plata[86]. To answer the received signals she used the lamp to send a message in Spanish: „Alemana Submarino", which means „German submarine". The U-Boot was flying the Kriegsmarine ensign. There was no black nor blue flag to signal the submarine surrendered. The U-Boot cast her moorings at a buoy outside the harbor, near the Argentine submarine *Salta* (Captain-Junior Grade Ramón) and the depot ship of the submarine squadron *General Belgrano*.

The U-Boot's oldest crew member was 45-year-old midshipman, one of the engineers was 32 years old. The average age of the rest of the crew was 22 years. The youngest seaman was 19. The living quarters of the submarine were dirty and neglected. After getting ashore, the seamen were given hot meals and a haircut in the military base. The German submariners were temporarily quartered in the harbor. The officers were accommodated separately but they remained in contact with the men. The U-Boot was interned. The submarine's condition indicated she had spent a long time at sea. Her tanks still had 6 t of fuel and 1.8 t of lubricating oil. During her last, seventh, cruise that lasted from February 19 to July 10, 1945, the U-Boot's crew spent 134 days at the high seas[87].

* * *

On July 17, 1945, a week after the capitulation and internment of *U 530*, a conference of the anti-Nazi coalition leaders in Potsdam began[88]. During one of the cocktail parties, the US secretary of state Jimmy F. Byrnes approached J. Stalin and asked: „Is Hitler alive?". Stalin answered: „Hitler didn't die. He escaped to Spain or Argentina".

Conspiracy theorists claim that Lt.Cdr. Wermuth's submarine entered Mar del Plata after she had „visited" one of the secret bases, as the submarine, despite travelling a dozen or so thousands of kilometers from Europe (over four months

---

[86] J. Salinas, C. de Nápoli, *Ultramar Sur. La última operacón secreta del Tercer*, Buenos Aires 2002, p. 424, based on Argentine intelligence reports: *"Wermuth testified that on July 9, 1945, at 3.00, from a distance of 18 miles, he saw lights of Punta Mogotes and he continued his jouney south towards the naval base in Mar del Plata. According to the lieutenant, the submarine's position gave him heading 240° towards the lights. Then, he submerged the U-Boot and waited for the dawn"*. He categorically denied taking part in a special, evacuation mission and having the Third Reich's key personnel on board and disembarking them on the shores of Argentina. It turns out, Wermuth decided to wait until sunset near Punta Mogotes, a town south of the Mar del Plata harbor. On the following day, after the first observation, he moved to about 3 miles from the shore, waiting for better light before entering the harbor. See: Resume of Interrogation of Lieut.(j.g.) Otto Wermuth, Commanding Officer of the German sumbarine *U 530...*, p. 3, typed. M. Ivinheim, *The Secret Alliance. The Unknown Alliance between the Third Reich and Argentina*, Hernando, Florida 2011, p. 115 revealed that Otto Wermuth wrote to him in one of his letters about his last cruise as „ein Reise" (journed), not as „ein Feindfahrt" (combat patrol). He also claimed all documents had been thrown overboard.

[87] From February 1943 to July 1945 *U 530* spent 504 days at sea. She sank 2 cargo ships (12,063 GRT) and damaged one tanker (10,195 GRT).

[88] The meeting was attended by the leadre of the Soviet Union Joseph Spalin, President Harry Tuman and the British Prime Minister Winston Churchill. The Potsdam conference lasted from July 17 to August 2, 1945.

at sea) was fully supplied[89]. How do we know that the submarine carried large amounts of food supplies? It is probable that the information came from a report made by the American intelligence officer, Major of Cavalry D. F. Gibbons, on July 13, 1945:

Large amounts of canned and condensed food are still on board. [I saw – M.B., P.W.] *something that looked like vitamin pills[90].*

Cdr. W.H. Fowler of the American intelligence headquarters in Buenos Aires, in his report from July 20, 145, to the Admiralty in Washington informed:

We received numerous reports talking about ships arriving at different parts of the coast up to San Julián. The issue is being investigated [...], so far there are no confirmations. Several reports concerning the Buenos Aires province were sent to the Argentine Navy and are being monitored with great vigilance.

I was able to take a glance at documents and books left on board, which are of the greatest interest to us. Everything that presented a certain value was thrown overboard. I saw things that were left: at least 2,000 cans of different food products and many other things, repair kits - everything in good condition. There is a lot of rubber among the equipment[91].

Igor Witkowski quoted earlier, writes:

The witness of the event - Cesar Genaro, a civilian employee of the Mar del Plata base, in 1945 responsible for provisions, testified that he had been surprised to see "U 530" fully supplied with food![92]

How did it really happened? It turns out, all German seamen were starved and exhausted when they reached Argentina. They were a mess - pale faces, long, dirty hair and thick beards. According to documents made by Argentine investigators, some of the men had first symptoms of scurvy. they were given oranges and other citrus fruit. It is interesting that at the time of their interment in Argentina, the crew had 4,000 cigarettes in 200 packs. The amount of tobacco was larger than expected. Then, who and why, intentionally departs from the truth?

---

[89] M. Ivinheim, *The Secret Alliance...*, p. 103-124; H.J. Kraft, *Submarinos alemanses en Argentina*, E-Book 1998, p. 13-35; C. Mey-Martinez, *La Base Antarctica de Hitler: Mito y Realidad. Vistaron la Antartida los Submarinos U-530 y U-977*, www.histarmar.com.ar.; I. Witkowski, *Supertajne bronie Hitlera...*, p. 41 and subsequent.

[90] Issued by The Intelligence Division Office of Chief of Naval Operations Navy Department. Intelligence Report, serial 195-45, No. 915-40, From Naval Attaché of Buenos Aires, 13 July, NARA, p. 3, typed.

[91] Reference Sheet. From Staff Officer (Intelligence) Buenos Aires, No.24/36/45, 20th July 1945, Special Activities Branch Op-16-Z, NARA, p. 2, typed.

[92] I. Witkowski, *Hitler w Argentynie...*, p. 44-45.

* * *

Argentine press smelled a hot topic - they immediately reacted to news of the U-Boot at Mar del Plata. Newspapers were full of excitement and speculations. According to the first information, *U 530* was spotted by a fishing boat crew who, on July 10, entered the base and notified the navy command of the enemy submarine presence near the harbor. As a result, surface patrol boats were sent to escort the U-Boot to the harbor.

Another "well informed" source claimed that the U-Boot was spotted by a transport ship of the Argentine Navy in... mid June and then followed. A reporter of one of the Latin American newspapers informed that two people were disembarked near Puerto San Julián around June 1. Then, they used a rubber dinghy to get on a sailing boat. The submarine was fuelled up from tanks hidden underwater (?) at a place marked by three big rocks. The other U-Boot - according to the author of the article - was also heading to Argentina to surrender. Assistant of the chief of the Investigation Department informed the chief of the national Police that capitulation of the German submarine was expected earlier than it actually happened. The reporter also claimed that... Eva Braun and Adolf Hitler landed in southern Argentina.

CREW OF *U 530* (AGE) WHO, ON JULY 10, 1945, SURRENDERED TO THE ARGENTINEANS AT MAR DEL PLATA
Officers: Otto Wermuth (CO) – 25, Karl Felix Schlüter (F/O) – 22, Karl Heinz Lenz (2/O) – 22, Peter Löffler (ChEng) – 22, Gregor Schlüter (1 A/E) – 32; Senior Non-Commissioned Officers: Rudolf Schlicht – 26, Rolf Petrasch – 26, Arno Krause – 25, Ernst Zickler – 24; Junior Non-Commissioned Officers and seamen: Johannes Wilkens – 30, Hans Söth – 26, Paul Hahn – 45, Jürgen Fischer – 27, Georg Rieder – 27, Heinz Rehm – 24, Rudolf Böck – 22, Günter Doll – 21, Viktor Woyzik – 27, Georg Mittelstaedt – 26, Werner Rothenhagen – 24, Robert Gerlinger – 24, Karl Kroupa – 25, Philip Kurt Wirth – 24, Herbert Pätznick – 22, Sigismund Kolasinski – 22, Fritz Mönkediek – 23, Harry Kolakowski – 21, Franz Hutter – 22, Georg Göbel – 24, Heinz Hoffmann – 20, Heinz Paetzold – 21, Georg Wiedemann – 21, Hans Bartel – 21, Joachim Krätzig – 20, Hans Wolfgang Hoffmann – 22, Ernst Liewald – 21, Gerhard Muth – 25, Engelbert Rogg – 20, Gerhard Schwan – 20, Artur Fritz Jordan – 21, Eduard Kalbach – 23, Rudolf Müller – 22, Franz Rothenbücher – 22, Johannes Oelschlüger – 20, Willy Schmitz – 21, Günther Fischer – 19, Walter Gerhard Nellen – 20, Gerhard Piesnack – 21, Friedrich Purcz – 21, Hugo Traut – 20, Arthur Engelken – 22, Reinhard Karsten – 22, Franz Jendretzki – 23, Josef Werner Zerfa – 20.

Later, conversations between officers of the Argentine naval base and American and British investigators proved none of the information above to be true. The German submarine turned up in the Mar del Plata base before anyone noticed her presence. It was revealed that heaps of sand partially blocking the entrance to the harbor channel and the city lights behind them, obscured the lights at the end of the breakwater which made it difficult to recognize the entrance to the base. Argentine submarine officers were impressed by outstanding navigation skills of the German seamen - for reasons mentioned above, they themselves never attempted to enter the harbor at night time. It is certain that Argentina participated in the war only in theory. The entrance to the harbor was never closed at night which would have prevented unauthorized ships from entering the naval base or raising alarm.

On August 7, 1945, the American intelligence officer made interesting remarks after visiting the Mar del Plata submarine base. He reported to the US Navy attaché in Buenos Aires:

There is proof that, in some cases, guards at the main entrance to the base are undisciplined. During the six-day-long stay at Mar del Plata, we paid many official visits and, every time, we were stopped at the entrance checkpoint. Having confirmed our identification, a guard would accompany us in our vehicle to prevent us from wandering around the base and to help us reach our destination.

With an exception of one rainy day when visibility was limited to 200 yards [182 m - M.B., P.W.]. In those conditions, none of the guards left their guardhouse and no one got into our vehicle.

It is almost certain that in case of heavy rain, even during day, the fence surrounding the base and the breakwater is left unguarded which makes entering the base in secret very easy[93].

* * *

The declassified FBI documents told us that reports of ... Hitler's presence in Argentina appeared as early as in May 1945! After the World War II ended in Europe, the Director of the Federal Bureau of Investigation, John Edgar Hoover began receiving sensational intelligence reports about Hitler and other people close to him who lived in Argentina. The reports were systematically verified. One of the memos was sent by the FBI field office in Los Angeles on August 14, 1945. The information came from an unidentified (the name was censored) agent or a secret cooperative (working as an actor). The content of the report is quite exciting:

[censored] *Hollywood, who was confirmed as a radio actor and as "playing small parts in movies", reported from confirmed sources that Adolf Hitler was hiding in Argentina. According to* [censored] *he met a man named* [censored] *of Spanish-Argentine origin in a club in Hollywood and, after a long conversation on general topics,* [censored] *told* [censored] *about a huge burden he had been carrying and wanted to know if* [censored] *was able to help him. He confirmed that* [censored]*, who was fluent in Spanish, was one of four men who met Hitler and his entourage when they arrived aboard a submarine two and a half weeks after the fall of Berlin* [about May 20-21, 1945 - M.B., P.W.].

---

[93] Intelligence Raport, 8 August 1945, Record Group (RG) 59, sign.862.30/7-1045 [information concerning *U 530* – M.B., P.W.], NARA.

The first submarine reported as arrived, appeared about 11.00 at night and the second one about two hours later. According to the report, Hitler was to be on the second submarine along with two women, a doctor and many other people. A total of 50 people disembarked the submarine. Horses had been prepared for them and, at dawn, the group began a one-day-long trip along the southern Andes. At dusk, they arrived at a ranch where Hitler and his men were to be hiding. According to [censored], *the enterprise had been arranged by six highest ranking Argentine officials in 1944 and* [censored] *and further reports had been prepared predicting/stating that had Hitler been captured, the names of the six officials would have been revealed to* [censored]. *Names of three other people that had helped Hitler reach his hideout* [deep inland - M.B., P.W.] *would also have been revealed.*

[censored] *confirmed receiving 15,000 dollars to help the enterprise and testified that apart from the fact that he was no longer willing to participate in the operation, he was convinced that capturing Hitler was just a matter of time and, in that case, he would have been forced to clear his name on his own.*

[censored] *informed that two interesting pieces of information were revealed during the expedition. One of them said that French harbors in the English Channel, after the fall of Berlin, were anti Allies and helped Hitler leave one of the ...* [end of the declassified document - M.B., P.W.] [94].

It turns out, that two weeks prior to *U 530* surrender, rumors circled Buenos Aires talking about the first (?) German submarine reaching the shores of Argentina. In the spring of 1945, the Allied military secret service gathered any information concerning U-Boots that probably arrived at South America. On the other hand, reporters wrote about Hitler and Bormann's alleged escape from besieged Berlin. The fact that Hitler and Braun died on April 30, 1945, in the German leader's office and their bodies were burnt at the bunker's evacuation exit by the Führer's closest men, did not present evidence hard enough to convince South American journalists.

In the first days of June 1945, the FBI office in Buenos Aires was informed by a secret collaborator that, on June 7, at 16.00, two unknown individuals were seen - one of them was a tall, balding man, over forty years old. They came off the seventeen-meter-long fishing boat *Juncal*[95] in the Mar del Plata harbor. The unidentified passengers left the boat and immediately headed to the capital of Argentina. The boat owner - according to the secret agent - spent a lot of time at sea but rarely brought any sharks.

The sensational reports, coming from informers who had allegedly seen German officials at the shore, were easy to impugn as they lacked authenticity.

A radiogram from the Federal Bureau of Investigation in Buenos Aires, declassified many years after the war, informs that about June 20, 1945, several weeks before

---

[94] FBI Messenger; Declassified FBI documents, Los Angeles, August 1945. Copy in the authors' collection.

[95] The boat was used to catch sharks; she had speed of up to 13 knots and was able to stay at sea for 3-4 days. The boat had five berths.

the first U-Boot surrendered at Mar del Plata, a German submarine had arrived to Argentina... with Hitler on board. The Third Reich chancellor's face was disfigured. The Argentine Army officer, Maj. Leon Dengoallamas (words come from a distorted message -M.B., P.W.)[96] escorted Hitler to a secret hideout in the Argentine province of Chaco, in the north of the country, close to the border with Paraguay.

The same report states that, about June 28, another submarine surfaced at the southern coast of the Santa Cruz province near the town of Puerto San Julián in Argentina and disembarked two unidentified individuals. A witness claims that one of them was a high ranking German Army officer and the other one was an even more important civilian. Who were the mysterious passengers? According to the declassified report No. 103 from July 14, 1945, which is being kept in the American National Archives in Maryland, all information came from a very unreliable source and both rumors were thoroughly investigated.

A report from July 18, was made by the USA military attaché in Buenos Aires The classified information was approved by Brig. Gen. A.R. Harris. Here are some of its extracts:

At 18.00, on July 5, 1945, the ocean going yacht "San Lorenzo" arrived at the Mar del Plata harbor with a person unknown to fishermen from the port area.

A Nazi agent, known to be employed in Pedro Ilvesto and considered to be the right-hand man of [SS captain - M.B., P.W.] *Juan Sigfriedo Becker[97], was seen in Miramar, south of Mar del Plata during the first week of July. It is very unusual for somebody to come to the resort during winter, unless one has some business there.*

On July 17, 1945, around 15.00, two submarines were spotted about three kilometers from General Lavalle, mid way between Buenos Aires and Mar del Plata. Visibility did not allow for identification but at 16.00 the ships were reported to be heading to Mar del Plata, escorted by aircraft of the Argentine Navy.

In the morning of July 18, the Argentine Navy denied presence of any other German submarines than „U 530" in the Argentinean waters.

The abovementioned rumors are being verified and a report will be made in the nearest future. Detailed interrogation of the crew (four of them have Polish sounding last names[98]) by the experts will probably provide evidence of anyone being left ashore[99].

---

[96] There is a hand written note next to the underlined name of the Argentine officer: "The Army should take efforts to explain this rumor".

[97] Becker lived in Buenos Aires; he was probably one of the most cunning and the most effective agents of the German intelligence on the Western Hemisphere until 1945. During the war, he conspired, along with Perón, to overthrow the Allies-backed Bolivian government. He helped the Nazis transfer money to Argentina. Himmler was very proud of him. Becker was considered, by the American intelligence, to be "the most important German agent" in South America.

[98] They were: Franz Jendretzki, Sigismund Kolasinski, Harry Kolakowski and Vicktor Woyzik,

[99] Military Intelligence Division W.D.G.S., Military Attache Report, Argentina, 18 July 1945; Report No. R-509-45, Record Group (RG) 59 (U.S. Departament of State Central Decinal Files), NARA, p. 2, typed.

We owe another clue connecting Hitler to Argentina to a declassified document No. 134 made by an FBI agent in August 1945. Part of the message was censored:

Data available in this document contain a report of a special agent [censored - M.B., P.W.] on July 18 and talk about the surrender of the German submarine "U 530" in Mar del Plata. It also concerns rumors about landing in San Julián in Argentina [censored - M.B., P.W.]. [The agent - M.B., P.W.] came across two sets of footprints leading in the same direction from water, through the wet and flat shore to an area near San Julián. Where the footprints ended , tire marks were found that led to the right of the coast. The footprints must have been left there on June 25 as flooding of the flat shore stops at that time. Attempts were made to establish the vehicle's route. The investigation led to the town of Veronica[100].

A radiogram from the FBI branch in Buenos Aires (there is no date of the declassified document) contained additional information concerning reports of the German fugitives (?) presence in the town of Veronica:

The local press informs about the Police department conducting searches [for Hitler - M.B., P.W.] in the German colony in the town of Villa Gessel. General Madariaga is conducting search for individuals who probably arrived there aboard a submarine. While combing through the terrain, transmitter equipment was found. Permission was given to conduct searches along the coast but no arrests were made. The investigation in the town of Veronica found many different forms [evidence - M.B., P.W.] of pro Nazi attitudes, however, no evidence was found to prove a recent arrival of any German personnel[101].

Evacuation aboard a U-Boot to South America in such a short time, was possible using a fast, large submarine (almost 90-meters long), for example the Type IX D2. The ocean going submarines reached speeds of 19 knots on the surface and about 7 knots submerged. Between 1942 and 1944 the Germans built 28 such submarines[102]. The Type IX D2 U-Boots needed about 17 days to travel 7,000-7,500 nmi (13,000-14,000 km). Such a trip to Buenos Aires was theoretically possible provided that the cruise would have began on the day of Berlin's capitulation (May 3, 1945).

---

[100] Report nr 134 from FBI in Buenos Aires, August 1945 (deciphered radiogram copy concerning U-Boot arrival to Argentina), NARA.

[101] S. Dunstan, G. Williams, *Grey Wolf...*, p. 222.

[102] *U 177, U 178, U 179, U 181, U 182, U 196, U 197, U 198, U 199, U 200, U 847, U 848, U 849, U 850, U 851, U 852, U 859, U 860, U 861, U 862, U 863, U 864, U 871, U 872, U 873, U 874, U 875, U 876.*

CHAPTER IV

INVESTIGATION AND CAPTIVITY

A lie is no different from the truth, except for the fact it is a lie.
Stanisław Jerzy Lec

In the morning of July 10, 1945, a representative of the Argentine Navy informed the chief of the American intelligence cell in Buenos Aires that a German submarine surrendered at the Mar del Plata base. The important fact was also shared with the British naval attaché in the capital of Argentina. Representatives of both allied countries were given permission to inspect *U 530*. The American military attaché in Buenos Aires, Maj. Gibbons wrote in his report:

I headed to Mar del Plata in a vehicle owned by the Argentine Navy, accompanied by Captain Villanueva (chief of the AN intelligence), Captain Loyd Hirst Ret. (assistant to the British naval attaché) and Captain Fowler (British intelligence). Immediately upon arrival we boarded "General Belgrano". Commander Julio C. Mallea, CO of the submarine base, accepted the surrender of the German submarine from her commanding officer. Captain Rogelio Perez, Chief of Staff of the Argentine naval squadron, was also present as the base was under his jurisdiction. Captain Perez flew all the way from Buenos Aires[103].

Unfortunately, right after the initial inspection, it turned out that, although the U-Boot had been painted green, most of the paint was worn off. The external appearance of the submarine was similar to her condition inside - she was rusty and neglected. Her conning tower was in a terrible technical state. On its surface, the Argentineans noticed penetration marks left by a strong caustic agent (acid?). The twin 37 mm anti-aircraft gun was corroded, covered with brown patina stained with characteristic greenish-blue patches. The weapon was out of commission. The bases of the four 20 mm anti-aircraft guns (two twin guns) were empty as the guns had

---

[103] Issued by The Intelligence Division Office of Chief of Naval Operations Navy Department. Intelligence Report, serial 201-39, No. 915-400…, NARA, p. 1, typed.

been thrown overboard. The torpedo tubes had only one faulty 533 mm torpedo. Ammunition for the anti-aircraft guns had been rendered useless as the crew had left it on the deck. The inspection revealed no firearms. None of the crew members had their documents. At the end if their cruise the crew got rid of the submarine's log, navigation log and all navigation maps. Only several navigation tables had been left to aid the crew in the last stage of the voyage. Two periscopes (search and combat) were in good technical condition. The snorkel's mast was undamaged. Some of the U-Boot's instruments were intact. The submarine was equipped with a very good and strong radio which was still operational[104]. There was no damage caused during combat engagement. The U-Boot had five deflated rubber dinghies, however, a large dinghy was missing.

Navy Lieutenant Archie W. Grenn Ret. from the American naval attaché office in Buenos Aires writes:

The life rafts were stored in a watertight container on the submarine's deck and were equipped with a bag containing yellowish chemical agent. The agent, upon releasing, would paint the surface of water very bright green. The rafts are orange so it is possible the chemicals were chosen to make them more visible from the air. It was noted that the locked container was in the front section of the conning tower when "U 530" arrived at Mar del Plata. There was no raft (rubber dinghy) in the container. It was filled with bright green liquid, probably colored by sea water. It is interesting that, if one raft (rubber dinghy) had been secretly used for some reason, it is possible that the chemical agent was left in the container and sea water could get inside[105].

When the crew of *U 530* disembarked, they were examined by the Argentine Navy doctor. Their general physical and mental condition was good. However, they were all pale, probably due to lack of daylight.

Rómulo Horacio Bustos, the Argentine Army officer and commander of a coastal gun battery near Mar del Plata, entered *U 530* three days after her crew had surrendered. His first impression upon boarding the submarine was an overwhelming stench (despite ventilating all rooms) and very little space in the crew compartments. He noticed that the U-Boot commander's cabin was also very small and modestly arranged. He did not see and Nazi symbols[106]. After many years, the retired Colonel Bustos remembered:

---

[104] The American investigator suspected that *U 530* had other reasons to come to Argentina. According to him, the U-Boot, during her cruise that had started in February 1945, was able to return to any of the European harbors to pick up special passengers and deliver them to Argentina. See: Issued by The Intelligence Division Office of Chief of Naval Operations Navy Department. Intelligence Report, serial 195-45, No. 915-400…, p. 3, typed.

[105] Issued by The Intelligence Division Office of Chief of Naval Operations Navy Department. Intelligence Report, serial 201-45, No. 915-400. From Naval Attaché at Buenos Aires, 24 July 1945, Source – Personal observation, Record Group (RG) 165 (War Departament General Staff), NARA, p. 3, typed.

[106] S. Dunstan, G. Williams, *Grey Wolf…*, p. 230.

I managed to have a conversation with the submarine commander, Otto Wermuth, who spoke French and English very well. He told me that, according to Admiral Dönitz's last order, they were to surrender to the Allies. At that time, the submarine was near the north-eastern coast of Brazil. He did not want to surrender to the Uruguayans. [...] Wermuth and other officers were quartered on the old armored cruiser "General Belgrano" [from 1899 - M.B., P.W.] and the rest of the crew was accommodated [temporarily in the base - M.B., P.W.] in tents on a football pitch. A navy doctor gave orders to regularly feed the German seamen with boiled potatoes and lemons.

I remember the German commander seemed very young and was very well mannered. [...] He was grateful to the Argentine Army for the good treatment he and his men received. He did not strike me as a fanatic Nazi. He said he missed his family very much[107].

Between July 13 and 15, 1945, officers of the Argentine intelligence interrogated nine crew members of *U 530* - five officers (Otto Wermuth, Karl Felix Schlüter, Karl Heinz Lenz, Peter Löffler, Gregor Schlüter) and four senior non-commissioned officers (Rudolf Schlicht, Rolf Petrasch, Arno Krause and Ernst Zickler). The remaining 45 submariners, after several days in the base, were, under guard, transferred to the navy maximum security prison on a small island of Martina Garcia (compared to the American Alcatraz Federal Penitentiary in San Francisco), where the Uruguay and Parana rivers meet. They remained there, waiting for their commanding officer and the rest of their comrades.

Although the American and British investigators reached the interrogation facility, they were not invited to take part in operations to confirm credibility of the German submariners' testimonies. Captain José A. Dellepiane, chairman of the Argentine Navy investigation committee, agreed to allow Navy Lieutenant Archie W. Green Ret. and John Meyer of the American legal attaché personnel (he spoke German) and Commander W. H. Fowler, staff officer of the British Navy intelligence in Buenos Aires, to participate in the interrogations but only as observers. José A. Dellepiane was afraid their presence could negatively influence the witnesses' testimonies. The investigation was conducted aboard the base ship *General Belgrano*.

Intelligence officers of the US and Royal Navy insisted to have the interrogation transcript read to them right after each interned seaman of *U 530* testified. The Argentineans translated the texts in a slipshod manner. Short notes were made in Spanish. Due to "political" reasons, the foreign military observers were asked not to share the fact of capturing the crew of the German U-Boot with the public, which was noted in one of the reports.

The Argentine investigation committee also included: Commander Carlos O. Ribera as a secretary and interrogation assistant, Lieutenant Olinto P. Berry as an in-

---

[107] Report in the authors' collection.

terpreter. Commander Patricio J. Conway and an interpreter Lieutenant Juan Caros Benisch got familiar with part of the U-Boot's documents.

The nine interned submariners were kept in separate cabins without being able to communicate with each other. During the interrogation, all questions and answers went via an interpreter. The questions had been prepared in advance[108].

On July 13, the first to testify was Lieutenant Otto Wermuth. When asked about his ties to Argentina, he stated that he did not have any relatives nor friends in South America, he had never been there before and he did not know anybody of the interned crew of *Admiral Graf Spee*. He emphasized that he knew of no one of his crew who would be related to the sailors of the battleship sunk near the Montevideo harbor[109]. He was not able to confirm his identity. During the interrogation (having thought for a while), not knowing whether it was relevant or not, he recalled that, when the submarine was in the open sea, one of his crewmen, Joachim Kratzig... married a girl from Kiel (probably on March 30, 1945). The U-Boot commander conducted the ceremony over a radio and signed the marriage certificate. He guaranteed, the certificate was in possession of one of the men. The formal record of the change of the 20-year-old submariner's marital status - as Wermuth explained - was certainly kept in the Kiel Registry Office.

Before the cruise, *U 530* commander had an opportunity to take 245 t of fuel but, upon the chief engineer's request, they only got 225 t. According to the first officer, it was done to achieve better stability of the submarine. Additionally, the U-Boot took 5 t of oil. Wermuth also claimed that, in Kiel, he loaded a week's worth of fresh food supplies (meat, vegetables, bread etc.) and special food supplies made for submarines for 17 weeks of combat patrol. The ship carried 14 torpedoes and ammunition but no naval mines. He then testified that later the submarine received no supplies.

When asked if *U 530* operated alone or in a pack, Wermuth refused to answer the question, but he admitted that orders came directly from Berlin. He was ordered to move to his area of operations to attack enemy shipping. He again refused to reveal his assigned AO.

The U-Boot commander revealed that, while in the area of operations, the submarines would not send radio reports about executed torpedo attacks nor would they report being attacked by enemy ships. Wermuth testified that his radio sent only daily weather reports. The last contact with the commanding officer in Berlin was on April 26 - the message concerned safety measures to be taken by the U-Boot.

When answering further questions of the investigators, he acknowledged that, on May 8, 1945, he received a non-coded message about ceasing all hostilities at sea.

---

[108] Issued by The Intelligence Division Office of Chief of Naval Operations Navy Department. Intelligence Report, serial 201-45, No. 915-400; From Naval Attaché at Buenos Aires, 24 July 1945..., p. 2, typed.

[109] It was not true. Lt. Karl Felix Schüller's (Executive Officer on *U 530*) brother Victor was the crewman of the battleship *Admiral Graf Spee* and, after she had been scuttled, was interned in Argentina.

Then, he corrected himself and testified that the message was received on May 10. He claimed that the message was received for several more days. According to it, the submarine was to seize hostilities, use navigation lights at night, fly a blue (?) flag on the periscope, move only on the surface and head to the nearest port to surrender to the Allies. Wermuth did not mention the fact that he was not authorized to destroy the diesel engines, anti-aircraft guns, radar, hydro acoustic or communication equipment. According to the high command orders they were to remove fuses from all torpedoes and throw all ammunition into the sea. Wermuth emphasized that he did not believe those orders were true. He suspected an enemy deception.

However, he decided to leave his sector of operations and head to a neutral harbor to have his submarine and crew interned. He said that Portugal and Spain were rejected as they were too close to the war zone. He knew that Argentina broke diplomatic ties with Germany, but not of the fact that the countries were formally at war. That is why he decided to sail to South America. He chose this place as it was far from war zones and he thought they would receive better treatment there. He found out that Argentina had entered the war after the U-Boot arrived at Mar del Plata.

Lieutenant Wermuth after Germany's capitulation - as he further testified during the interrogation - initially intended to go to Miramar to surrender, but later decided to head to the Argentine submarine base in Mar del Plata. He told the investigators that 54 men aboard *U 530* was the standard complement of that type of the ocean going submarine[110]. He added that, during the last patrol, the U-Boot did not carry any additional passengers - neither civilian nor military.

Wermuth was asked about prisoners of war (?) and answered that there were no such passengers during the cruise. He also testified that not a single person or any kind of treasure had been unloaded at the Argentine coast or anywhere else before the submarine surrendered. There were no valuables aboard *U 530*.

When answering further questions of the Argentine Navy officers, Wermuth said that he was unaware of any other submarines heading to Argentina and his had no contact with any U-Bootwaffe ships. However, he also said that if there had been any U-Boots on course to Argentina, they would have reached their destination within a week from his arrival. Wermuth did not give a reason for such a statement which gave the investigators something to ponder about.

Already at the beginning of the investigation, the U-Boot commander testified that the submarine's main engines were worn out and in poor technical condition. However, later he admitted to giving orders to sabotage the diesels by not lubricating them. Later, a liter and a half of caustic mixture containing nitric, sulfuric and hydrochloric acid was added to oil and ran through the engines. Wermuth confessed that the acid mixture was also added to all oil tanks.

---

[110] Several weeks later, Wermuth told the investigators in the USA, that *U 530* had the ability to carry even 60 people but the crew was reduced due to difficult situation of the German submarine fleet (because of lack of trained submariners).

The German officer confirmed that the following were thrown overboard: ship's log, navigation log and classified documents, five torpedoes, gyroscope and warhead of a faulty torpedo, torpedo guidance system, 20 mm and 37 mm anti-aircraft ammunition, some components of the 37 mm gun, dynamite charges, gauges, three devices of the anti-radar system, complete radar equipment along with the antenna.

When asked about the amount of fresh water aboard the submarine, he answered he had no knowledge of that, since the distillation facilities' efficiency exceeded the daily consumption of the 50-men crew. Lieutenant Wermuth said:

I divided the journey into four areas. The weather was as follows: Area 1 (North Pole to Bahia in Brazil), strong east winds, visibility 5 miles up to 5 m above sea level, waves 3 m regular; Area 2 (Bahia to 20° south latitude), south winds 6 m per second, visibility 3 to 4 miles to 5 m above sea level, waves 3 m regular; Area 3 (20° south latitude to Rio Grande do Sul in Brazil), wind changeable from south to north 3 m per second, visibility 8 miles to 5 m above sea level, small waves; Area 4 (Rio Grande do Sul in Brazil to Mar del Plata in Argentina), north winds up to 28 m per second, visibility 4 to 5 miles to 5 m above sea level, occasional showers, waves from 4 to 5 m[111].

Then, the Argentine investigators accused the commanding officer of *U 530* of torpedoing the Brazilian light cruiser *Bahia* (3,150 t) near the Penedo de Sao Paulo islands on July 9, 1945[112]. The accusations were withdrawn when it was proved that the submarine was too far from the place of the cruiser's tragedy[113].

The statement of reasons reads:

In the case of the alleged sinking of the Brazilian cruiser "Bahia" by the [German - M.B., P.W.] *submarine: distance, time frame and speed of the submarine make the event highly improbable. A constant speed of 18 knots would have been required and the submarine would have to stay on the surface taking the shortest route, close to the shore. It is doubtful that the submarine was able to maintain such speed, moving on the surface for six days, unspotted*[114].

According to the official report, the tragedy of *Bahia* was caused by a 20 mm Oerlikon round that, while conducting target practice, hit depth charges stored on the

---

[111] Resume of Interrogation of Lieut.(j.g.) Otto Wermuth, Commanding Officer of the German submarine *U 530...*, p. 4, typed.

[112] Map analysis shows that those are the hardly visible, 18 meters above sea level, Saint Peter and Saint Paul Rocks, almost on the equator, about 1,000 km from the Brazilian Natal harbor, coordinates - 00°55'02"N and 29°20'44"W.

[113] Issued by The Intelligence Division Office of Chief of Naval Operations Navy Department. Intelligence Report, serial 201-45, No. 915-400; From Naval Attaché at Buenos Aires, 24 July 1945..., p. 2, typed.

[114] Issued by The Intelligence Division Office of Chief of Naval Operations Navy Department. Intelligence Report, serial 195-45, No. 915-400..., p. 4, typed.

deck of the cruiser. A huge explosion destroyed the ship. Two hundred ninety four crewmen lost their lives (other sources give a number of 336). Thirty six (?) men were rescued. Four American radio operators who served on the ship - William Joseph Eustace, Andrew Jackson Pendleton, Emmet Peter Salles and Frank Benjamin Sparks died (the US Navy mentions those men as missing in action).

* * *

Lieutenant Otto Wermuth, at the beginning of his stay at Mar del Plata, appeared - according to the Argentine investigators - completely depressed and stripped of all hope for the future, after Germany had lost the war. However, a few days after the investigation was concluded, during private conversations with Argentine officers, he looked more lively. At one occasion Wermuth said that "he likes the country - it is a good place to live" and "when all this is over" he would bring his family and settle in Argentina[115].

LIGHT CRUISER *BAHIA*
Light cruiser *Bahia* (pennant number C 12) was built by the Armstrong Whitworth shipyard in Elswick, Great Britain. The ship was laid down on August 7, 1907, launched on April 20, 1909, commissioned in 1910. General characteristics: displacement – 3,150 t; dimensions: length oa- 122,4 m, beam – 11.9 m, draft – 4.2 m; Maximum speed – 27 knots; Range: 6,600 nmi at 10 knots; propulsion: 3 turbines, 6 boilers = 22,000 hp; fuel: 640 t of mazout; armor: deck 38 mm; armament: 10 (x I) guns cal. 120 mm L/50 Armstrong pat. 06, 4 (x I) anti-aircraft guns cal. 76 mm, 8 (2 x IV) anti-aircraft Vickers Mk.III cal. 12.7 mm guns, 4 (2 x II) torpedo launchers cal. 533 mm. In 1926 the cruiser Bahia was modernized - additional ? (x I) cal. 20 mm and 2 depth charge launchers were installed.

What did 22-year old Lt. Karl Felix Schlüter, executive officer on *U 530*, testify?

He abstained from giving answers to a lot of questions or was completely indifferent, not willing to cooperate. He testified that he entered service in the Kriegsmarine in January 1941, and two years later received his first officer's commission. In February 1945, he was promoted to the rank of lieutenant (his awards included the Knight's Cross Second Class for his participation in combat). Although he admitted to be the executive officer, he refused to give the date he was assigned the position. He also did not give any details concerning the last patrol of *U 530*. He did answer questions about additional cargo carried on the submarine.

Schlüter claimed the main engines were in poor condition because they were worn out and the crew had had problems with them four days prior to entering Mar del Plata. Similar version was presented by other crew members interrogated

---

[115] Resume of Interrogation of Lieut.(j.g.) Otto Wermuth, Commanding Officer of the German submarine *U 530*..., p. 5, typed.

in Argentina. The submariners did not reveal the true reasons of the engine trouble. The investigators learned about the real cause of damage to the diesels only thanks to Wermuth's testimonies. Lieutenant Schlüter refused to sign the interrogation protocol but did not give any rasons for his decision[116].

Ensign (Leutnant zur See) Karl Heinz Lenz was the artillery officer on *U 530*. He told the investigators that before entering service in the navy he had studied medicine. He testified that all men on the submarine were members of the same crew that had left Kiel and no other people (prisoners of war or civilians) were on board of the U-Boot during her last cruise. He either did not remember or purposely witheld the truth about the number of large life ratfs (rubber dinghies) aboard the submarine. He refused to say whether the crew was aware of Germany's capitulation. He claimed, he did not know of any other German submarines heading to Argentina. When asked detailed questions, he refused to answer or claimed he did not remember. He was one of the few witnesses who signed their testimonies[117].

The chief engineer on *U 530* was Lieutenant Peter Löffler. He testified that he was transferred to the submarine at the end of January 1945. For his service, he was awarded two medals and the Knight's Cross Second Class. Löffler said he knew about Germany's capitulation but refused to answer particular questions. He added that, during the cruise, the commanding officer called a meeting of officers. Löffler avoided answering questions concerning the subject of their conversation. They decided to head to Argentina because they thought they would receive better treatment there. The chief engineer confirmed that, when the submarine began her patrol, there were six life rafts (rubber ones) but they left one in Norway as it was in a very bad condition[118]. When the Argentine investigators asked about the place where the engine oil was loaded, the Lieutenant said that the barrels with the lubricant were brought onto the ship in Norway. After reaching Mar del Plata, the U-Boot had 6-7 t of fuel and 4 t of lubricating oil in her tanks. Löffler confirmed the fact that the commander had ordered the crew to destroy all valuable things and documents or throw them into the sea. The German, however, was not willing to say when it happened or to point the location on a map. He refused to sign the document.

32-year-old Lieutenant-Junior Grade Gregor Schlüter, first assistant engineer, was the oldest officer aboard the U-Boot. He was married and had a two-year-old daughter. Before entering service in the Kriegsmarine, he had studied engineering. For a year and a half he had served on patrol boats and mine layers as engineering

---

[116] Resume of Interrogation of Lieut. (j.g.) Karl Felix Schlüter, Executive Officer of German submarine, *U 530*, 24 July 1945, Special Activities Branch Op-16-Z, NARA, p. 1, typed.

[117] Resume of Interrogation of Ensign (j.g.) Karl Heinz Lenz of the German submarine, *U 530*, 24 July 1945, Special Activities Branch Op-16-Z, NARA, p. 1, typed.

[118] Typ IX C/40 submarines were equipped with one large rubber dinghy made by the "Metzler" company and five smaller ones. According to the manufacturer's manual, one 2 m long and 1.05 m wide rubber dinghy could carry four men.

petty officer until being assigned to *U 530* (it was his first submarine). As an officer, he received two medals for his service at the sea and the Knight's Cross Second Class for his patrol service. He testified that *U 530* had been cleaned and painted for the last time in the middle of January 1945. His testimonies were similar to those of the other witnesses. Schlüter refused to give details concerning the time of the commander's decision to head to Argentina. He said they celebrated crossing the equator but he withheld all the details. Like his comrades, he avoided answering many questions and refused to sign the interrogation protocol[119].

It was time to interrogate and test the credibility of the U-Boot's senior non-commissioned officers. The mechanics Rolf Petrasch and Ernst Zickler were the first ones to testify. The former volunteered for the Kriegsmarine in 1938. In 1940, he was transferred to submarines. Feldwebel Petrasch participated in all seven patrols of *U 530*. For distinguished service on the sea, he was awarded the Knight's Cross Second Class and two medals. The Petty Officer confirmed the officers' testimonies concerning the fact that the submarine, during her last patrol, did not sustain any damage, however, the U-Boot had been rammed by a tanker during one of the previous missions. He claimed they left Kristiansand in March 1945, and, for some time, travelled submerged to avoid aerial attacks. Then, they took course for England. At its northern shores, they entered their assigned sector where the submarine was to attack Allied ships. At night time they would use the snorkel to charge the batteries. Petrasch told the Argentine investigating officers that the U-Boot began her journey with 240 t of diesel fuel and later did not refuel. Regarding the rubber dinghies, he testified that the submarine carried four or five life rafts and each crew member had a rubber life vest.

The diesel engineer, Petty Officer Ernst Zickler was the most cooperative witness. He said he volunteered for the navy (he was single) in the middle of October 1939. After almost six months of training, he was transferred to submarines. After completing the theoretical course, he was assigned to the training flotilla used to prepare U-Boot crews. He had served on other submarines before he was assigned to *U 530* at the end of July 1943. He received four medals - the Knight's Cross First and Second Class and two naval medals. According to him, the submarine was in a dry dock for the last time in the Deutsche A.G. Werft in Hamburg, at the beginning of January 1945. Zickler testified that, at the beginning of March, the U-Boot left Kristiansand escorted (for two hours) by another ship but he did not remember what vessel it was. Later, they travelled alone. During the following days (three weeks), they sailed submerged due to the threat of aerial attacks. They used the snorkel to charge the batteries. He said that, during the last cruise, the submarine's diesel and electric motors were used constantly. The maximum speed they were able to reach while using the snorkel was 6 knots. The Petty Officer testified:

---

[119] Resume of Interrogation of Ensign Gregor Schluter, 2nd Engineer of the German submarine, *U 530*, 24 July 1945, Special Activities Branch Op-16-Z, NARA, p. 1, typed.

One day, during the cruise, the captain said over the speakers that the fighting had ceased. Several days later, also via the intercom, he informed the crew that they were going to Argentina to surrender. He said that they were heading there to receive better treatment and that he had chosen Mar del Plata as their destination. He thought they were able to sail farther but it was doubtful due to poor condition of the engines. The engines were "knocking" and that was why they had to move slowly.

Before the cruise we had loaded 243 t of diesel fuel [! - M.B., P.W.] and 13 t of lubricating oil. [...] During the cruise we used two to three tons of diesel fuel a day. [...]

"U 530" was sailing better on two electrical and high-pressure engines. When the submarine was new, it had maximum speed of 19 knots on the surface but now she was not able to reach more than 16 knots. Her maximum speed underwater was 8 knots. The submarine was able to sail submerged for over two days at 2 knots.

Each crew member was equipped with individual rubber life vest[120].

The America investigators, after getting familiar with the documents, were convinced that the 24-year-old Petty Officer Zickler (he did not sign the document), with use of proper interrogation procedures, would have had revealed more about the events that took place during the last patrol.

25-year-old Petty Officer Arno Krause was the underwater weapons officer on *U 530* from August 3, 1942. He was a volunteer and entered service in 1941. His first submarine was the Type VII, middle size U-Boot (he did not reveal the ship's pennant number). He confirmed that they began their last combat patrol in Norway but he did not know the planned route. During the last patrol they did not sink any ships. Several days after the commander informed the crew about the end of the war, they were ordered to throw torpedoes and ammunition overboard. Krause testified that they saw lights on the shore a day or a day and a half before entering Mar del Plata; they were submerged, about seven miles (13 km) from the submarine base.

Petty Officer Schlicht was the least cooperative. He refused to answer most of the questions. He only testified that he volunteered for the Kriegsmarine in 1939. After a year of courses and exercises at sea in the training flotilla, he spent the rest of his time in the U-Bootwaffe serving on several submarines (he did not reveal the U-Boots' numbers). Schlicht said that, at the beginning of May, the commander told the men that the war had ended.

The interrogation of the German submariners, who, after several days, were transported to the prison on the Martina Garcia Island, ended with no significant results. The Argentine investigating officers concluded that *U 530* did not carry any Nazis nor military officials and that no one had been disembarked on the Argentine shore before the submarine surrendered. The Argentineans gave the complete

---

[120] Resume of Interrogation of Ernst Zickler, Engineering Petty Officer of the German submarine, *U 530*, Special Activities Branch Op-16-Z, NARA, p. 1-2, typed.

documentation of the interrogation of U 530 crew to USA and Great Britain military services in Buenos Aires.

The American and British observers were disappointed by the way the Argentine investigators handled the case. They thought the interrogators conducting the hearing of the German submariners, did not make any effort to get more information. Not for one moment were the U-Boot crewmen under crossfire of questions which would have made their testimonies more detailed and interesting - that was the opinion given by Maj. Gibbons on July 24, 1945, after he had got familiar with the complete set of documents. The analysis of the documents from the interrogation revealed that the senior non-commissioned officers were not very cooperative and none of them signed their testimonies.

Captain Dellepiane, chairmen of the Argentine investigation committee, maintained friendly relations with the Allied representatives in Mar del Plata. All officers that participated in the interrogation of the German prisoners were invited to a farewell dinner. The Argentine investigators told their allies - after a few shots of whisky - that they had talked to the interned seamen privately. Allegedly, they revealed details which were not included in the reports - that was Cpt. Fowler's short note put into the report sent to the Admiralty Office in Washington[121]. However, what the crewmen of U 530 revealed, remains unknown.

On July 18, Dellepiane appeared at the press conference and informed journalists about the results of the investigation. The captain denied the latest rumors that had been circling for some time, talking about mysterious submarines carrying Nazis, landing in Argentina and other places in South America. He said that the crew of U 530 could not be considered to be considered pirates (war criminals) although the American US Navy attaché thought otherwise. Dellepiane also told the journalists that the German seamen were being kept in the maximum security prison without a possibility to communicate with each other. That was not true. In the official statement, he claimed that the Argentine Navy had full control over the detainees and, in case of escape, they would face serious consequences[122].

At the beginning of the second half of July 1945, the German submarine along with her crew and full documentation of investigation concerning the last patrol of U 530 were handed over to the Americans[123].

On July 24, 1945, the US Navy intelligence officer, Lt. C.R White, flew from the United States to Argentina. However, upon his arrival, he found out that it was a mistake to begin the inquiry in Buenos Aires. The prisoners were not being held in individual cells, they had not been separated, contrary to what the Argentine Navy

---

[121] Reference Sheet. From Staff Officer (Intelligence) Buenos Aires, No.24/36/45, 20 th July 1945..., p. 1, typed.

[122] The Americans feared to lose the U-Boot. They thought that, after sabotaging the diesels, the Germans were able to do more harm to the submarine - damage the fuselage or open the bottom valves (Kingstones) which would result in scuttling of the U-Boot.

[123] See also: From: The Officer in Charge [Glen Jacobsen – M.B., P.W], U 530. To: The Commander Submarines, Atlantic Fleet; 29 August 1945, Naval Intelligence Papers, syign ADM 199, p. 1, typed.

claimed. Life of those more „talkative" could have been in danger. That was why, beginning the investigation in Argentina when all preparations to transfer the crew of *U 530* under the American jurisdiction had already been made, was just a waste of time. There were 45 junior non-commissioned officers and seamen waiting to be confronted by the investigators. Lt. Otto Wermuth and his subordinates had to be ready to give their statements again, in an internment camp.

✷✷✷

At the end of July 1945, *U 530* left Mar del Plata accompanied by an Argentine tugboat and torpedo boats *Misiones* and *San Juan* and headed to the Argentine Navy base in Rio Santiago. Two days later the U-Boot entered a dock. Meanwhile, a crew of 33 American submariners came to Argentina. Until the end of August, all compartments of the U-Boot were 60% ready to be used. Three technical teams, assigned to repair the diesels, worked 24 hours a day. The submarine was supplied with fuel, water and provisions.

✷✷✷

On July 30, the German seamen from Mar del Plata were transported to Santa Cruz and then, on two Douglas C-54 Skymaster aircraft, were flown to Miami, Florida[124]. Several Argentine soldiers went along with them, as guards.

At the beginning of August, Lt. Otto Wermuth and the other submariners of *U 530* were placed in Fort Hunt high security military base in Virginia[125], a dozen or so kilometers south from Washington, near Mount Vernon. The investigation of *U 530* combat operations was supervised by the Special Operations Department in the Office of Naval Intelligence from the start . The crewmen of the German submarine were interrogated individually and in groups until September 1945. Lieutenants Wermuth (gave his statement under officer's oath) and Schlüter[126] were subjected to

---

[124] See also: Memorandum for Commander in Chief, US Fleet. Subject: German Submarine and German Prisoners of War in Argentina, 17 July 1945 r. (a letter to the US Navy commander was perpared by Thos B. Inglis), Record Group (RG) 165 (War Departament General Staff), NARA, p. 1, typed.

[125] During World War II, Fort Hunt was a top secret investigation center of the American intelligence services where German submarine officers (mainly) were held and interrogated. Until the end of 1943, over 700 U-Bootwaffe POWs had been interrogated in the facility. On June 15, 1944, Captain Werner Henke, commanding officer of *U 515* - the highest ranking Kriegsmarine officer in the fort - was shot and killed by the Americans while "attempting to escape".

[126] R.C. Newton, *Actividades Clandestinas de La Maina Alemana en Aguas Argentinas, 1930-1945, Conferencia especial a La Rendicion de dos Submarinos Alemanes en Mar del Plata en 1945* ; www.histarmar.com.ar/InfHistorica/BusquedasUBoats/5-InformeCeanaCastellano.htm, p. 5; idem, *The „Nazi Mence" in Argentina, 1931-1947*, Stanford 1992.

long questioning. Documents found on the U-Boot in July 1945, were also helpful during further investigation[127].

On August 9, 1945, an extended list of questions was prepared by the chief of the US Navy Department in Washington, Gould H. Thomas and the chief of the US Navy War Crimes Department in Washington, Lieutenant Commander James O'Malley Jr. Ret[128].

Seamen of U 530 were quartered in barracks bugged with listening devices. Their conversations were recorded by the investigating officers fluent in German language. The gathered material turned out to be of little use. Lieutenant Wermuth was interrogated by Captain Halle, expert in international law, accompanied by Mr. Duevell, as an observer[129]. The American investigators were not able to undoubtedly ascertain if U 530 had participated in organized escape of German Nazis or if she had carried any valuables (gold bars, cash, jewelry of tremendous value and documentation of strategic weapons) to Argentina[130].

In fall of 1945, submariners of U 530 were taken to Fort George G. Meade in Maryland and to Papago Park in Arizona, the US Army camp for German seamen.

---

[127] The following documents helped the investigators: album documenting the submarine's launching and commissioning, with entries made by different people giving their best wishes to the crew; a list of officers and the crew of U 530; receipts for purchase of maritime equipment; diesels' maintenance log kept until July 8, 1945; world's merchant ships register for 1941-1942; copies of orders for the technical staff; chronometer log; map of the North Sea, geographical atlas - property of Lt. Schlüter - with a map recording U 530's last journey from Germany to Argentina (the investigators were certain the map had been falsified - there was a continuous line leading straight to Mar del Plata, not a day by day route); sea map with a route to Guyana; diary of Ensign Lenz with interesting entries but some pages had been torn out (the diary contains the proof the crew was aware of the lost war and the unconditional surrender, the Führer is referred to in the present tense) and documents belonging to Lt. Wermuth - payment book and identification card, notification of his mother's death, certificate of crossing the equator on U 530 with a date of October 23, 1943, and a check book. There were many more books and documents in German. See: Documents which might be of interest which were found on board the German submarine U 530, Record Group (RG) 165 (War Departament General Staff); Records of the G-2 (Intelligence) Division MIS-Y, NARA, p. 1-2, typed.

[128] The questions prepared by the investigators were about: contacts between the crew and passengers with people on land in Argentina; disembarking the SS soldiers in Argentina; informations concerning escape of German Nazis and war criminals; transfer of secret funds from Germany to South America; contacts with surface ships from the day of departure from Germany; special cargo – gold in bars, cash and strategic materials; information about surface ships and warships that could have run the blockade – details of the journey, cargo etc.; help received from a U-Boot or from a neutral country (including Argentina during its neutrality); information concerning shipping routes. See: Navy Department. Office of the Chief of Naval Operations. Memorandum, 9 August 1945 (document signed by director Gould H. Thomas), Special Activities Branch, NARA, p. 1, typed.; Memorandum for LT. Commander S. R. Hatton – Navy Department, Questions suggested for use in interrogation of German submarine personnel received from Argentina (document signed by Lt.Cdr. J. O'Malley Jr. Ret.), Special Activities Branch, NARA, p. 1-2, typed.

[129] The investigators asked tricky questions to prove Wermuth was lying, e.g. the Lieutenant was asked several times about 58 people aboard U 530. The U-Boot's commander consequently emphasized there were 54 crewmen on the submarine.

[130] We know that only a small amount of documents of conversations between the German submariners (including Wermuth, Schlüter and Wiedemann), that had been secretly recorded by the American investigators is kept in the National Archives and Records Administration in College Park. See: Records of the G-2 (Intelligence) Division MIS-Y – U 530, NARA.

After a dozen or so months spent in captivity in the USA, all members of the ocean going submarine Type IX C/40, who had caused quite a commotion on two continents with their arrival to South America, were released and returned to... Argentina. Veterans of *U 530* who wanted to join their families... were not allowed to return to Germany.

* * *

On September 8, 1945, *U 530*, repaired and in working order, was manned by an American crew. A few days later, tugboat USS *Cherokee* led the U-Boot from Rio Santiago - with a four day stop in Rio de Janeiro - to the United States of America. In the first days of October, *U 530* was in the US Navy submarine base in New London, Connecticut, near New York. On October 12, the U-Boot was sent to the Long Island naval base. On November 5, *U 530* entered the Key West base. From November 11 to December 12, she sailed, accompanied by the destroyer escort USS *Thomas*, the, so called, Victory Tour through Texas. Over a period of one month the ships visited the following harbors: Port Arthur, Houston, Galveston, Corpus Christi, Brownsville, Beaumont and Orange. After their return to the north, the submarine was in the US Navy bases in Key West and Norfolk.

On November 21, 1947, at 11.48, *U 530* was sunk during test, hit amidships by a torpedo fired by the American submarine USS *Toro*, in the North Atlantic at the shores of New England, north east of the Cod Peninsula at coordinates 42°39'N and 69°32'W. The U-Boot's wreck lies at a depth of 260 m[131]. She rests accompanied by *U 234, U 805, U 889, U 977* and *U 1228*, captured and sunk by the US Navy.

* * *

In 1947, Peter Hansen, the U-Bootwaffe veteran who, during the war, had participated in a combat patrol on *U 226* (before she was sunk in November 1943) and later worked on land for the Abwehr (he knew Admiral Dönitz and Admiral Canaris), was sent on a journey from Germany to Argentina. He was ordered to translate documents concerning the internment of *U 530*. His opinion on the documentation is unknown.

In 1990, 70-year-old Wermuth (he died in 2011), told Harry Cooper (an American supporter of conspiracy theories concerning escape of Hitler, Bormann and other Nazis to Argentina) that when the U-Boot left Kiel in February 1945, there

---

[131] See: A. Niestlé, *German U-Boat Losses...*, p. 127. However K. Wynn, *U-Boat Operations of the Second World war...*, v. 2, p, 17 writes that *U 530* was sunk during tests of a new type of an American torpedo on November 28, 1947.

were 56 people on board. Two "passengers" left the submarine in Horton. From then on, until her internment, *U 530* had 54 crewmen. They did not carry any special cargo (just food, torpedoes and six rubber dinghies).

As Wermuth said 45 years after the events in question, on May 12, 1945, they decided to sail to Punta Arenas in Chile (earlier he had never told anyone about that fact) but, at the beginning of July, the chief engineer informed him that they had not enough fuel - there were about 10 tons in the tanks. They were sailing along the Argentine coast. On July 8, at night, they were about 50-100 km south of the Miramar lighthouse (in a straight line, it is 46 km to Mar del Plata)... and there, they lost (?) a rubber dinghy, however, only the chief engineer and the watch officer were aware of that fact[132]. Wermuth gave no more details. Near Miramar, due to lack of fuel, *U 530*'s commanding officer decided to turn back and head to Mar del Plata[133].

In March 2008, the Argentine Navy allowed the American Sharkhunters Foundation and its chairman, H. Cooper, to get familiar with the archives about *U 530*, created in July 1945. The boxes did not contain any sensational materials. However, it turned out that the Argentine government had decided that all documents concerning the final mission of *U 530* on other submarines would remain classified until 2020. It is difficult to say what source materials are hidden in the old files.

* * *

In the introduction, the authors talked about the unexplained story of a high ranking SS officer and police official, Lieutenant General Heinrich Müller, who escaped justice several dozen hours before the fall of Berlin. For many years, historians and hunters of German war criminals claimed that the chief of the Gestapo in years 1939-1945[134] had disappeared at the end of the war covering all his tracks. Müller gained notoriety with his cruel attitude towards his political opponents and Jews. He was suspected to cooperate with the Russians or the CIA however, there is no trace of such contacts[135].

Hitler's personal pilot, Hans Baur, testified many years after the war that:

Those who knew Müller, were afraid of him although he had never been as powerful as Himmler or Kaltenbrunner. I am deeply convinced that his fate is not a mystery or,

---

[132] S. Dunstan, G. Williams, *Gref Wolf...*, p. 224 write: "*Wermuth interrogation report, translated from German to Argentine language and then, to English by the US Navy says that, he contemplated going to Miramar before making the decision to surrender in Mar del Plata*".

[133] H. Cooper, *More to U 530 skipper Wermuth*, KTB Nr 292, p. 11-12 (The Official History Publication of the U-Bootwaffe), www.sharkhunters.com

[134] A. Ramme, *Służba Bezpieczeństwa SS*, Warszawa 1975, p. 280.

[135] J. Mayo, E. Craigie, *Ostatni dzień Hitlera...*, p. 348.

in any case, there is nothing secret about it until the evening of May 1, 1945[136]. About an hour before the planned breakout, soon after sunset, I met Müller on the first floor of the Reich Chancellery. We used a lull in the Russian barrage to have a conversation. I thought Müller had come to join one of escaping groups. When I asked him about that, he answered: „Baur, my friend, I'm a realist and I know the end is coming. I can imagine how the Russians would play with the chief of the Gestapo if they got him. I have no illusions about that. No, I am staying here and when the time comes I will use my pistol and I think it will happen tonight..." Although I strongly opposed all the constant talking about suicide that had been going on in the last days, I did not try to talk him out of it. He knew about the Russian methods more than everybody else combined[137].

If 45-year-old Müller was planning his suicide, why was his body not found? When, on May 2, 1945, the Red Army soldiers captured Hitler's bunker, they found bodies of generals Wilhelm Burgdorf - Chief of the Army Personnel Office, one of Hitler's closest associates and Hans Krebs - the last Chief of Staff of the High Command of the German Army. They both had taken their own lives. Among their and other officers' bodies there was no trace of Müller.

The Gestapo chief disappeared and, from then on, nobody heard about him nor saw him. After the war, German officials considered him deceased. The government documents include his death certificate and in September 1945, his family held a funeral ceremony on the Kreuzberg (district of Berlin) cemetery. The general's relatives paid for his grave maintenance for a long time and his tomb was always decorated with flowers. The mystification was successful for many years...

In the 1960s, agents of the Israeli intelligence (Mossad), after capturing and bringing Adolf Eichmann before the court in Israel, began hunting other war criminal hiding in South America. According to Paul Manning, an American journalist, who worked for the CBS during the war, the chief of the Gestapo faked his own death. His gravestone bears an inscription: "Our beloved Daddy, Heinrich Müller, B. 28.4.1900, D. in Berlin on May 15, 1945"[138]. After exhumation conducted in 1963, it turned out that Müller's grave contained mixed remains of three different bodies (probably prisoners of war)[139]. The Berlin prosecutor's office confirmed the fact that the remains in the grave were not those of General Müller.

In 1967, the German government asked the authorities of Panama for extradition of a man named Francis Willard Keith with appearance so similar to Müller's, his own wife was convinced it was him. Fingerprint analysis proved it was not true.

---

[136] P. Manning, *Martin Bormann. Nazi in exile...*, p. 175 writes, that the last time Müller was in Hitler's bunker was on April 28, 1945.

[137] U. Bahnsen, J. O'Donnel J., *Katakumba. Ostatnie dni w bunkrze Hitlera...*, p. 236.

[138] P. Manning, *Martin Bormann. Nazi in exile...*, p. 179

[139] The exhumation was conducted after an article in one of the German newspapers; a journalist notified by an informer (his name was never revealed) questioned the authenticity of H. Müller's remains.

Did the chief of the Gestapo manage to escape aboard *U 530* to Argentina as Witkowski suggests[140]? If the war criminal arrived at South America aboard a U-Boot, it could not have been the submarine commanded by Lt. Wermuth. We know that *U 530* did not carry any of the German fugitive war criminals.

Müller probably lived in Cordoba from the spring of 1948 but disappeared after the kidnapping of Eichmann. Then he moved to a town of Natal in Brazil. Müller supposedly lived in Argentina in 1980, however, there is no evidence to prove it [141].

---

[140] I. Witkowski, *Supertajne bronie Hitlera...*, p. 142.

[141] S. Dunstan, G. Williams, *Grey Wolf...*, p. 291 write about H. Müller's life after the war in Patagonia. See also: H. Thomas, *SS-1. The Unlikely death of Heinrich Himmler*, London 2001, p. 183.

CHAPTER V

U 977 - BEARING FREEDOM

Every myth is a version of the truth
Margaret Atwood

In April 1945, Kiel, one of the main naval bases, shipyard centers and a place where the Third Reich submarines were produced, was the target of mass bombings conducted by heavy bombers of the Bomber Command. The Royal Air Force began systematical destruction of the Kriegsmarine warships and submarines. The operations were executed simultaneously with bombing raids deep in German territory. In the "Tirpitz" wet dock, an artificial fog was generated to guarantee safety for U-Boots (it was a place for almost 40 submarines) anchored at the pier.

People reacted nervously to huge explosions of aerial bombs, they anticipated further bombings in anxiety. The Luftwaffe long range night fighters, that were supposed to protect the cities, had practically ceased all their operations. Losses and damage to the harbor installations necessary to service U-Boots were substantial. Shipyards in the Kiel Bay, specializing in submarine construction, often had to stop production and the downtime would last several weeks. Submarine crews preparing for their last patrol of the war faced many difficulties. All necessary repairs were made in haste and, when the harbor was free from bombing raids, submarines were supplied with ammunition, fuel and provisions.

On April 1, supply operations on *U 977*, commanded by 24-year-old Lt. Heinz Schäffer, began. The U-Boot was loaded with provisions and ammunition (torpedoes and rounds for a single 37 mm and twin 20 mm anti aircraft guns) for a two-month-long mission. She was one of 568, mid-size, sea-going Type VII C attack submarines - the "work horses" of the Great Admiral Karl Dönitz. The ship was 67 m long with a beam of over 7 meters. Her hull was light gray. The Type VII submarines were reliable and dangerous. They were quite fast and maneuverable on the surface. The U-Boots had good underwater characteristics. A major flaw of the first series of the "sevens" was their short range due to smaller fuel capacity. Later versions of the most used German submarines received enlarged fuel tanks.

GENERAL CHARACTERISTICS OF THE TYPE VII C SUBMARINE	
Length	67.1 m
Beam	6.2 m
Draught	4.7 m
Height	9.5 m
Pressure hull length	50.5 m
Pressure hull beam	4.7 m
Pressure hull thickness	18.5 mm
Displacement surfaced	762 (769) t
Displacement submerged	869 (871) t
Combat displacement submerged (max)	1,070 t
Propulsion surfaced	2 x 1,400 hp, six cyllinder, four-stroke, Type F46, boosted Germaniaw-erft diesel engines
Propulsion submerged (without the snorkel)	2 x 375 KM Algemeine Elektricitäts Gosellschaft (AEG) 175 electric motors Typu GU 460/8-276
Batteries	2 accumulator batteries, 62 cells each (in containers without protective rubber coating) Type AFA 33 MAL 800 E with 9,160 Ah capacity and total weight of 62 t
Fuel capacity	113.47 t (maximum, using Nr 1 and Nr 3 torpedo tubes as tanks – 121,5 t)
Speed surfaced	17 knots
Speed submerged	7.9 knots
Range surfaced	8,500 nmi at 10 knots 3,250 nmi at 17 knots
Range submerged	80 nmi at 4 knots 120-130 nmi at 2 knots
Maximum depth	165 m
Collapse depth	280 m
Propellers	2
Crash dive time	30 s
Periscopes	2 – combat and search
Armament (since 1944)	Twin anti aircraft gun cal. 20 mm Flak C/30 and a single anti aircraft gun cal. 37 mm, 4 bow torpedo tubes and 1 stern. 14 cal. 533 mm tor-pedoes
Complement (since 1943)	4 officers, 53 non-commissioned officers and seamen

Although *U 977* had been commissioned on May 6, 1943, she did not participate in a combat patrol until several weeks before the end of the war. The first command-ing officer of the submarine was 25-year-old Lt. Hans Leilich (born in 1918) who came from a medium sized town of Pirmasens in the southern Rhineland. On April 3, 1937, he joined the Marineakademie (Naval Academy) in Kiel. On May 1, 1938, he was promoted to Fähnrich zur See (Officer Candidate) and on July 1, 1939, he received the rank of Oberfähnrich zur See. A month before the beginning of the

Second World War, on August 1, 1939, he was promoted to the first officer rank in the Kriegsmarine - Lieutnant zur See (Ensign). From August till November 1940, he worked in the Kriegsmarine office in Boulogne, France. From November 1940 until September 1941, Leilich was a company commander and a submarine warfare lecturer in Mürwik. On September 1, 1941, he was promoted to the rank of lieutenant. He trained submariners from September 1941 to March 1942. From March 1942 to February 1943, he was a trainee and a watch officer on training ships of the 24. U-Flottille in Memel (now Klaipėda) and 4. U-Flottille in Stettin (Szczecin). He was trained in a combat unit of the 10. U-Flottille in Lorient. During his short service on training submarines, he was a watch officer.

Shipyards across Germany built more and more different types of submarines. The U-Bootwaffe command needed well trained officers. The men of certain character would later become U-Boots' commanders creating the backbone of the submarine fleet. Ships participating in fast, intense operations, fighting against convoys, needed young, energetic and aggressive commanders full of optimism, with the ability to quickly adapt to unexpected situations. The way to a commanding officer's position was very long.

Leilich had several months of combat experience. As Ensign Ausbildungsoffizier (officer lecturer), he acquired practical knowledge of combat at sea since November 1939 to August 1940, from Kapitän zur See (captain) Bernhard Rogge, commanding officer of the first German auxiliary cruiser *Atlantis – Schiff 16*. She was almost 150 meters long, ex freighter *Goldenfels* (7,862 GRT, built in the Vulcan shipyard in Bremen) that, after two years of civilian service in the Hansa Line in Bremen, in fall of 1939, was requisitioned by the Kriegsmarine and converted into a disguised raider. During her raider operations, the cruiser *Atlantis*[142] sailed over 102,000 nmi (188,904 km) in 622 days, sank 16 and captured 6 allied cargo ships (freighters and tankers) of a total volume of 145,697 GRT. At that time she changed her appearance and colors ten times. *Atlantis* was the third most effective German auxiliary cruiser of World War 2. On November 22, 1941, the raider was sunk by the British heavy cruiser HMS *Devonshire* in the south Atlantic.

Let us go back to the beginning of *U 977* service. After raising the German Navy Ensign, the submarine was sent to the technical training center for submariners in Kiel. For over four months, until September 30, 1943, the U-Boot was part of the 5. U-Flottille until her crew reached full operational readiness. The crewmen had to get familiar with the ship's construction, inspect - literally - every rivet and washer, know the purpose of every one of thousands pipes, wires etc. All this, to make them able to localize every valve in the darkness of the submarine's steel heart in the most extreme combat situation. That was more. The men were put in simulated combat situations, taught to fire torpedoes and trained on every aspect of diving proce-

---

[142] Leilich left the Kriegsmarine ship after boarding a prize of the Norwegian motor vessel *Tirranna*, which was taken to Saint-Nazaire in France, by a German crew.

dures. The submariners familiarized themselves with operation of diving planes, trim tanks and the hull's strength. Their tasks fulfilled during the demanding training included trials of diesels and electric motors, weapon systems tests, radio and sonar checks. It was also the time when the men got to know each other and slowly became one, well functioning organism. The training was conducted during day and night time in the Bornholm Deep in the Baltic Sea. The crew learned the tactics for attacking convoys. Their effort would be put to use during the Battle of the Atlantic. The training was very intensive. The commanding officer demanded obedience and high level of proficiency from his crew. All their skills would determine success of operations against merchant ships and allow them to return home safely.

From the beginning of the training, the submarine was ill-fated. According to the Allied intelligence records, *U 977* commanded by Lt. Leilich, during her cruises on the Baltic Sea three times rammed other ships or was rammed by others. A series of accidents occurred during diving maneuvers. Either the equipment or the commander and crew's lack of experience were to blame. We need to remember that the Type VII C was a very stable submarine in good weather but during a storm, she would become a "wild pig"! Some sections of the pressure hull were damaged in the last collision so severely (there were problems making them watertight again) that the U-Bootwaffe command decided to withdraw *U 977* from combat service and turn her into a training submarine.

On October 1, 1943, after several months spent in Kiel, *U 977* was assigned to Pillau (Baltiysk) at the Gdansk Bay, the training center of the 21. U-Flottille. The U-Bootwaffe needed specialists like mechanics, electricians and radio operators. In 1944, Germany lacked specialized technicians. Qualified cooks were also desired. Sailors, after basic training and practical seamanship in one of the Kriegsmarine centers at the Baltic Sea, were assigned to U-Boots that returned from combat missions (partial change of crew was required) or were sent to newly commissioned submarines.

At the beginning of March 1945, Lt.Cdr. Hans Leilich passed the command of *U 977* to Lt. Heinz Schäffer who, for over a year, had been in command of a small submarine *U 148*. The procedure of taking over a U-Boot commanding officer's responsibilities lasted a few weeks. During that time *U 977* participated in short, several-day-long training cruises on the Baltic Sea. The submarine would enter harbor only for several hours. At the end of the year, a group of a dozen or so seamen left the submarine for a two-week leave. They were late assigned to front line ships. Their positions were manned by recruits after basic training.

Near the base of Pillau (Piława), Lt.Cdr. Leilich and Lt. Schäffer put their crew through hard training drills. When practicing diving procedures, defects and weak points were discovered. Knowledge on tactics and torpedo attacks was perfected. Discipline on the U-Boot was very strict, which allowed the young submariners to keep cool under stress. One maneuver was practiced regularly - the crash dive. According to Leilich, through constant training at sea, the 40 submariners had a chance to familiarize themselves with the equipment, perfect their particular skills and get used to the hard living conditions on a submarine.

LIEUTENANT HEINZ SCHÄFFER
– THE SECOND AND LAST COMMANDING OFFICER OF *U 977* [143]

He was born on April 28, 1921 in Berlin. During his last year in high school, he decided to continue his education in a naval school. He wanted to join the Kriegsmarine – he made a decision to become a cadet in the naval school in Kiel. At the end of December 1939, he arrived at the Kiel alma mater and passed all the exams. He became the Kriegsmarine cadet with a rank of a seaman. In winter of 1940, Schäffer was sent to a military camp on a small island of Dänholm, at the German northern coast of the Baltic Sea, near Stralsund. In March 1940, after completing the first stage of his training, he was sent back to Kiel where he was assigned to the training sailing ship *Gorch Fock* and took part in his first training cruises. In May of the same year, he returned to school and participated in practical training and several trial cruises on the battleship *Schlesien* in the Baltic Sea. Then, he was transferred to the Marineschule in Mürwik-Flensburg. For several months he was trained in navigation, tactics, gunnery and torpedo warfare, communications and history of the navy. He wanted to serve on U-Boots – he took his seamanship on a training submarine in the Baltic Sea. In November 1941, he was promoted to ensign. From the spring of 1941 to May 1942, he participated in 6 combat cruises on *U 561*. On May 1, 1942, he was promoted to the rank of lieutenant-junior grade and, at the end of the month, joined the crew of *U 445* as the executive officer (participated in four combat patrols). From October to November 1943, he attended a course in the base of the 23. U-Flottille in Danzig (Gdańsk). From November 30, 1943, to December 15, 1944, commanding officer of *U 148* (Type II D) – the submarine was used to train submariners in the centers in Pillau and Wilhelmshaven. On December 1, 1943, promoted to the rank of lieutenant. Received the Iron Cross 1st and 2nd class and the U-Boot War Badge. He participated in 10 combat patrols before taking command of *U 977* (formally, he became the submarine's CO at the beginning of March 1945, in Pillau).

During the practical course, U-Boot commanders had the chance to get to know their individual crew members' skills, abilities and experience. A commanding officer had to rule his submarine with an iron fist and lead his crew to the highest level of combat efficiency possible, gaining their trust and devotion. Boastful officers using theatrical gestures, full of excessive self confidence and contempt in face of the enemy, were held in low esteem. There was little time so dynamic trainings were necessary. Lying on a berth was a luxury. A crew's full combat readiness was a priority.

The officers of *U 977* were complemented by two watch officers - 30-year-old Lt. Karl Reiser (executive officer) and 22-year-old Lieutenant-Junior Grade Albert Kahn (second watch) and the chief engineer, 22-year-old Lieutenant-Junior Grade Dietrich Wiese.

In January 1945, a disaster struck on the eastern front. A decision was made to dissolve the submarine crews training center in Pillau. The war was lost, there was no doubt about that. Further military activities at the sea were unnecessary. People

---

[143] R. Busch, H-J. Röll, *Der U-Boot-Krieg 1939-1945...*,v. 1, p. 203.

were sent to their deaths. However, U-Boot commanders had no courage to demonstrate their dissatisfaction. They were soldiers. They did not want to be treated as
mutineers. They did not want to abandon their crews and - trusting their fate - wait
for the end of the war.

The last commandant of the 21. U-Flottille Lt.Cdr. Herwig Collmann appointed
Lt. Schäffer as commander of the convoy escort. The group comprised four Type
VII C U-Boots, all armed with anti-aircraft guns. The submarines were ordered to
move to Wesermünde. During the several-day-long cruise, they were not attacked
by enemy aircraft. On its way, the convoy had an unplanned stop at Swinemünde
(Świnoujście). *U 977* had her underwater hull section damaged. The Baltic Sea was
still partially ice-covered. The "sevens" were fitted with profiled steel plates which
were to protect the covers of the bow torpedo tubes. The protection on *U 977* was
not durable enough. The plates bent. The commander of the small convoy refused to
continue the cruise with the damaged submarine. In those circumstances, the other
U-Boots left the base and *U 977* was sent to a dry dock. Meanwhile, it turned out
that the harbor depots had no protective collars for the bow torpedo tubes. Waiting
for them to be delivered would have taken too much time.

Lieutenant Schäffer waited for instruction while his submarine was anchored at
Swinemünde. Finally, *U 977* received orders to leave her whereabouts and move to
the Howaldtswerke A.G. shipyard in Hamburg. Workers were supposed to make
all urgent repairs. The route led from Swinemünde via Kiel, Kaiser Wilhelm Canal
(now the Kiel Canal), Cuxhaven to Hamburg and ended on February 20.

The overhaul began with a delay of almost one week. The U-Boot was put into a
dry dock. All necessary repairs were planned for a period of several weeks. When
spring came, *U 977* was awaiting orders. The training submarine was approved for
combat operations - by people who did not have to spend weeks patrolling high seas
on such a ship. The hurray optimism was not shared by Schäffer and his men who
had participated in combat operations in the North Atlantic. It was an absurd to risk
the crew's lives and send the submarine to certain destruction. However, the commanding officer did not opt for a mutiny, keeping high morale even when *U 977*'s
situation seemed to be hopeless. The seamen did not want to lay down their arms,
faithful to their oath and their admiral till the end.

The Hamburg shipyard made all urgent repairs. Most of the work was, unfortunately, not finished. Two old batteries of accumulators were not replaced, still showing 70% capacity (they were necessary while operating the electric motors). There
had been situations when excessive amounts of hydrogen, carbon dioxide, nitrogen
oxide and hydrogen antimonide made the crew's life even harder. The first officer reported cases of headache, difficulty breathing and allergic reactions among the seamen. Couplings, that had been in use for over a year and were prone to chafing, were
not replaced. Due to the lack of time it was impossible to install armored plating for
the twin 20 mm Flak C/30 anti-aircraft guns mounted in the conning tower, behind
the gangway. The single 20 mm anti-aircraft gun was not mounted on the deck.

What is interesting, at the end of the war, *U 977*, without combat record, was equipped with the latest radio technology. She was fitted with a modern radiolocation equipment - passive device called "Naxos", detecting enemy radars. The radiolocation devices that were installed on all U-Boots operating on the Atlantic were to detect approaching enemy aircraft, at a longest distance possible, by detecting its radar impulses. *U 977* was also fitted with a new antenna for the "Naxos" system, designated FuMB Ant.24 "Fliege", which allowed to increase the detection range to 20 km, minimizing the danger of unexpected aerial attack. The rotating antenna, also designated "Cuba I", operated on 8-20 cm waves. The submarine was also equipped with a cone antenna FuMB Ant.25 "Mücke" that operated on 3 cm waves. Its detection range was 60 km. From May 1944, the "Fliege" and "Mücke" antennas were mounted together on a single mast, placed in the middle of the conning tower, near the periscope or separately, along with a round radio antenna. Although not many such devices were produced, they were installed on a training submarine! It was not a coincidence. Among the crew members there were four seamen who had graduated from specialized courses for radio operators, wireless operators and hydroacoustics specialists. Apart from the aforementioned equipment, the U-Boot was fitted with the snorkel. There was a special bay for storing the snorkel mast and its lifting mechanism. Lieutenant Wiese had no experience operating the snorkel. Fast introduction of the crew to operation procedures of the device, that allowed the air in and out of the submarine at periscope depth, would affect the U-Boot's operation on diesel engines. The overhaul and fittings lasted from February 26 to March 31, 1945.

Then, Schäffer received orders to relocate *U 977* to the Kiel harbor and to achieve full combat readiness. The stop was to last for a dozen or so days. Standard fuel capacity of a U-Boot was 113.47 t, 121.5 maximum with torpedo tubes 1 and 3 used as fuel tanks. However, *U 977*'s large fuel tanks were not filled to maximum, which is strange considering the fact that the submarine was to be prepared for a long journey.

At the beginning of April, Grand Admiral Karl Dönitz called a briefing for U-Boot commanders from Kiel. The meeting was held aboard the base ship *Patria*. The Kriegsmarine commander in chief assured the seamen that their spirits should be high as the final victory was imminent! The submarine commanders were surprised by their superior's unmotivated enthusiasm. After the meeting, Dönitz invited Schäffer to his cabin. *U 977*'s commanding officer complained about the submarine's poor technical condition. Dönitz tried to calm the young submariner down, emphasizing that he was the recipient of the Iron Cross (Class I and II) and had the necessary combat experience! He was one of those who would fight to the end. The admiral insisted Schäffer should take his submarine on a combat patrol despite her condition. In face of those arguments, he was helpless. He had a mission to fulfill and there was no place for unnecessary discussions.

Soon, Schäffer took a train to Berlin to meet his mother. However, it was not the only reason for his short visit in the damaged German capital. The U-Boot's commander probably met an unknown officer in the Waffen-SS headquarters. The officer told Schäffer about the Third Reich's new wonder weapon! It was to change the course of the war. He claimed victory was still possible (!) in a longer run due to development of the most modern and spectacular German constructions that were being created in secret SS research facilities. The officer presented photographs showing an unknown device. Schäffer received a proposition to join an elite Nazi unit. On the next day, he witnessed tests (either field or laboratory) of the mysterious weapon! Was it a device producing so called death rays (with use of electromagnetic waves)? There is no evidence that the fantastic wonder of unconventional defensive technology (in history of the Third Reich) was later loaded onto the deck of *U 977*. The story is so improbable, it is hard to believe it was true[144].

When Schäffer returned to his ship, Kiel was being plastered with bombs. Atmosphere aboard *U 977* was like on the front line. Day and night, the harbor was under aerial attack. *U 977* hastily left the port and dropped anchor in one of little bays, far from exploding bombs.. The submarine was not the primary target of the RAF bombers. Other U-Boots were not so lucky. They were destroyed by the B-17 Flying Fortresses and B-24 Liberators of the 8. Army of the United States Air Force. On April 3 and 4, bombs seriously damaged (which resulted in their decommissioning) or sank *U 1221*, *U 2542*, *U 749*, *U 237* and *U 3003*.

At that time, the crew of *U 977* witnessed an air raid of the American B-17s during which, the German passenger ship *New York* caught fire, capsized and sank. The submarine was anchored near the liner that had been requisitioned for the Kriegsmarine. The floating "barracks" were ablaze, sounds of exploding ammunition could be heard. Aerial bombs fell behind the stern of *U 977*, dangerously close. The crew started the engines, mooring lines were cast away and the U-Boot moved full ahead to get as fast and as far away from the tragedy as possible. The rest of the night was uneventful.

The submarine was being loaded until the last day of her stay in Kiel. Shortly before her departure, the U-Boot received supplies of fresh food. The crew was constantly aware that their submarine was an easy prey for the American, long range B-17 bombers. The four-engine aircraft carried a bombload of 2,200 kg.

On April 9, at night, 576 aircraft of the 1., 3. and 8. RAF Squadrons, destroyed submarines Type XXI – *U 2516* and Type IX C/40 - *U 1227*, in docks of the Deutsche Werke A.G. shipyard in Kiel. Only the U-Boots kept in shelters under several meters of reinforced concrete and behind huge armored doors, were safe.

The command HQ of the U-Boot arm (Befehlshaber der Unterseeboote) issued an order to create a group of three U-Boots. They were to sail to one of the German naval bases on the southern coast of Norway. One of the submarines waiting to

---

[144] Such insinuations appeared in the United States. The authors do not know if the owner of the sensational news had any hard evidence to prove the hypothesis. All this is based on circumstantial evidence. See: M. Ivinheim, *The Secret Alliance...*, p. 160-161.

depart from Kiel was the new Type XXI *U 2502* (Lt.Cdr. Heinz Franke). The other U-Boots of the group were *U 977* and *U 287* (Lt. Heinrich Meyer). The commanders of both "sevens" were to lead their crews to a combat patrol for the first time. During a meeting called by the officer in charge of the flotilla, Lt.Cdr. Franke, the recipient of the Knight's Cross talked in superlatives about the most advanced operational submarine of the Second World War.

The trip to Norway that was ahead of them, was very dangerous. The Kattegat Strait (between the Jutland Peninsula and the Scandinavian Peninsula) was controlled by the RAF aircraft. All U-Boots leaving for patrols had to cross the strait to get to the German bases in Norway. In the first quarter of 1945, over half of the U-Boots, lost in that sector, were destroyed after striking a mine while moving submerged through the narrow section of the strait. Submarines tried to cross the dangerous zone on the surface but they were easy prey for aircraft. They stood little chance against fast and nimble RAF planes. U-Boots had long lost their freedom of movement, observation and certainty of action. Even the cloak of night did not guarantee their safety when crossing the Kattegat.

At the end of the war, the U-Boot evacuation route led to the harbors of Norway, where they delivered material goods, documentation of military research programs and people who were not able to travel with false documents aboard passenger ships. In the summer of 1944, the German U-Boot bases in France were captured by the Allies while Norway remained in German hands until the end of the war.

Submarines were one of transportation means used on transfer routes. In the last weeks of the war, aircraft carrying the most valuable cargo landed in the Bodö military air base and other places. Their precious load was then transported by U-Boots, long range aircraft and, after the war, by merchant ships of neutral countries like Argentina, Brazil or Chile.

In 1945, Norway was practically the only safe place for U-Boots (Norwegian harbors operated for almost 5 years) and the Germans realized that the main war front would pass the country.

Only a day before the departure of *U 977*, an order was given to replenish fresh food supplies - bread, fruit, vegetables, eggs, meat and sausages. It was also time to fill the fresh water tanks - drinking water was kept separately from water used for washing and washing up which was taken directly from the harbor hydrants. Lieutenant-Junior Grade Albert Kahn (second watch) was responsible for the loading and proper stowage of the provisions.

In the evening, on April 12, *U 977* was ready to begin her cruise. According to the official orders from Dönitz, Schäffer was to begin the Operation "Southampton" in the British coastal waters. At this stage of the war, the mission was a suicide for any German submarine, especially for the Type VII C. We have to remember that *U 977* was a submarine with "history". Despite their heroic efforts, the mechanics were able to make only the most urgent repairs. The submarine was seaworthy but with limitations.

On April 13, *U 977* cast her moorings away and slowly moved through the harbor waters accompanied by an escort ship. Only a few brothers in arms were standing on the pier. U-Boots' glory days were long gone, there was no orchestra, no cheering crowd. Nurses from the local hospital did not come to wave goodbye. Dönitz, who liked to talk to commanders and their crews before a patrol, also did not arrive. The Kriegsmarine commander in chief himself and his words boosted submariners' morale. For the crew of *U 977*, the ceremony was disheartening. Some of them were standing on the deck, leaning against the railings, smoking cigarettes, chatting and catching the last rays of the spring sun. They left the pier of the "Tirpitz" wet dock behind. They departed Kiel.

Schäffer, who had commanded a submarine only during training, intended to accomplish his mission. After several days of sailing, they were supposed to enter the Horten base where a two-day training exercise on the use of the snorkel was planned.

How did the other U-Boots do? *U 287* left Kiel on April 15, and five days later arrived at Horten. Later she sailed to Kristiansand and moved to her patrol area in the North Sea. The submarine remained in her sector of operations until May 4. She did not sink any ships. On May 16, the U-Boot was scuttled by the crew on the Altenbruch roadstead near Cuxhaven, as part of the Operation "Regenbogen".

U 2502 was damaged on April 19, by the Mosquito aircraft, while passing the Kattegat Strait, en route from Kiel to Horten. Despite the damage, Lt.Cdr. Franke managed to nurse his submarine to Horten where she remained until the end of the war. Finally, the U-Boot came to the Lisahally harbor in Northern Ireland on August 2, 1945. She was sunk on January 3, 1946 by the Polish destroyer ORP *Piorun* as part of the Operation "Deadlight" (coordinates 56°06'N and 09°00'W).

During day, *U 977* moved at periscope depth and at night the submarine remained on surface to recharge the battery of accumulators and air the compartments. When the radio location devices detected an RAF aircraft, the submarine submerged immediately. After crossing the Sund Strait, the U-Boot sailed to Frederikshavn in Denmark. What was the reason for the submarine's short stay in the harbor of the north east Jutland?

Heavy cargo was loaded onto the U-Boot. Dimensions of the payload made it difficult for the crew to move between the submarine's sections. From then on, life on the ship - according to reports of the crew members - was even more comfortless. The load packed into several or a dozen or so boxes, was valuable. The crew had to find space to store the boxes. The submarine was ready for a cruise planned for six or eight weeks at sea. She was filled with provisions and ammunition to the maximum. There were 48 crewmen aboard. There was no additional space due to narrowness of the living quarters.

Some armament was removed from *U 977*. The submarine carried 10 instead of 14 torpedoes. Five torpedoes were in the bow tubes (4) and stern tube (1). Four "steel eels" were stored beneath the floor in the bow torpedo room. The remaining "cigar" was placed under the floor of the stern torpedo compartment. The bow torpedo room had two torpedo racks, above the floor, between the berths. Torpedoes were replaced by boxes. Free cargo space was over 14 meters long. There was also additional space for two torpedoes in containers on the pressure hull, under the outer skin. The containers were filled with canned provisions. Some of the cargo loaded in Frederikshavn was crammed into all available nooks and crannies.

Operational capability of *U 977* was weakened by reducing her torpedo load by 4 units. The U-Boot also carried reduced amount of fuel. The decision to take only 85 t of diesel fuel for such a cruise was made by The German technicians after giving the issue serious thought. In Frederikshavn, the amount of provisions was so high, the first officer-engineer protested against the excessive weight that could have made the diving procedures dangerous. We have to remember that German fuel reserves were almost non-existent, railway infrastructure and factories producing synthetic fuel were destroyed.

Everything could be logically explained if one did not take into consideration the fact that, in August 1945, Lt. Schäffer told the Armada de la República Argentina (Argentine Navy) investigators that he had room for 130 t of fuel, but his chief engineer demanded to take 85 t to optimize the submarine's stability - the subject is discussed in the next chapter. It is hard to believe that the U-Boot was filled with large amount of provisions at a cost of lowering her combat readiness. During her first patrol, *U 977* was to attack cargo ships in the Southampton harbor.

In the last year of the war, attack of a single U-Boot against Allied ships or warships was a suicide mission. Probability of sinking a U-Boot during a combat patrol was 40% but there was one in eight of a chance that the sustained damage was an excuse to abort the mission. What was worse, a submarine commander had only 10% chance to sink an Allied ship. In the last months of the war, the main target of the Germans were merchant ships moving in convoys through the Irish Sea.

Shipping on the English Channel was also in danger. The British Admiralty was prepared to meet the enemy. Sending *U 977* for this kind of mission was a mad decision.

Shipyards and the Kriegsmarine ships were decorated with propaganda slogans: "The enemy shall find in Germany nothing but rats and mice", "We will never capitulate", "Better death then slavery".

The U-Boot commanded by Schäffer, was escorted by a mine-sweeper (heavily armed with anti-aircraft guns) whose task was to lead the submarine through the mine field laid near the base. After reaching the deeper Frederikshavn roadstead, *U 977* was able to hide underwater from aerial attacks. Already while leaving the harbor, *U 977*'s passive radar detected enemy patrol aircraft. There were twelve of them, approaching fast. After 30 seconds, the submarine submerged to a periscope depth. Soon, aerial radars detected the ship. If *U 977* had stayed on the surface, she would have been lost. Despite the danger of hitting one of the mines, the commandant decided to submerge to a depth of several dozen meters. Every time they raised the FuMB anti-radar device, it detected the enemy aircraft.

To sink the a submarine, aerial bombs would have to be dropped with high accuracy (2.5 m from the hull). The aircraft tried to hunt the U-Boot down. It is interesting that none of the dozen RAF aircraft circling *U 977*'s position, attempted to engage the submarine with depth charges or missiles.

Similar situation occurred several weeks later when a single RAF patrol aircraft saw the surfaced *U 977*, made a circle above the submarine but did not attack. The plane followed them for a while and flew away.

Schäffer waited for initial deployment of the snorkel. The snorkel's operating procedure, without high level of proficiency, was difficult during a combat cruise. Had the valve of the air intake pipe been flooded by waves, the diesel engines would have started taking oxygen from inside of the submarine.

Before reaching Horten, when crossing the Skagerrak, combat alarm was sounded at least four times on *U 977* due to the threat of aerial attack by the RAF patrol aircraft. The radio operator's responsibility was high. He operated devices that allowed communication on three frequency ranges - on short, medium and long or very long waves. The latter were especially useful at the end of the war - these waves are able to penetrate water and can be received by on periscope depth. Since 1944, U-Boots spent most of the day submerged due to the threat of aerial attack.

At the end of the first stage of the cruise, *U 977* remained at a depth of 50 m for 6 hours in the waters of the Oslofjord. A time came to deploy the snorkel. The snorkel's cover was difficult to detect for the enemy radar. The device was raised hydraulically from the depth of 20 m. The submarine was sailing at a speed of several knots. There were no other ships in vicinity.

On April 20, *U 977* arrived at Horten. After consulting with the BdU, Schäffer ordered several days of rest before beginning the main stage of the mission. The crew conducted training exercises on the use of the snorkel. The submarine entered a training lane and submerged to begin the exercise.

The crew's morale was low - the battle for Berlin was in progress. Everything was falling apart. The end of the Third Reich was near. Engineer Wiese was in especially low spirit as, a few days earlier, he had learned of his father's death (he served in the Volkssturm - a militia used during the last phase of the Second World War, established by Adolf Hitler on October 25, 1944).

On April 30, at 5.00, *U 977* left Horten and headed to Kristiansand. Later, the submarine submerged to perform trimming procedures. On the same day the U-Boot reached her stop at a well equipped harbor and anchorage used by the Kriegsmarine warships and submarines. The Kristiansand harbor fulfilled operational tasks for the U-Bootwaffe until the end of the war. There were no German submarines in the harbor, which Schäffer celebrated opening a bottle of champagne.

On May 1, while listening to the radio, the crew of *U 977* learned that Admiral Dönitz issued a statement (in the Hamburg radio station) to the German people: "Hitler died fighting «along his troops» in Berlin". He also informed of the fact that he had assumed the leadership of the country and all Wehrmacht forces. On the following day, a simple ceremony was held on the U-Boot. The Kriegsmarine ensign was lowered at half staff to mourn Hitler's death. The crew realized that the day of the "thousand-year" Reich were over. It was not hard to believe, since the Führer, in face of the inevitable defeat, assured he would not leave Berlin even despite demands of his followers who wanted him to flee to the south of Germany.

The submarine was ready to depart. Not all mechanical equipment of the U-Boot was in perfect order. Couplings of the diesel engines were chafing and an intense combat cruise was ahead of them (after Hitler's death, no one anticipated a long trip). In face of the difficult conditions, discipline was crucial. The crew would soon feel the effects of prolonged stress and constant anxiety which always accompanied submariners on the day of their departure for a combat patrol.

On May 2, at 22.00, the U-Boot dropped her moorings. Under the cover of darkness *U 977* began her first and last combat patrol. As soon as it was possible, the submarine submerged. For over two hours, the U-Boot sailed at periscope depth. Before midnight, Schäffer ordered to deploy the snorkel. On the days that followed, they used the snorkel for about 3-4 hours per day to recharge the batteries. Soon, they left the coast of Norway.

When Dönitz became the last Führer of the Third Reich, the 48-men crew began their most incredible frontline missions of a German submarine. *U 977* was to operate on the waters of the English Channel near Southampton and, if possible, enter the harbor. The other option was to secretly sneak into the Plymouth harbor. Due to the overwhelming supremacy of the Allied forces with their thousands of aircraft and ships equipped with the latest devices able to detect and destroy a submerged submarine, the mission was madness.

At night from May 4 to 5, the crew of *U 977* received orders for all Kriegsmarine submarines to cease all hostilities. It was a hard moment for the seamen. It was over. At that time, the submarine was sailing submerged at some distance from the Norwegian coast. Schäffer considered the radio message to be fabricated by the British[145]. He suspected that some radio stations had been captured by the enemy. After long and intense discussions with his fellow officers, the commander decided to ignore the order to stop fighting. The other crew members were not informed of the message. A decision was made to continue the cruise. According to the message, all the U-Bootwaffe frontline submarines were to return to Norwegian harbors.

At that time, reports were sent sporadically due to tactical reasons. The enemy would have been able to establish the U-Boot's position. The snorkel was deployed only every now and then. *U 977* remained submerged for long hours. Schäffer and other officers decided not to raise the capitulation flag. According to his secret orders, the commanding officer only accepted the instructions.

---

[145] Statement of Schaeffer, C.O. of U-977, NARA, Record Group (RG) 59 (U.S. Department of State Central Decimal Files), sign. 862.30/8-445 – 8-2145, p. 1, typed.

U-Boots that continued their patrols, were ordered to abort all missions and surrender. The instruction included information about harbors where the submarines
operating in different areas, were supposed to surrender. The order was signed by
the Allied Committee.

U 977 continued her mission, submerged at daytime, at periscope depth at night.
During the next two days, they did not notice neither an enemy aircraft nor a cloud
of smoke. The sea was calm and seemed to be empty.

On May 7, during crash dive, Lt. Reiser forgot to lower the search periscope. At
a depth of 100 m the steel lines were not able to endure the pressure, the periscope
mast hit the deck breaking its prisms. The device could not be repaired at sea. The
optical mechanism was crucial for sailing with the snorkel. The U-Boot was blind.
The commanding officer was not able to use the observation periscope to see if the
engines were producing smoke or search for the Royal Navy warships. It was not
possible to substitute the search periscope with the combat periscope. The latter was
too short when the submarine used the snorkel. The combat periscope was utilized
for underwater torpedo attack at night with cloudy skies. The search periscope was
fitted with special optics and could be used for observing aerial targets.

The commander decided not to return to one of the German harbors in Norway.
All U-Boots received news of Germany's capitulation. According to new rules, the
Kriegsmarine ships were forbidden to use coded messages. U-Boot commanders
were ordered to destroy old codes and to turn all current code books over to the
Allies.

Making a decision to abort the mission and to surrender to the enemy meant giving the crew a prison sentence. All men were very anxious. Sailing with the snorkel,
not being able to observe the submarine's surroundings was a huge challenge. With
the changing season, nights in the north became brighter and shorter. The batteries
were recharged at night since the snorkel mast would create a visible trail of white
foam on water. Adding the clouds of exhaust fumes, detecting the U-Boot was much
easier.

The inside of *U 977* was tight and uncomfortable, there were no coolers for provisions, air conditioning, head or a mess hall. People would sleep on narrow berths
placed on torpedo tubes or other equipment. When the sea was rough, waves hitting
the deck caused a submarine to roll which created additional problems to crews
already exhausted by a long patrol. Stress also lowered the morale of the seamen.

The Type VII C's strength lied in its thin and low profile which made the U-
Boot hard to detect even on surface and allowed the submarine to conduct surprise
attacks giving it an edge over the enemy. Meanwhile, *U 977* was approaching the
blockade zone. The submarine was sailing at periscope depth. At the end of the war,
Hitler's submariners got used to the British propaganda broadcasts informing that
a U-Boots maximum life span was 40 days. *U 977* crew had survived eight days and
had 32 days before their expected demise. However, they could meet their end on
any day, maybe tomorrow, maybe the next day or the day that would follow.

CONFIDENTIAL
NA   BAires   R-201-45   24 July 1945   915-400
- -

3.   The interrogation consisted merely of questions and answers and was conducted through an interpreter, hence little of importance was learned. A set of questions had previously been drawn up and these questions were asked each of the men examined, regardless of his rank and duties aboard the sub.

4.   In lieu of sitting in on the actual interrogation, our representatives insisted that the transcripts of the interrogations be read to them immediately following the termination of each one of them. Enclosures (A) to (I) inclusive are resumes of the principal points brought out. It should be borne in mind that the enclosures were worked up from very hasty spot translations and brief notes made during the reading, which was in Spanish, and hence they are subject to some slight errors. However, on the whole, and particularly on the more important points, they are substantially correct. The Naval Attaché has not yet been given an official copy of the interrogation, although one is expected soon.

5.   The following officers of the Argentine Navy constituted the Interrogation Board:

   (a)   Interrogation:

          Captain José A. Dellepiane, in charge and interrogator.
          Commander Carlos O. Ribera, Secretary and assistant
                                      interrogator.
          Lieut. Comdr. Olinto P. Berry, Translator.

   (b) Examination of Documents:

          Commander Patricio J. Conway, in charge.
          Lieut. Comdr. Juan Carlos Benisch, Translator.

6.   The examination of the documents revealed that many important ones had been destroyed and that those remaining have been thoroughly censored. Enclosure (J) is a list of some of those remaining which are of interest and possible value.

7.   Our representatives were treated with courtesy and consideration and at no time were any facilities refused them in the fulfillment of their duties.

8.   The U-530 was short one large rubber life raft. These are carried in waterproof containers on deck and are equipped with a sack of yellowish chemical that when loosened in sea water dyes it a very bright green. The rafts are orange colored and the dye is presumably used to make them more visible from the air. It was noted that the container just forward of the conning tower, which was closed when the U-530 arrived at Mar del Plata, did not contain a life boat but was filled with a bright green liquid, presumably dyed sea water. Attention is called to the fact that if one boat were used for some purpose clandestinely, it might be assumed that the dye would be left in the container and sea water could easily have splashed into the container.

9.   It has been pretty well established that the U-530 could not have sunk the Brazilian cruiser BAHIA because of distance, time, and maximum speed of submarine. It is believed that the Brazilians are convinced of this.

An excerpt (page 2) from the report prepared by Lt. Archie W. Grenn (Reserve) from the office of U.S. Naval Attaché in Buenos Aires. The document is in the collection of the National Archives and Records Administration at College Park, Maryland, USA.

Long Overdue U-Boat Takes Secret to Argentina

Another photograph of *U 350* at Mar del Plata, taken on July 12, 1945.

Another article about the surrender of *U 530*, published by one of American newspapers after July 10, 1945.

An excerpt from a note prepared by the U.S. intelligence agent in Buenos Aires.

U 530 at Mar del Plata, July 1945.

Peter Wytykowski, the co-author of the book, during his search for documents at the National Archives and Records Administration at College Park, Maryland, USA.

CONFIDENTIAL

Resume of Interrogation of Lieut.(j.g.) Otto
WERMUTH, Commanding Officer of the German
submarine U-530.

- -

WERMUTH stated that he is a native born German, aged 25
years, and the Commanding Officer of the submarine U-530. He
stated that he had joined the German Navy in April 1941 and
was sent immediately to the submarine school from which he was
graduated in October 1941. He was then sent to the officers
school from which he was graduated in March 1942.

He stated that he had no friends or relatives in Argentina,
that he had never been here before, and that he knew none of
the internees of the ex-battleship GRAF SPEE, though he had met
some of the escaped officers of that ship in Hamburg, Germany,
in 1941. He stated that as far as he knew none of his crew
were related to or had friends among the internees here.

He stated that he was the holder of four decorations, they
being: The Kreigs Abzeichen, a service medal; the Front
Abzeichen, for U-boats; and the 1st and 2nd Class Iron Crosses.
He had received both of these latter for service in another
submarine, the number of which he would not give.

He stated that the U-530, on the present voyage, was his
first command. He had been selected by Admiral Hans Von
FRIEDEBERG, Chief of the German Submarine Division, about the
middle of 1944, to command a submarine then in Lorient, France,
for repairs. These repairs were delayed, though, and he had
later been sent to Hamburg, Germany, to take command of the
U-530.

He had no identification of any kind to support his
statement that he was actually in command of the submarine and
upon being questioned as to whether or not he c_ould substan-
tiate this he, after much reflection, recalled that one of his
seamen, Joachim KRATZIG, had married a girl in Kiel, Germany,
by proxy and radio during the voyage and that he, as commanding
officer of the submarine, had signed the marriage document.
He thought that KRATZIG still had the certificate and was sure
that it would be registered in the Civil Registry of Kiel.

WERMUTH stated that his rank, which corresponds to lieutenant (j.g.) was the minimum for command of a submarine and
that such officers were usually of that rank or the next higher.
However, he stated, officers of higher rank (equivelant to our
lieutenant commander) were allowed to command submarines if they
specially requested it.

He said that after being in dry dock around the first of
the year 1945, the U-530 went to Kiel which, he said, was the
supply base for all submarines operating out of Germany proper.
Here it was supplied and on 19 February 1945 sailed for
Christiansand (Skaggerak), Norway, where she was fueled.

He said that the U-530 had a fuel oil capacity of 245 tons,
but at the request of the Chief Engineer he took aboard but 225
tons. This request was made for reasons of better stability.
In addition to this the craft had 5 tons of lubricating oil on
board. He stated that in Kiel he had taken on board a one week's
supply of fresh provisions including meat, vegetables, bread,
etc., and a 17 weeks' supply of special submarine foodstuffs.
A normal supply of torpedoes and ammunition were on board, but
no mines. He further stated that at no time did he receive
further provisions.

Enclosure (A)
NA BAires R-201-45   -1-   CONFIDENTIAL

Transcript (page 1) of the interrogation of the commander of the German submarine
U 530, Lt. Otto Wermuth.

The commanders *U 530* and *U 977* were both accused of sinking the Brazilian light cruiser *Bahia* in May 1945. A thorough investigation concluded that German submarines had nothing to do with that event. The Brazilian vessel sank as a result of a tragic accident.

BASIC PERSONNEL RECORD
(Alien Enemy or Prisoner of War)

7G - 178 - NA
(Internment serial number)

SCHUELLER, Carl Felix
(Name of internee)

Male
(Sex)

F. P. C.* ....

Reference * ....

Height **6** ft. .... in.

Weight 68 kilograms

Eyes .... brown

Skin .... fair

Hair .... brown

Age 22

Distinguishing marks or characteristics:

None

INVENTORY OF PERSONAL EFFECTS TAKEN FROM INTERNEE

1. ....
2. ....
3. ....
4. ....
5. ....
6. ....
7. ....
8. ....
9. ....
10. ....

The above is correct:

Carl - Felix Schüller
(Signature of internee)

1 Aug. 1945, DIO-7ND, Miami, Florida
(Date and place where processed (Army enclosure, naval station, or other place))

Right Hand

1. Thumb	2. Index finger	3. Middle finger	4. Ring finger	5. Little finger

Left Hand

6. Thumb	7. Index finger	8. Middle finger	9. Ring finger	10. Little finger

W. D., P. M. G. Form No. 2
December 9, 1941   16—25525-1

Note amputations in proper space

* Do not fill in.

ID card of the 22-year-old Lt. Karl Felix Schlüter, second-in-command of the submarine *U 530…*

1. ⟨Oberleutnant zur See der Reserve⟩ (Grade and arm or service)	10. **10 July 1945** (Date of capture or arrest)
2. **U-530** (Hostile unit or vessel)	11. **Mar del Plata, Argentine** (Place of capture or arrest)
3. (Hostile serial number)	12. (Unit or vessel making capture or arresting agency)
4. Duisburg, Rheinprovinz, Germ. :2 Aug. 1923 (Date and country of birth)	13. None (Occupation)
5. ⟨Wildpoldsried, Allgau, Bavaria, Germ.⟩ (Place of permanent residence)	14. ⟨Realgymnasium Duisburg (Graduate⟩ (Education)
6. ⟨Father: Carl Felix Schneller⟩ (Name, relationship of nearest relative ¹)	15. **German, English** (Knowledge of languages)
7. same as 5 (Address of above)	16. good (Physical condition at time of capture or arrest)
8. None (Number of dependents and relationship)	17. single (Married or single)
9. — (Address of above)	18. Roman cath. (Religious preference)

ADDITIONAL DATA:

Transferred from	Date depart	Transferred to	Date received	Official signature of receiving officer	Personal effects not transferred ²
Santa Cruz	30 July	Miami, Fla.	1 Aug.	*W.W.Mehrtens*	
DIO-7ND USN	1 Aug.	PM U.S.Army	1 Aug.	*Robert ? Pope*	

REMARKS:

¹ If no relative, name person to be notified in case of emergency.
² If personal effects taken from individual are not transferred, note exceptions and place of storage or depot.

GPO 16—25525-1

… second page of that document. The photograph was taken at the National Archives and Records Administration at College Park, Maryland, USA.

On 19 July 1945, the Argentinian daily "Critica" published news about another U-Boot which "surrendered to the Argentinian Navy ship 30 miles from the coast, near Mar de Ajó" to the north of Mar del Plata. However, nothing more has been written about that incident.

CONFIDENTIAL
NA BAires Rpt. 201-45 of 24 July 1945

Enclosure (B) Resume of Interrogation of Lieut. (jg) Karl Felix
SCHULLER, Executive Officer of German Submarine,
U-530.

Lieutenant SCHULLER stated that he was a native-born German
subject, age 21 years, single. He declared that he was the second
in command of the U-530 but refused to give information as when
he assumed that post.

He stated that he has three decorations - 2 service decorations and the Iron Cross, 2nd Class, for action against the
enemy.

He stated that he had entered the German Navy as a volunteer
in January 1941, and was commissioned an officer in January 1943.
He said that he had been promoted to his present rank in February
1945.

SCHULLER stated that he had a brother, Victor SCHULLER, who
was a member of the crew of the ex-pocket-battleship "Graf Spee"
and who is interned in Argentina. He stated that the brother
had been in Cordoba, Argentina when he last heard of him.

Subject refused to give any details regarding the last
journey of the U-530. He stated that the engines were in bad
condition due to use and that they had developed trouble some four
days before arriving at Mar del Plata.

He stated that all of the men on board the submarine were
crew members and that they were the same as at the time of the
beginning of the voyage. He said that no person had been landed
anywhere and that no passengers had been aboard the ship during
the voyage. He stated that there had been no prisoners of war
aboard during the voyage.

He refused to answer a question as to possible cargo which
may have been aboard, other than that regularly carried by ships
of that type.

He stated that he did not know that Argentina had declared
war, that he'd only known that the country had broken relations
with Germany.

He refused to answer as to whether or not they (the officers
and crew) knew of the surrender of Germany, at the time of their
arrival in Mar del Plata.

He stated that they had decided to come to Mar del Plata
for internment because they thought the country to be neutral and
because they thought they would get better treatment here. He
said that the Captain of the submarine would have gone on to
Puerto Belgrano Naval Base but put into Mar del Plata when the
motors began to go bad.

SCHULLER refused to sign a transcript of his interrogation.

COMMENT: There were a great many questions that SCHULLER, who was
very non-cooperative, refused to answer and which are not mentioned
in the foregoing. The same questions were asked him that had been
asked the Captain of the U-530. In general, the above is only
designed to present the information given, not all answers.

CONFIDENTIAL

Summary (page 1) of Lt. Karl Felix Schlüter's interrogation.

BASIC PERSONNEL RECORD
(Alien Enemy or Prisoner of War)

7G – 179 – NA
(Internment serial number)

F. P. C.* ....

LENZ, Karl-Heinz
(Name of internee)

Reference * ....

Male
(Sex)

Height __6__ ft. .... in.

Weight __64 kilos__

INVENTORY OF PERSONAL EFFECTS TAKEN
FROM INTERNEE

Eyes ....brown....

Skin ....fair....

Hair ....brown....

Age ....22....

Distinguishing marks or
characteristics:

stiff little finger
right hand

1. ....
2. ....
3. ....
4. ....
5. ....
6. ....
7. ....
8. ....
9. ....
10. ....

The above is correct:

Karl Heinz Lenz
(Signature of internee)

1 Aug. 1945, DIO-7ND, Miami, Florida
(Date and place where processed (Army enclosure, naval station, or other place))

Right Hand

1. Thumb	2. Index finger	3. Middle finger	4. Ring finger	5. Little finger
				unable to straighten out

Left Hand

6. Thumb	7. Index finger	8. Middle finger	9. Ring finger	10. Little finger

W. D., P. M. G. Form No. 2
December 9, 1941   16—25525-1

Note amputations in proper space

* Do not fill in.

U 530 artillery officer, Sub-Lieutenant Karl Heinz Lenz's ID card (page 1). A photograph taken at the National Archives and Records Administration at College Park, Maryland, USA.

U.S. Navy sailors on deck of the German submarine *U 530* in Houston in 1945.

CONFIDENTIAL
NA BAires Rpt. 201-45 of 24 July 1945 - - - - - - - - - - - - - - -

Enclosure (C) Resume of Interrogation of Ensign Karl HEINZ
                LENZ of the German submarine U-530.

    Ensign LENZ stated that he was a native-born German subject
and that he was Battery Officer and in command of the Command room
aboard the submarine U-530.

    He stated that he was the holder of one decoration - a service
medal.

    He said that he had no friends or relatives in Argentina and
he had never before been in that country. He stated that he had
no friends or relatives who had been members of the crew of the
ex-pocket-battleship "Graf Spee".

    He stated that he had been studying medicine prior to his
entry into the German navy.

    LENZ stated that the U-530 had left Kiel, Germany on 19 Feb.
1945 on her present voyage and had left Christiansand (Skaggerak),
Norway, on 3 March 1945.

    He stated that the men aboard were the same crew that they
had left Kiel with and that no other persons had been aboard
throughout the voyage. They had had no prisoners of war aboard
during the trip, nor had they carried any passengers.

    He stated that he was not sure as to the number of large
rubber life-boats that had been carried aboard but that each man
on the ship had one individual rubber life-boat and that none had
been lost.

    LENZ refused to state whether or not they knew that Germany
had surrendered.

    He stated that he knew of no other submarines which might be
coming to Argentina to surrender. LENZ signed a transcript of his
                                        interrogation.

COMMENT:

    The same questions that had been asked the Captain were
asked the subject. With the exceptions noted above, he refused
outright to answer them, pleaded ignorance or evaded answering.

Summary of Sub-Lieutnant Lenz's interrogation.

BASIC PERSONNEL RECORD
(Alien Enemy or Prisoner of War)

7G - 181 - NA
(Internment serial number)

F. P. C.* _____

LEFFLER, Peter
(Name of internee)

Reference * _____

Male
(Sex)

Height __5__ ft. __10__ in.

Weight __62 kilos__

Eyes __brown__

Skin __fair__

Hair __brown__

Age __22__

Distinguishing marks or characteristics:

__None__

INVENTORY OF PERSONAL EFFECTS TAKEN FROM INTERNEE

1. _____
2. _____
3. _____
4. _____
5. _____
6. _____
7. _____
8. _____
9. _____
10. _____

7G-181-NA   7G-181-NA

1 Aug. 1945, DIO-7ND, Miami, Florida
(Date and place where processed (Army enclosure, naval station, or other place))

The above is correct:

(Signature of internee)

Right Hand

1. Thumb	2. Index finger	3. Middle finger	4. Ring finger	5. Little finger

Left Hand

6. Thumb	7. Index finger	8. Middle finger	9. Ring finger	10. Little finger

W. D., P. M. G. Form No. 2
December 9, 1941   16—25525—1

Note amputations in proper space

* Do not fill in.

First Engineer, Lt. Peter Leffler's ID card.

At the beginning of August 1945, Lt. Otto Wermuth (on the right in the photo) and other crew members were placed at the U.S. military base, Fort Hunt in Virginia.

CONFIDENTIAL
NA   BAires   Rpt. 201-45 of 24 July 1945.

- -

Enclosure (D) Resume of the interrogation of Lieutenant (jg)
               Peter LEFFLER, Engineer Officer of the German
               submarine U-530.

     LEFFLER stated that he was a native-born German subject,
22 years of age, single, and the Chief Engineer Officer of the
Submarine U-530. He stated that he had been transferred to the
submarine near the end of January 1945. He is the holder of three
decorations, 2 service medals and the Iron Cross, 2nd Class.

     He declared that the crew aboard the submarine was the same
with which she had left Germany without additions or subtractions
and that no passengers or prisoners of war had been on board
at any time during the voyage.

     LEFFLER stated that they had known that Germany had sur-
rendered but refused to give any further details. He said that
there had been a council of officers but refused to give any further information on the subject. He stated that they had decided
to come to Argentina because they thought that they would receive
better treatment here.

     He said that they had originally had six large rubber
life-boats aboard but that one had been left in Norway because it
was in bad condition (see comment).

     LEFFLER stated that the oil had been put aboard the submarine
in Norway in barrels. He said that on arrival in Mar del Plata
there were from 6 to 7 tons of fuel oil remaining in the tanks
and 4 tons of lubricating oil.

     He stated that the motors were in bad condition, that they
had been knocking badly for sometime before their arrival. He
stated that this was possibly due to poor oil.

     He said that by orders of the Commanding Officer all valuable
things and papers had been destroyed or thrown overboard but
refused to state at what time this had taken place.

     LEFFLER refused to sign a transcript of his interrogation.

COMMENT:

     Though LEFFLER was a reluctant and evasive subject and re-
fused flatly to answer many of the questions asked him, his
answer regarding the number of large rubber lifeboats aboard is
very interesting in that it contradicts a statement made by the
Captain of the U-boat to the effect that there was a shortage of
one boat when they were loaded aboard the submarine. See the
covering report for this enclosure for further discussion of
the missing lifeboat.

Summary of Lt. Laffler's interrogation.

BASIC PERSONNEL RECORD
(Alien Enemy or Prisoner of War)

7G – 180 – NA
(Internment serial number)

SCHLUETER, Gregor
(Name of internee)

Male
(Sex)

F. P. C.* _____

Reference * _____

Height **6** ft. **2** in.
Weight 90 kilos
Eyes blue
Skin fair
Hair blond
Age 32

Distinguishing marks or characteristics:
None

INVENTORY OF PERSONAL EFFECTS TAKE
FROM INTERNEE

1. _____
2. _____
3. _____
4. _____
5. _____
6. _____
7. _____
8. _____
9. _____
10. _____

1 Aug. 1945, DIO-7ND, Miami, Florida
(Date and place where processed (Army enclosure, naval station, or other place))

The above is correct:
Gregor Schlüter
(Signature of internee)

Right Hand

1. Thumb	2. Index finger	3. Middle finger	4. Ring finger	5. Little finger

Left Hand

6. Thumb	7. Index finger	8. Middle finger	9. Ring finger	10. Little finger

W. D., P. M. G. Form No. 2
December 9, 1941   16 25095 1

Note amputations in proper space

* Do not fill in.

ID card of the thirty-two-year-old Second Engineer, Sub-Lieutenant Gregor Schulter, who was the oldest officer aboard *U 530*.

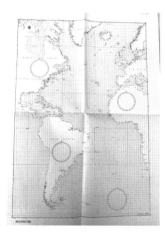

The map (which came from Lt. Schlüter's atlas) which shows the *U 530* last journey from Germany to Argentina. The investigators were of the opinion that the map was falsified - there is a continuous line leading straight to Mar del Plata and not a day by day route. Photograph from National Archives and Records Administration at College Park, USA.

CONFIDENTIAL

Resume of interrogation of Ernst ZICKLER,
Engineering Petty Officer of the German
submarine U-530.
- -

ZICKLER stated that he is a native born German subject,
age 24, single, and a Diesel Machinists Mate on the submarine
U-530.

He stated that he entered the German Navy as a volunteer
about the middle of October 1939. He entered the submarine
service about six months after his enlistment, serving on another submarine before being transferred to the U-530, which
transfer took place about the end of July 1943.

He is the holder of four decorations: two service medals
and the 2nd and 1st Class Iron Crosses. The 2nd Class Cross
was given for service in another submarine and the 1st Class
for service aboard the U-530.

He said that the U-530 had last been in dry dock about
the first of the year in the yards of the Deutsch Werke, in
Hamburg.

He stated that while operating out of Lorient the U-530
had belonged to the 10th Submarine Flotilla, but that operating
out of Kiel (as was the case on this voyage) she belonged to
the 33rd, under Commander KUHNKE. He did not know when or
where the others had surrendered.

ZICKLER stated that they had sailed from Christiansand
(Skaggerak), Norway, during the first days of March and that
for the first two hours they had been escorted by another craft
but he did not know what it was. He said that after that they
were alone.

According to Subject, they navigated for the next three
weeks submerged at all times due to fear of air attacks, using
the Schnorkel apparatus for charging the batteries. He stated
that the maximum speed that they could make using this device
was about six knots.

He said that the motors, diesel or electric, had been continuously in operation during the whole of the trip.

He stated that the U-530 had suffered no battle damage
during this voyage, but that on her third trip she had been
rammed by a tanker. He said that they had sunk no ships on
this trip.

ZICKLER stated that one day during the voyage the Captain
of the submarine had announced over the loudspeaker that
fighting had ceased. Several days later, by the same means,
he advised them that they were headed for Argentina to surrender
themselves. He had said that they were going there for better
treatment, that he had chosen Mar del Plata as the port to enter,
that he wished to go further but could not on account of the bad
condition of the motors.

He said that the motors knocked and that on account of
this they had to run at slow speed.

Summary of the interrogation of diesel engine mechanic aboard *U 530*,
Boatswain Ernst Zickler.

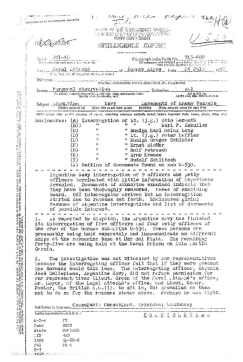

U.S. Intelligence Services Report concerning *U 530*, a document held at the National Archives and Records Administration at College Park, USA.

U 503 during her few days' stay in Rio de Janeiro, on the way to the United States.

CONFIDENTIAL

COPY No. _____
(For Record Section only)

MILITARY INTELLIGENCE DIVISION W. D. G. S.

MILITARY ATTACHE REPORT   Argentina
(Country reported on)

Subject German Submarine Surrenders to Argentine Navy   No. 0501.0207
(Brief descriptive title)   3123.0404

From M. A. Argentina   Report No. R-509-45   Date 18 July 1945

Source and degree of reliability:

Confidential   Rating: As indicated

SUMMARY.— Here enter careful summary of report, containing substance succinctly stated; include important facts, names, places, dates, etc.

1. (A-1) At 7.30 am on 10 July 1945, the 700-ton 50-meter German submarine U-530 surfaced in the harbor at Mar del Plata and surrendered to the Argentine Navy. The U-530 was commanded by 25-year old Captain Otto WERMUTH and carried a crew of 54 men. The oldest member of the crew was a 45-year old warrant officer, one of the engineers was 32 years old, and the rest of the crew averaged 22 years of age, with the youngest 19. The Argentine Ministry of Marine issued a communiqué the evening of 11 July, stating that interrogation of the crew and inspection of the submarine proved that:

   a. The U-530 had nothing to do with the sinking of the Brazilian cruiser "Bahia".

   b. She did not carry any German politicians or military officials.

   c. No persons were landed on the Argentine coast prior to the surrender.

   d. All personnel aboard were bona fide crew members.

On 16 July, the officers and crew were taken under guard to Martín García, a small detention island in the Río de la Plata. Details on crew members and their fingerprints have been or will be turned over to United States and British authorities. A special committee appointed by the Ministry of Foreign Affairs recommended on 16 July that the submarine and crew be placed at the disposal of the United States and British authorities. The question was discussed in a Cabinet meeting held on 17 July and it was decreed that both submarines and crew with reports and findings of Argentine naval authorities would be turned over to United States and British authorities.

2. (B-3) Local newspapermen have reported the following:

Distribution by originator   MIS — Chancery

Routing space below for use in M. I. D. The section indicating the distribution will place a check mark in the lower part of the recipients' box in case one copy only is to go to him, or will indicate the number of copies in case more than one should be sent. The message center of the Intelligence Branch will draw a circle around the box of the recipient to which the particular copy is to go.

AGF	AAF	ASF	AC of S G-2	Chief I G	Eur.-Afr.	Far East	N. Amer.	Air	Dissem.	AIC	FLBR	OSS
M A Sec.	CIG	Rec. Sec.	ONI	BEW	CWS	ENG.	OPD	ORD	Sig.	State	QMG	

MIS 183115

CPM 1
Mil 2
*Pol 2
   Route
   Lib
WW 1
W Eur Spc 1
Dir Inf 1
HQAAF 1
ONI 3
State 3
" ES 1
FBI 1

Enclosures:

Copy of report of Naval Attaché
of 13 July 1945

Pol 1
   Route
   Lib
WW 1

CONFIDENTIAL

CONFIDENTIAL
(Classification)

WAR DEPARTMENT
O.C.S.17 (2nd Rev.)

A copy of the document from the surrender of the German submarine *U 530* to the Argentinian Navy. On July 16, 1945, officers and crew were transported under guard to prison on the island of Martin Garcia. Photograph from the National Archives and Records Administration at College Park, USA.

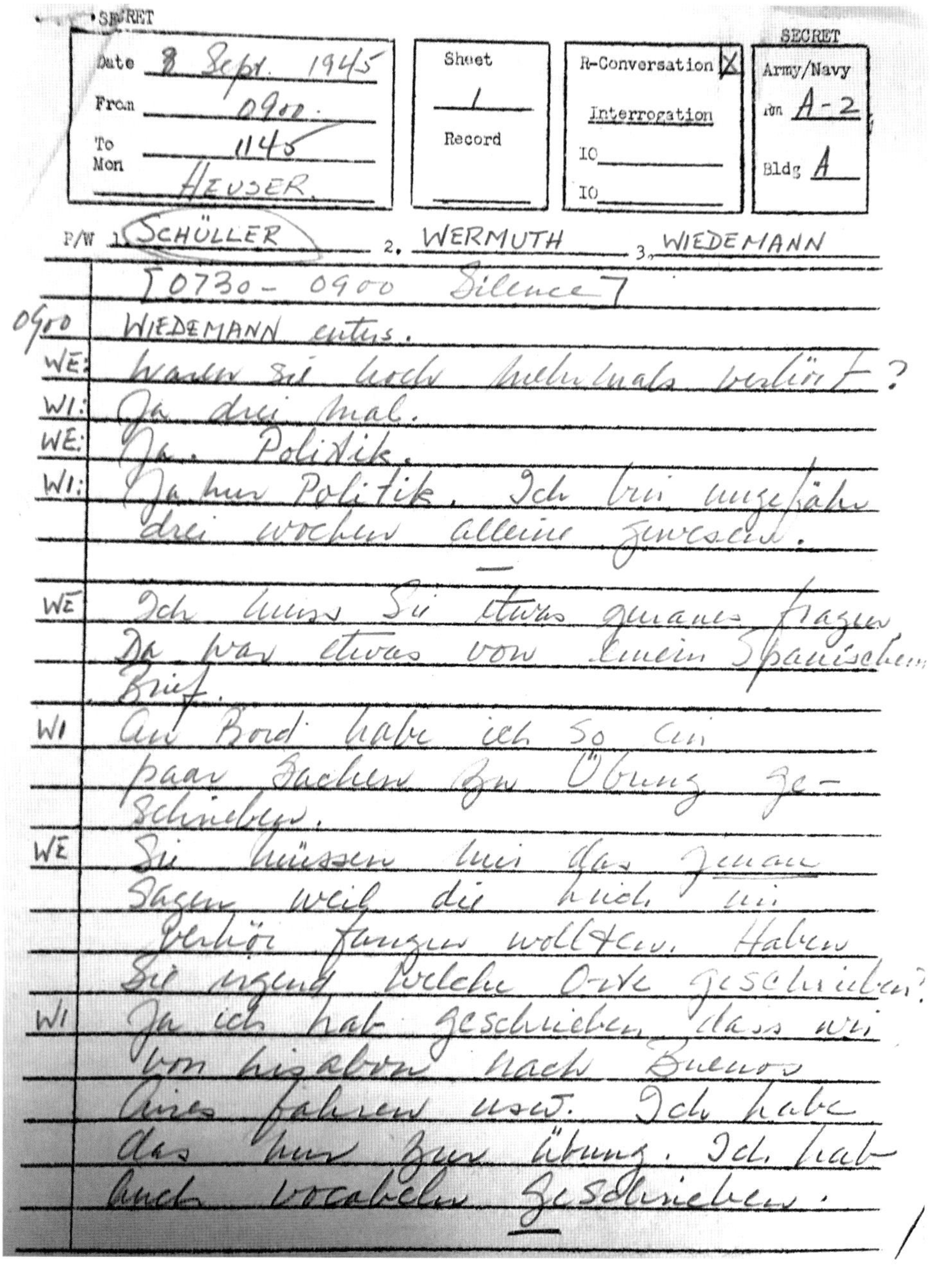

SECRET

Date 8 Sept. 1945	Sheet	R-Conversation ☒	SECRET
From 0900	1	Interrogation	Army/Navy
To 1145	Record	IO	for A-2
Mon HEUSER		IO	Bldg A

P/W 1. SCHÜLLER 2. WERMUTH 3. WIEDEMANN

[0730 - 0900 Silence]

0900 WIEDEMANN enters.

WE: Waren sie noch mehrmals verhört?

WI: Ja drei mal.

WE: Ja. Politik.

WI: Ja nur Politik. Ich bin ungefähr drei wochen alleine gewesen.

WE: Ich muss Sie etwas genaues fragen. Da war etwas von einem spanischen Brief.

WI: An Bord habe ich so ein paar Sachen zur Übung geschrieben.

WE: Sie müssen mir das genau sagen weil die mich nie verhör fangen wollten. Haben Sie irgend welche Orte geschrieben?

WI: Ja ich hab geschrieben, dass wir von higabron nach Buenos Aires fahren usw. Ich habe das nur zur übung. Ich hab auch vocabeln geschrieben.

Prisoners from the submarine *U 530*, who were imprisoned in the U.S. Navy barracks, were subjected to surveillance.

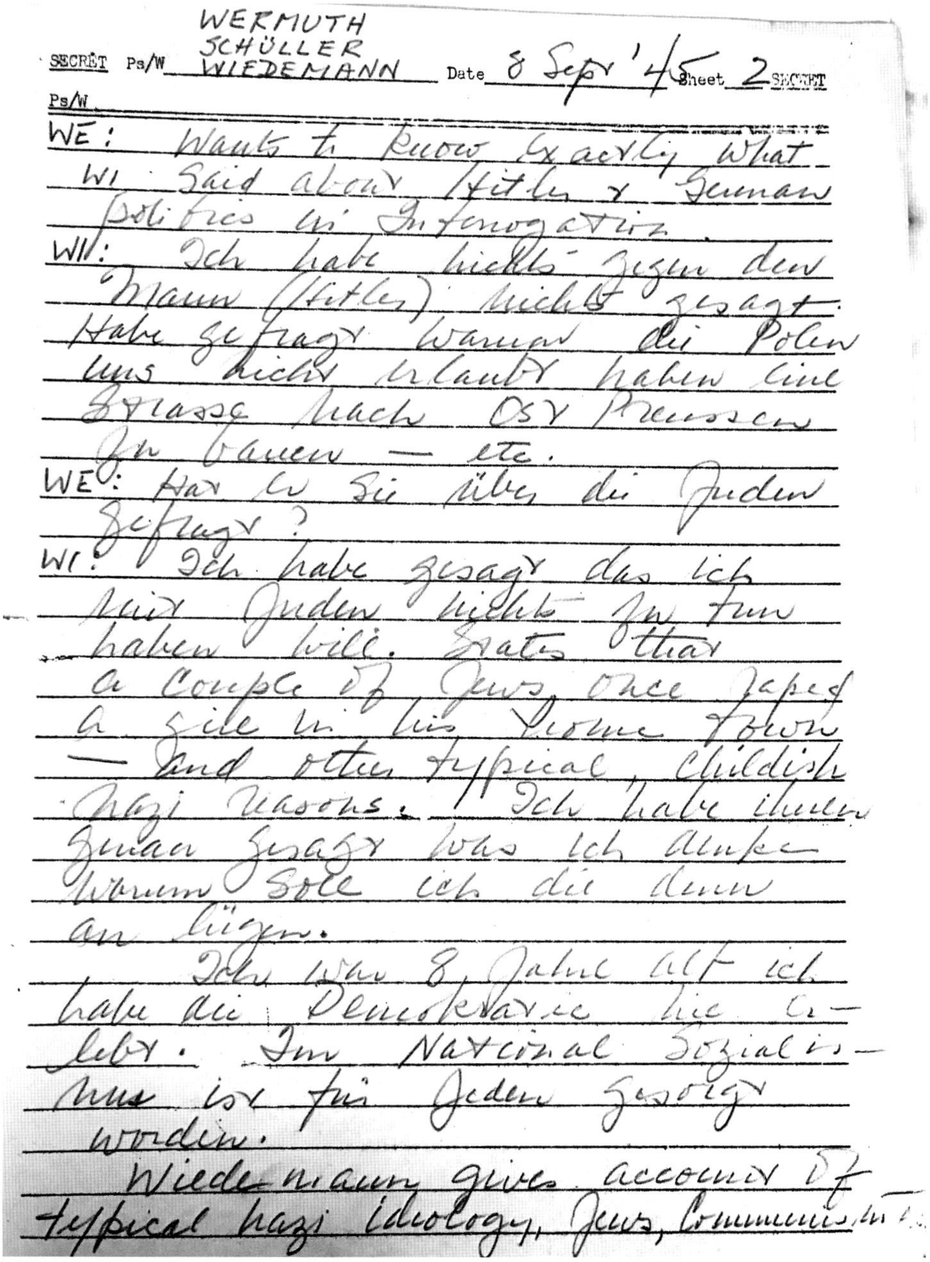

WERMUTH
SCHÜLLER
SECRET Ps/W   WIEDEMANN   Date 8 Sep '45   Sheet 2   SECRET
Ps/W

WE: Wants to know exactly what
WI said about Hitler & German
politics in interrogation.

WI: Ich habe niehts gegen den
Mann (Hitler) nicht gesagt.
Habe gefragt warum die Polen
uns nicht erlaubt haben eine
Strasse nach Ost Preussen
zu bauen — etc.

WE: Hat er Sie über die Juden
gefragt?

WI: Ich habe gesagt das ich
mit Juden nicht zu tun
haben will. States that
a couple of Jews once raped
a girl in his home town
— and other typical, childish
Nazi reasons. Ich habe ihnen
immer gesagt was ich denke
warum soll ich die denn
an lügen.
    Ich war 8 Jahre alt ich
habe die Demokratie hier er-
lebt. Im National Sozialis-
mus ist für jeden gesorgt
worden.
    Wiedemann gives account of
typical Nazi ideology, Jews, Communism.

The College Park archives near Washington keep documents dating back to September 8, 1945, which are a summary of the surveillance of three *U 530* prisoners staying in the same cell.

(U-530

NAVY DEPARTMENT
OFFICE OF THE CHIEF OF NAVAL OPERATIONS
WASHINGTON, D.C.

Op-414-G/rn
Serial: 00267P414
(SC)F41-10

~~S-E-C-R-E-T~~
~~DECL~~ASSIFIED   18 September 1947

From: Chief of Naval Operations.
To :   Chief of the Bureau of Ordnance.

Subject: Submarines - Obsolete U. S. and Ex-German - Disposal of.

Reference: (a) CNO restr ltr Op-414-G/rn ser 2408P414 over SS/L11-3
                of 12 Aug. 1947.
            (b) BuShips restr ltr SS/L11-3(5315-806) over EF30/SS
                of 6 Aug. 1947. Encl. (A) of ref. (a).
            (c) Fifth "Joint NOL-BuOrd" Torpedo Conference of
                4 April 1947. Conf. NOLM EF6-27/S75-1 (1-1199) of
                11 April 1947.
            (d) BuOrd conf ltr (Re6a) SS of 29 Aug. 1947.
            (e) BuOrd secret ltr (Re6)-OLL:al EF30, serial 004292 of
                3 July 1947, with end. thereto.

    1.   The proposal contained in reference (d) that four of the
obsolete Ex-German submarines be allocated to a torpedo exploder testing
program, is approved.

    2.   The Ex-German submarines, the U-234, U-505, U-530 and U-889
are designated for this project.

    3.   In reference (e) the Bureau of Ordnance requested that
the Naval Ordnance Laboratory be authorized to conduct certain underwater
electric potential (UEP) measurements on German submarines.

    4.   Prior to conducting the tests outlined in reference (d),
the Chief of the Bureau of Ordnance is authorized to conduct the underwater
measurements of these submarines as requested in reference (e).

    5.   By copy of this letter, Commander Submarine Force, U. S.
Atlantic Fleet is directed to assist in the accomplishment of these two
projects. A report of ultimate disposal is desired. This report should
include time and location of final sinkings.

    6.   By separate correspondence, the Commandant, First Naval
District is being requested to tow these submarines to firing areas
designated by Commander Submarine Force, U. S. Atlantic Fleet.

Document dated September 18, 1947, which refers to the use of *U 530* as a target for
torpedo tests.

On November 21, 1947, *U 530* was sunk during tests by a torpedo fired by the U.S. submarine USS *Toro* (in the photo) in the North Atlantic, north-east of Cape Cod.

... one of the final photos of *U 530*.

A bird's eye view of *U 530*.

Lieutenant General Heinrich Müller, chief of the Gestapo in 1939-1945. At the end of the war he disappeared, covering all his tracks. Traces lead to Argentina.

According to American reporter Paul Manning, chief of the Gestapo faked his death.

U.S. historian Chris Kraska is checking declassified documents concerning German submarines in South America in 1945. Photograph taken at the Archives and Records Administration at College Park near Washington.

Lt. Hans Leilich, the first commander of *U 977*.

Lt. Heinz Schäffer (1921-1979), during World War II he was the
commander of Type II D submarine *U 148* and Type VII C - *U 977*.

Type VII C submarine,
U 977 is being
commissioned.

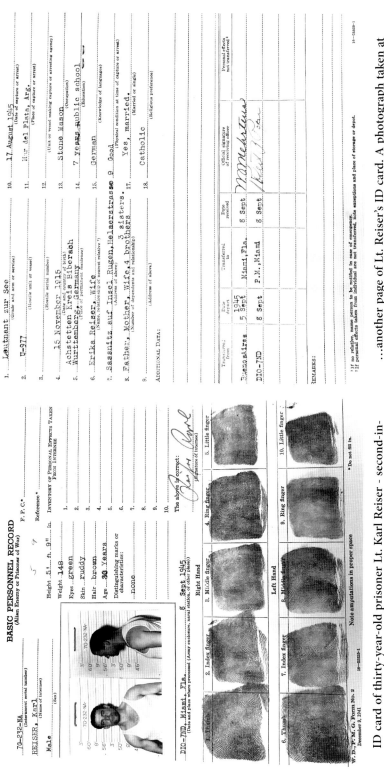

ID card of thirty-year-old prisoner Lt. Karl Reiser - second-in-command of *U 977* submarine. The document was prepared by request of the U.S. military intelligence in September 1945.

...another page of Lt. Reiser's ID card. A photograph taken at the Archives and Records Administration at College Park near Washington.

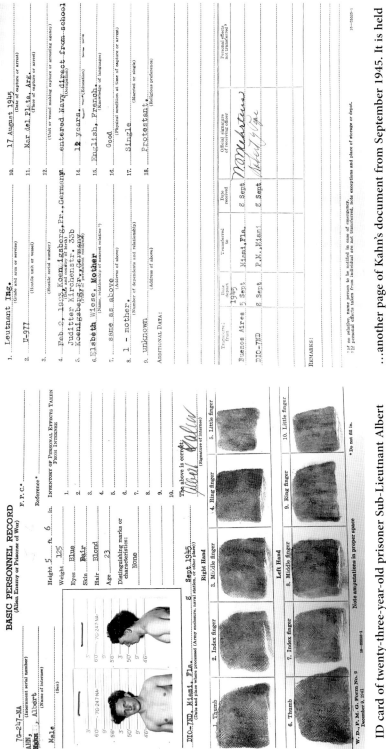

ID card of twenty-three-year-old prisoner Sub-Lieutnant Albert Kahn, *U 977*'s second mate.

...another page of Kahn's document from September 1945. It is held at the Archives and Records Administration at College Park near Washington.

BASIC PERSONNEL RECORD
(Alien, Enemy or Prisoner of War)

IQ-231-MA
(Internment serial number)

WIESE, Dietrich
(Name of Internee)

F. P. C.*

Reference*

Male
(Sex)

Height 6 ft. 0 in.

INVENTORY OF PERSONAL EFFECTS TAKEN FROM INTERNEE

Weight 145

Eyes blue

Skin fair

Hair blond

Age 22

Distinguishing marks or characteristics:
mole on right knee

The above is correct:
(Signature of Internee)

8 Sept 1945
(Date and place where processed (Army enclosure, naval station, or other place))

DIC-7ND, Miami, Fla.

1. Thumb
2. Index finger
3. Middle finger
4. Ring finger
5. Little finger

Right Hand

Left Hand

6. Thumb
7. Index finger
8. Middle finger
9. Ring finger
10. Little finger

Note amputations in proper space   * Do not fill in

W. D., P. M. G. Form No. 2
December 9, 1941

1. Leutnant zur See
(Grade and arm or service)

2. U-977
(Hostile unit or vessel)

3.
(Hostile serial number)

4. 25 July 1922 Strausfurt
(Date and country of birth)

5. Gebesee Ringleber Str. 82
(Place of permanent residence)

6. Wilhelm Kahn
(Name, relationship of nearest relative *)

7. Same as 5.
(Address of above)

8. None
(Number of dependents and relationship)

9.
(Address of above)

10. 17 August 1945
(Date of capture or arrest)

11. Mar del Plata, Arg.
(Place of capture or arrest)

12.
(Unit or vessel making capture or arresting agency)

13. Student
(Occupation)

14. 1/12 yrs Military School
8 yrs high school 4 yrs punblic sch.
(Education)

15. Little of French and English
(Knowledge of languages)

16. Good
(Physical condition at time of capture or arrest)

17. Single
(Married or single)

18. Evanglist
(Religious preference)

ADDITIONAL DATA:

Transferred from	Date depart	Transferred to	Date received	Official signature of receiving officer	Personal effects not transferred[1]
Buenos Aires	1945 5 Sept	Miami,Fla.	8 Sept		
DIC-7ND	8 Sept	P.M.,Miami	8 Sept		

REMARKS:

[1] If no relative, name person to be notified in case of emergency.
[2] If personal effects taken from individual are not transferred, note exceptions and place of storage or depot.

...another page of the same document held at the Archives and Records Administration at College Park near Washington.

ID card of twenty-two-year-old prisoner Sub-Lieutenant Dietrich Wiese, chief engineer aboard *U 977*.

A view of *U 123* in the harbor basin at the "Tirpitz" pier in Kiel, in the far background the depot ship *New York* is visible. At night of April 3-4, 1945, the former German passenger liner was sunk during bombing raid on the harbor of Kiel conducted by the U.S. B-17 Flying Fortress and B-24 Liberator bombers. The wreck was raised in 1948 and in the following year towed to a shipyard in Dalmuir, near Clydebank in Scotland, where she was broken up.

A bird's eye view of *U 977*, a photograph taken in September 1945.

The conning tower of *U 977*, a photograph taken in August 1945, at Mar del Plata.

Argentinian submarine *Salta*.

U 977 in Argentina, August 1945.

U 977 on her way
to Argentina.

Lt. Schäffer, the second and last
commander of the submarine
U 977.

German submarines *U 530* and
U 977, which officially
arrived in Argentina
in July and August 1945.

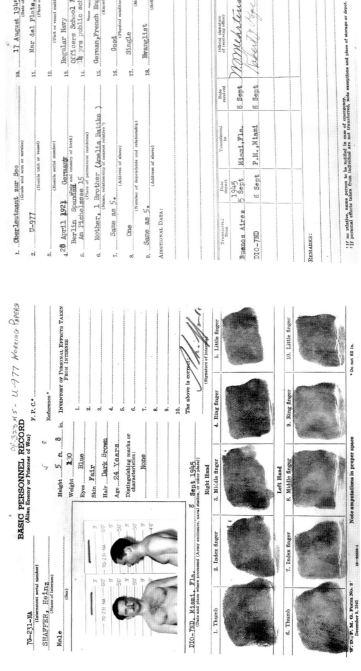

ID card of twenty-four-year-old prisoner Lt. Heinz Schäffer, commander of U 977…

...another page of Schäffer's ID card, held at the Archives and Records Administration at College Park near Washington.

República Argentina
Ministerio de Marina

Dokument der Übergabe.

In Mar del Plata, am siebzehnten August des
Jahres neuzehnhundert und fünf und vierzig, durch dieses Schriftstücks
und in Gegenwart des Kommandanten der U-Bootsdivision der argentinisch
Kriegsmarine, Fregattenkapitän JULIO C. MALLEA, übergibt bedingungslos
der Oberleutnant zur See HEINZ SCHAFFER, das Schiff unter seinem Kommando und die Besatzung nach Liste die diesem Schriftstück beigefügt
ist.-

Das U-Boot U-977 ist in den ussengewässern
von Mar del Plata am Siebzehnten August neunzehnhundert fünf und vierzig um zehn Uhr aufgebracht worden durch den Minensucher "PY" und
wurde in den Hafen unter dem Kommando des Oberleutnant zur See der
argentinischen Kriegsmarine RODOLFO SAENZ VALIENTE gebracht.-

Der Oberleutnant zur See HEINZ SCHAFFER bezeugt,
dass das U-Boot U-977, an dem die gesammte Mannschaft ausgebootet wurden ist, sich in sicherem Zustand befindet, dass sich an Bord Munition
für die Schnellfeuergeschüzte und Sprengstoffe befinden, dass von den
zehn Torpedos an Bord, die fünf die sich in den Rohren befinden, mit
Gefechtspistolen versehen sind; dass alle diese Materalien sich an
den dafür bestimmten Pläzten befinden und entsprechend gesichert sind;
und erklärt ausdrücklich dass sich an Bord kein Gegenstand oder Vor-
richtung befinden die das U-Boot versenken oder gänzlich oder teil-
weise zerstören könnte.-

Von diesem Schriftstück vier Kopien in spanisch
und ebensoviele in deutsch ausgestellt worden; von der beigefügten
Liste sind vier Kopien in beiden Sprachen ausgestellt worden. Der spa-
nische Text ist der allein gültige. Es unterzeichnet dieses Schriftstück und die zugehörige Liste die beiden zuständigen Kommandanten
Argentiniens und Deutchlands.-

JULIO C. MALLEA
Fregattenkapitän
Kommandant der U-Bootsdivision

HEIN SCHAFFER
Oberleutnant zur See
Kommandant "U-977"

Documents which confirm the transfer of *U 977* to the Argentinian Navy on August 17, 1945.

DECLASSIFIED
Authority NND B73041

Agregado al Acta Rendición U-977
Dem Schrift Stük der Übergabe des U-97 7
beigefügt

República Argentina

Ministerio de Marina

ROL "U-977"
BESATZUNG "U-977"

1	Oberleutnatt z.S	Tte. de Fragata	Schaffer Heinz
2	Leutnant z.S.	Tte. de Corbeta	Reiser Karl
3	" " "	" " "	Kann Albert
4	" Ing.	" " "	Wise Dietrich
5	Obermaschinist	Subof.Mayor MaQ.	Krebs Hans (x)
6	Oberstedermann	Subof.Mayor de Naveg.	Klinger Leo
7	Bootsmaat	Subof.2do. de Mar	Dudek Erich
8	Matrosen Hauptgefreiter	Cabo Principal Mar	Meyer Gerhard
9	" Obergefreiter	Cabo Primero Mar	Kullack Karl
10	" "	" " "	Husemann Wilfried
11	" "	" " "	Lehmann Heihreich
12	" "	" " "	Schöneich Rudi
13	" "	" " "	Maier Walter
14	" "	" " "	Meuwirther Rudolf
15	" Grefeiter	Cabo 2do. Torpedista	Bäumel Hans
16	Matrose	Marinero de Mar	Haupt Heinz
17	"	" " "	Risse Hermann
18	Maschinen Ob.Gefreiter	Cabo Primero MaQ.	Plontasch Johannes
19	" "	" " "	Blasius Heinz
20	" "	" " "	Kraus Alois
21	" "	" " "	Nittner Kurt (x)
22	Mahinengefreiter	Cabo Segundo MaQ.	Böttger Heinz
23	"	" " "	Wurker Heldfried
24	"	" " "	Waschk Heinz
25	"	" " "	Nashan Kurt
26	"	" " "	Höfler Gerhard (x)
27	Funkobergefreiter	Cabo 1ro.Radiotelg.	Hentscnel Harry (x)
28	Fungefreiter	Cabo 2do.Radiotelg.	Maros Helmth
29	Matrose IV	Mar.Radiotelegrafista	Knoblich Alois
30	Mechanikers Ob Gefr.	Cabo 1ro.MecánicoTorp.	Franke Heinz
31	" Gefreiter	Cabo 2do.MecánicoTorp.	Komorek Marl
32	" "	Cabo 2do.Mecácino Art.	Baier Adwin

Los marcados con asterisco, Curso Especial de Electricidad.-
Die Bezeichneten haben den U-Bootelektrolehrgang.-

El Comandante alemán que suscribe, deja expresa constancia de haber desembarca-
do los dieciseis hombres que se indican y que completan su dotación de guerra
en la isla Hellesoy (Noruega) el día diez de mayo de mil novecientos cuarenta
y cinco.-
Der Kommandant welcher unterzeichnet bezeugt ausdrücklich, dass die übrigen sec
sechzehn Mann, die hier angedeutet sind, die Kriegsbesatzung vervollständigen
und dass dieselben auf der Insel Hellesoy (Norwegen), am zehnten Mai des Jahres
1945 ausgeboot worden sind.-

1	Obermaschinist	Subof.Mayor MaQ.	Kethner
2	Oberbootsmaat	Subof.1ro. de Mar	Hilgeland
3	Bootsmaat	Subof.2do. de Mar	Persch
4	Maschinenmaat	Subof.2do. de MaQ.	Kempf
5	"	Subof.2do. de MaQ.	Völkel
6	"	" " "	Hackbart
7	"	" " "	Großmann
8	"	" " "	Blaser
9	Obermaschinenmaat	Subof.1ro. de MaQ.	Hirsch
10	Oberfunkmaat	Subof.1ro.Radiotelg.	Dämmig
11	"	" " "	Kötter
12	Obersanitätsmaat	Subof.1ro.Enfermero	Brouvers
13	Mechanikersmaat	Subof.2do.Mecan.Torp.	Steinmsior
14	Maschinen Ob.Gefreiter	Cabo 1ro.MaQuinista	Gersten
15	Maschinengefreiter	Cabo 2do.MaQuinista	Kötter
16	"	" " "	Heuer

Mar////////// ....

U 977 crew list during the internment in Argentina and a list of 16 crew members who left
the ship at night of May 10-11, 1945, in vicinity of Bergen. Document held at the Archives
and Records Administration at College Park near Washington.

Appendix To Interrogation Report on U-977

Statement of Schaeffer, C.O. of U-977

I left Kristiansand S. on 2 May 1945, normally equipped, and under orders to proceed to the Channel *(i.e. English Channel)*.

A few days later I picked up fragments of signals, which I suspected of being the work of enemy deception. When, however, these signals were not cancelled, I had to assume that the radio stations had fallen into enemy hands and that we had lost the war. The fact that uncoded signals signed "Allied Committee" were coming through, convinced me that the orders contained in these signals were illegitimate and not in agreement with the German High Command. When we began our patrol, an official slogan had been posted on all Naval establishments and ships which said: "The enemy shall find in Germany nothing but rats and mice. We will never capitulate. Better death than slavery."

It must be remembered that radio reception on board the U-977 was only sporadic since, for tactical reasons, we only occasionally came to Schnorchel depth. However, enough signals had been received so that I felt that I no longer had any superiors, and that I was relieved of my oath. In any case, I did not feel obligated without direct orders from my own government to accept enemy orders.

I no longer considered my ship as a man-of-war, but as a means of escape, and I tried to act for the best interests of all aboard. I respected the wishes of members of my crew insofar as they did not imperil the ship or cause damage to it.

One of my main reasons in deciding to proceed to the Argentine was based on German propaganda, which claimed that the American and British newspapers advocated that at the end of the war, all German men be enslaved and sterilized. Another consideration was the bad treatment and long delay in return home suffered by German prisoners-of-war held in France at the end of World War I. Then again, of course, the hope of better living conditions in the Argentine.

It was absolutely my intention to deliver the boat undamaged into Allied hands, while doing the best I could for my crew. I felt that the ship's engines might be a valuable adjunct to the reconstruction of Europe. I carried out these intentions and delivered the boat in perfect condition.

U 977 commander, Lt. Schäffer's August 1945 statement. Document held at the Archives and Records Administration at College Park near Washington.

A view of the conning tower and the 20 mm anti-aircraft guns of *U 977* in Argentina, August 1945.

On May 8, a message was decoded. The decoding process was done by the elec-tromechanical Enigma machine (type Marine) which was very easy to use. The message was decoded by Lieutenant-Junior Grade Kahn, who used a current Enigma system key called "Triton" (the code was used by U-Boots in the Atlantic, Baltic and North Sea), and handed to Lt. Schäffer. The author of the message thanked U-Boots' crew for their heroic six-year service on the sea. He assured all submariners they would go down in history. Their hardest task was still ahead of them. They were to capitulate and to follow the Allies' orders. There was no signature under the message because, before it was received, the antenna mounted on the snorkel went under water.

Schäffer found it hard to control himself, his patience was running low. As the U-Boot commander, he had no combat experience. He participated in 10 combat patrols as a watch officer - on Type VII C submarines - *U 561* and *U 445* from June 1941 to September 1944 - which made him a seasoned warrior in the Battle of the Atlantic. Most of his crew had not taken part in any combat missions. Only several senior non-commissioned officers had tasted the bitterness of sea combat. The easi-est option was to surrender the submarine to the Allies. Schäffer ignored the order to cease all hostilities. He had a plan and wanted to present it to the crew. With the exception of the officers, the crew was unaware of the latest decisions made by the Führer, Karl Dönitz. Capitulation became a fact.

The submarine had already left Norway and was heading towards the northern shores of Great Britain. Schäffer informed his crew of the German capitulation and presented a risky plan that would lead them to freedom. He decided to sail to Argen-tina. They had several thousand nautical miles to go. The commander had acquain-tances and friends there. It turned out that one of the seamen of the engineering room knew the South American country well and kept in touch with friends who lived there. He also had extensive knowledge about this South American republic which, following the end of the war, had bright future ahead.

Many German immigrants lived in Argentina. From the historical point of view, due to its friendly relationship with Germany, Argentina was an obvious choice. Argentina was one of the most developed countries in South America, in the south-ern part of the Atlantic. It had huge natural resources, large agricultural areas and unlimited development possibilities.

The men had doubts - there was a long and intense discussion. There was no unanimity. The commander managed to convince the most doubtful members of his crew that they had enough fuel (?) and provisions for three months which made them self-sufficient. Some seamen considered the plan preposterous. Lieutenant Schäffer hoped that in a friendly country he would be able to build new future.

The Goebbels' propaganda of the time, claimed that the American and British press demanded that, after the war, all captured German males should be steril-ized and treated as slaves. It was one of the key arguments to convince the men to continue their cruise. Schäffer also reminded them of the bad treatment German prisoners received from the French after the Great War. He presented them with a vision of a huge camp guarded by merciless enemy who would heap abuse at them, treat them with brutality and starve them to death. Escape was the only way to avoid humiliation. They had the means to realize the plan - their submarine.

After the German capitulation, the commanding officer considered *U 977* to be the means for escape not a combat submarine. He was not going to use torpedoes. If they had not managed to reach Argentina due to lack of fuel, engine failure or sickness of the crewmen, in face of the alternative, the commander would have headed to Brazil.

On the following day, the crew had a vote - of 48 men, 30 decided to flee to Argentina, two men wanted to be disembarked in Spain (which promised a quicker return to the Fatherland), 16 - mainly the married ones - wanted to return to their loved ones as soon as possible. It was a huge loss as thirteen of those who wanted to leave were the oldest and most experienced crewmen. They thought the decision to escape the trap on a submarine was madness. They did not believe in the success of such an undertaking.

The commander suggested disembarking the men near the coast of Norway. The easiest solution was to find a small ship and convince its captain to sail to the closest port in Germany. The plan was naive but the men were desperate. A dozen or so non-commissioned officers were provisioned for four weeks' trip. The farewell with the commanding officer was a sad one. The U-Boot headed back to Norway.

In the late 1950s one of the Argentine tabloids informed that the commanding officer ordered the disembarking of sixteen people because.... the U-Boot was overcrowded! Meanwhile, in the course of investigation conducted by the Argentine and U.S. investigators in mid-August 1945, it turned out, as the authors present on the following pages of the book, that *U 977* was to take sixteen German specialists, scientists and Nazis from Norway to Argentina. These passengers were to take part in a secret mission to Japan and sail on board of a large and modern Type IX D2 ocean-going submarine. When it turned out that the submarine could not continue her journey and was in needed repair, the BdU decided to embark those special passengers on *U 977*. What was it really like?

It turns out that the size of the mysterious cargo hindered the free movement of the crew on board the ship. It is interesting, that in his published memoirs, Schäffer describing the events related to disembarkation of one third of his crew, wrote that the ship was still cramped. Even with only thirty-two people left on board, the journey was unbearable!

On the dark night of May 10/11, *U 977* came to the surface. For several days they had been continuously underwater. They had been unable to find a good position for days. They could not take bearings from even a single star, let alone the Sun or the Moon, which they had not seen for a long time. The special direction finding equipment on board the submarine was not working. They did not precisely know where they were. The easiest solution was to enter the nearest port. But such a course of action was out of question, as the crew would have been surely made prisoners.

The petty officers were packed and ready to leave the ship. Their personal belongings could not interfere with their escape. They were equipped with detailed maps. The evacuation began in quite an unfortunate way, before they left the ship it turned out that one of the three large dinghies was damaged and there was no time to fix it. Sixteen people had to cram into two rubber dinghies. They were all wearing life jackets.

They were a few nautical miles away from the coast and the fog made accurate navigation difficult. It was shortly after midnight and the ship arrived near the island of Holsenöy, in the vicinity of Bergen. The commanding officer gave the orders in a quick and decisive manner. The day would dawn in just a few hours. The U-Boot moved slowly, because there were numerous underwater rocks around, protruding slightly above the surface. The depth was being sounded all the time. Ten, eight, fifteen meters, the reports changed all the time. The ship was running on electric motors, one at the "slowest forward" speed, the other prepared for "full speed astern".

Suddenly, the U-Boot's bow heaved dangerously out of the water, without first hitting or grazing against underwater rocks. The depth gauge was showing 5 m under the keel. The commanding officer immediately gave an order "Emergency full speed astern!", but it was oo late. The entire bow as far as the forward hydroplanes rose out of the water at a sharp angle of about 30 degrees.

Diesel engines were running at full speed astern, pushed to their limits, but the ship just would not budge. Those who were not on duty moved to the bow section. The engines were then turned one ahead and the other astern, but to no avail. The situation was hopeless. The U-Boot could not move, she was stranded on the rocks. She could have been detected at any time. Schäffer had to make a decision: surrender the ship intact or blow her up.

The evacuation of sixteen non-commissioned officers was at risk. There was no time to wait any longer. At 02.30 the sailors gathered on the deck, getting ready to leave the ship. Hand shakes were the sign of sincerity and the expression of solidarity with comrades and tears were shed. The rubber dinghies were launched. Unfortunately, one of them capsized. Fortunately, the situation was quickly brought back under control. A moment later another misfortune stuck. The ship heeled and two men fell into the sea. They were quickly hauled in, but there was no time for them to change their clothing. After a while the dinghies moved away from the submarine. An hour had just passed from the beginning of the disembarkation, when the flashlight signals from the mainland were observed. The Morse code message said "Bon voyage!"

U 977 had to quickly leave the dangerous area. Schäffer was responsible for the safety of the ship and the remaining crewmen. A prudent commander always dived two hours before the dawn. He would do so for two reasons. First of all, it allowed

for the use of hydrophones, so that the submarine could avoid an attack of the enemy ship approaching unnoticed in the dark. Secondly, it allowed for the crew to
rest, eat a meal in peace and use the toilet.

The crew comprised 32 men, including four officers and twenty-eight ordinary
and able seamen and non-commissioned officers. It was a skeleton crew, which
would face a rough time. Schäffer lost the most experienced men. Each crash dive
had since been a risky maneuver, but a necessary one if they wanted to continue
their voyage.

How many of these men believed in the success of their commander's plan? The
ship had a damaged search periscope and a skeleton crew only. The most pressing
matter was taking the ship of the rocks. They put all their faith in the knowledge
and skills of the first engineer and the commander of the ship. Water from the tanks
was pumped, first to the starboard and then to the port and back again. The engines
were running at full speed. But the ship would not budge. The only hope was to let
the compressed air into all diving tanks. Again, both engines were working at full
speed. Finally, the U-Boot began to throb and then, she finally moved. U 977 began
to moved away from the dangerous area.

At about 04.00, the U-Boot, slipping past the steep rocky cliffs, luckily avoided
a brush with death in vicinity of the island of Holsenöy. The appearance of an
unidentified submarine so close to the shore did not escape the attention of the
Norwegians. The searchlights flashed and illuminated the place where U-Boot had
been before. At that very moment, her crew noticed the first muzzle flashes of
coastal battery guns. U 977 was their target, but fortunately, the fire was inaccu-
rate.

Despite the fact that the U-Boot was constantly within the range of the
searchlights and under fire of Norwegian coastal battery, she managed to escape
the danger. There were still shallows, unknown to the Germans, as well as un-
charted rocks protruding above the surface of the water, which threatened the
safety of the ship. The engineers opened the ballast tanks valves. Water flooded
the tanks with a loud roar, pushing out the air. The U-Boot began to dive, going bow down fast at the angle of 35°. No internal leakages were reported to the
commander and the submarine descended smoothly. Finally, the depth was over
20 m and U 977 became invisible to the enemy, disappearing under the surface.
The commander decided they would travel for a few miles and then remain at
the bottom, like a ghost in calm water. The safety of the deep brought time for
reflection.

What was the fate of those 16 sailors who decided to leave the ship? It turned out
that they safely reached the shore in the vicinity of Bergen. But they only briefly
enjoyed their freedom. They were captured by the Norwegians, who handed them
over to the British. During the interrogation, they unanimously testified that they
were the only survivors from a U-Boot which had struck a mine. In that way, U 977
was considered lost and the submariners were taken prisoners.

The list of 16 crewmen of U 977, who disembarked on the night of May 10/11, 1945, in the vicinity of Bergen and decided to return to Germany.			
1.	Birsch	9.	Hilgeland
2.	Blaser	10.	Kempf
3.	Brouvers	11.	Kethner
4.	Dämmig	12.	Kötter
5.	Gerstan	13.	Kötter
6.	Grossmann	14.	Persch
7.	Hackbart	15.	Steinmeier
8.	Heuer	16.	Völkel

Let us go back to the "grey wolf's" voyage to Argentina. Those on duty were at their stations and those off duty were awaiting orders. Despite the fact that the young crew had no combat experience, they carried out the orders of their superiors to the letter. The most difficult conditions were in the diesel engine room, where there were practically no men to spare. That situation was a real challenge for the 22-year-old engineer Wiese. Steady and failure-free march depended on the change in the engine compartment's rhythm of life, set by subsequent watches.

Those who served on deck fared better. The crews of Type VII boats were divided into three watches commanded by officers: the deputy commander, the watch officer and the navigation officer. Each deck watch performed its duties for four hours and then was replaced by the next one, hence the conclusion, that each watch was in charge of the ship twice a day in the 4/8 hour system (4 hours on duty, 8 hours off). As the number of engine room personnel was smaller, it was usually divided into two watches and worked in six-hour shifts, under command of its own non-commissioned officers and under the supervision of the chief engineer (officer). Due to the shortage of personnel aboard *U 977*, the watch timetable was being altered.

The U-Boot submerged to 100 m. Then it was time for the crew to have some rest and relax after hours of tension, when the ship was stranded on the rocks. To ease the tension, the deputy commander gave the radio operator permission to play a record. A supply of records was prepared before departing for patrol. The loudspeakers played German songs. It was easy, entertaining music. The most famous was *Lili Marleen*, one of the greatest German hits of the period, known on both sides of the front line. They did not listen to the radio, because they knew that any special announcement had always brought bad news. All the more so then, when the Germany had already surrendered.

One week following the capitulation, the following message was transmitted on all U-Boot frequencies: „Any ship that does not surrender immediately will be considered a pirate and will be sunk".

The submarine had already left the coast of Norway and headed towards the northern coast of Great Britain. They sailed submerged all the time. According to the plan, their journey would take them along the European coasts, then, they would sail parallel to the coast of Spain and Gibraltar. On the way, there was North Africa and Portuguese Cape Verde. They were to pass the equator and continue south along the east coast of South America to Argentina.

The U-Boot's commander made an important decision. With a supply of fuel, provisions and fresh water, he decided to embark on a voyage unheard of in the history of submarine warfare. He had to stay calm and cautious, to maintain order and discipline. It would be a difficult journey, as for the most part of it, they would sail submerged.

Schäffer knew that the Royal Navy patrol ships, Allied forces and the RAF planes controlled the waters off the coast of the United Kingdom. *U 977* was ready to face enemy ships, but the commander decided to cease military operations, as such would have resulted in the destruction of the submarine anyway.

It was May 17. A week had passed since the 16 crew members left the ship and more than two weeks since the ship left the Norwegian harbor of Kristiansand for a combat patrol in the English Channel. The struggle for freedom continued, but how long could one travel submerged without a search periscope? During the day, the ship was moving at the depth of 50 m. At night they were running at periscope depth, using the snorkel and diesel engines charged, which were charged two large and heavy battery of accumulators. It was half-dark and humid inside the ship. The voyage, despite its numerous inconveniences, went on smoothly. Presence of aircraft or ships was rarely reported by the listening watch.

After several days of sailing, people started to look miserable due to the limited supply of fresh water, which was basically used only for cooking and drinking. Nobody was bothered by matted, greasy hair, unshaven beards and rarely changed underwear. Shaving was forbidden during the voyage as the water was strictly rationed. The skin was sprayed with cheap French cologne of intense fragrance to get rid, at least for a moment, of the unpleasant smell of the unbathed body. The fresh water ration was half a cup every second day for brushing teeth. As the voyage progressed, the interior of the ship, filled with rumbling of diesels, smelled of diesel oil, sweat and rotten food. The stench of urine, vomit and feces was ever-present. The potatoes, packed in bags, began to rot and stink immediately after the first dive. That was their everyday life.

U 977's route south was often crossed by the Royal Navy anti-submarine forces. After days of living under constant tension and in uncertainty, the U-Boot's crew was roused by an amplified, almost buzzing tone - "Alert"! The diesel engines were immediately shut down and the snorkel lowered. *U 977* dived into the abyss. The sound of turning propellers could not be heard. The listening devices were silent. An airplane flew directly above the submarine, but it did not drop bombs. That time they were lucky. There was no air attack. The voyage was more and more tiring. Tension was rising high inside the ship. People were in a bad mood and they were quickly annoyed. The crew did not breathe fresh air for a long time, neither did they see the sun or the blue sky. They joked that too much fresh air would make them unconscious. However, there was not much to joke about. The first symptoms of gum disease were found. People were taking vitamin tablets that were supposed to protect them from scurvy. Some had black rings under their eyes. Green mold started to cover pale faces of the sailors, slowly turning them into living dead. It was the result of a long, almost three-week-long underwater voyage. They were still in the area of the Atlantic, which was controlled by the Royal Navy and the RAF 24 hours a day. The bunks were damp from sweat or condensation dripping from the cold steel of the bulkheads. The rising temperature turned the ship into a stuffy greenhouse. Dampness was omnipresent aboard the ship. It was like that every day. Thick layer of intrusive, green mold began to grow on the sides and metal parts were covered with rust.

The cook was busy. The pile of refuse grew larger every day. It could not be jettisoned overboard, because the ship was permanently submerged. Horrible stench could be felt in every compartment. The pile of dirty laundry was growing at an alarming rate. Dirty underwear was stuffed in the corners, because tiny cabinets holding personal belongings were too small. There was no way to wash it. They almost ran out of soap, which according to the manufacturer's assurances should work in salt water (sailors did not confirm that fact). It turned out, that things washed in salt water never dried inside the ship and they caused painful itching and abscesses. Clothes became stuck to the skin. The ship had a desalination plant, but it was rarely used because one liter of diesel oil was needed to produce a liter of fresh water. The engine room personnel had to endure extremely painful suffering: their hands, faces and the other parts of their bodies were covered with a layer of lubricant that they could not get rid of.

The crew completely lost their sense of time, they did not know what the time of day it was. Life in a several-dozen-meters-long steel cylinder was regulated by the watches. The fact that they were powerless was terrifying. The first symptoms of hysteria were observed among the youngest sailors. There was a suspicion that submariners would start screaming and cursing, feeling powerless. Life became unbearable with every passing day. As the voyage continued, Schäffer and other officers were under more and more stress, hence they visited the diesel engine compartment more frequently. Since they did not want to give reasons to weaken the morale of the remaining crewmen, they had to get a grip on themselves and stay calm. They were as terrified as the rest of the men, because they were aware of the fact that the U-Boot could be discovered at any time. They were prepared for a load of depth charges. It was the end of the war, but they did not want to surrender. The depth was their advantage and the only protection.

Despite the commander's negative opinion, diesel engines were running flawlessly. People began to believe that the diesels would be able to withstand the hardships of the voyage. Unfortunately, it was only true up to a certain moment. *U 977* was running at periscope depth. At some point, the diesels started to work under full load. Lieutenant Wiese ordered to turn off one of the engines. After checking its condition, it turned out that the main couplings had been chafing and got overheated. The engines required a quick overhaul. The chance for successful escape was at risk.

Under these conditions, the malfunction had to be repaired by themselves. The chief engineer could not guarantee the commander that the couplings would not start chafing again. Schäffer was quite worried. Not only did he lose his search periscope, but what was worse, his ship with one diesel inoperational was in the area under strong control of the enemy. The risk was high. With one engine they now needed five hours to charge the battery.

After two days of repairs, the problem was fixed. But they seemed in for a run of ill-luck. The second diesel broke down soon. It was the same malfunction and the same repair procedure had to be repeated. With time, the engineers gained practice in repairing malfunctions. People were afraid that there would be some serious malfunction of the engines or other mechanical devices, which they would not be able to repair on their own and there would be no hope for victory. Luckily, they had a qualified mechanic who had a knack for that. Every day, the U-Boot travelled for eight hours using snorkel, because for some time diesels were incapable of working under full load.

Surfacing and ventilating the ship was out of question until they passed Gibraltar. People had to remain inside. It was only after leaving the dangerous area that they could expect Allied patrols to be less active. In order to avoid the danger, Schäffer had no other option but to stop the engines at short intervals (at least every 30 minutes) and move to listening depth. Such a maneuver was carried out in a flash.

June 21 was the fiftieth day of U 977's underwater odyssey. The beginning of summer was warmer. Mold became a real plague. If they had not scraped it off the sides, it would have covered them with green layer within a few days. Some sailors had a rash or ulcers on their hands. Rubbish and dirt were piling up and the crew had enough of it. There was only one possible way of getting rid of that garbage while being submerged - load the waste into a torpedo tube and fire it out by compressed air. The U-Boot was near Gibraltar.

Over the next few days the submariners fought fatigue and resignation. They were at the end of their tether. Their breathing became shallower and their movements slower. The stench, swept some of the seamen off their feet. It was difficult to maintain discipline. People started to murmur in the corners. They avoided eye contact with the commander. Schäffer lost good contact with his crew. Penetrating smell of fuel vapor soaked their clothes, not to mention food, which had the taste of oil and grease. They lost their appetite and became apathetic.

The noise, squeaking and unpleasant smell could be heard. These were the symptoms of a worn out coupling. Even with the increased speed of diesel engines, the U-Boot was unable to accelerate. Since the clutch plate lining was completely worn out, the diesels could stop working at any time. Under these circumstances, the ship would have to surface and the escape would be impossible. The chief engineer nailed the new lining to the plate. That field repair extended the coupling's service life.

On the ship's commander initiative a modest ceremony was prepared. The mood improved and hopes among the crew were revived. People were again of one heart and one mind. Nobody said that the U-Boot commander's decision had been that of a madman. They admired the lieutenant for his audacity. The non-commissioned officers, who had wanted to be disembarked near the coast of Spain, gave up the idea. The excitement hit the crew.

On July 1, almost two months had passed since U 977 began her voyage to Argentina. The crew almost literally began to grow moldy. The last patches of colors vanished from the faces of the submarines. People had lost their appetite and they went on coughing. Following the latest socializing event, the crew's faith and optimism was gone after only a few days of the voyage. The ship resembled a floating coffin. It did not take much time for a mutiny to break out on board. Sailors who were not on duty were lying on their wet bunks waiting for death.

On the night of July 6/7, after sixty-six days of traveling underwater, the commander of U 977 finally gave the order to surface. They were somewhere north of the Azores, about 1,500 km from the coast of the Iberian Peninsula. A new spirit kicked in. Smile, not observed for a long time, could again be seen on people's skinny and unshaven faces. It was the end of the hellish experience. The ship returned from the underworld.

The U-Boot was in the Mid-Atlantic. The U 977 ran on one engine running at full power; the other was used to charge the batteries. After more than two months of staying inside the ship, each of the sailors dreamed of finally being able to breathe in the sea air. Schäffer could not deny his men the pleasure. They did not resemble proud sailors who had gone out to sea two months ago. Lieutenant Reiser's hair had gone completely grey.

The fuel supply shrank by half. That was one of the reasons why some of the sailors had doubts about the success of their escape to South America. Their prospects looked pretty bleak. The U-Boot had covered 1,800 nmi so far (slightly over 27 nmi daily), i.e. about 3,340 km. There were about 40-45 tons of diesel fuel left in the tanks and they still had over 5,500 nmi (10,186 km) ahead of them.

The commanding officer ordered the crew to ventilate and thoroughly clean the living quarters and to preserve and paint the most corroded mechanisms aboard the ship. It was necessary to stop even the slightest leakage in the hull. However, the men were discouraged and tired, some even openly rebellious. Those dissatisfied were led by the 30-year-old Lieutenant Reiser, who tried to convince the crew that there was not enough fuel in the tanks for the U-Boot to reach Argentina, and that it would be scuttled earlier anyway. He was also in favor of getting rid of all torpedoes (10 altogether) in order to have more space in the compartments. The commander categorically rejected the proposal of the second in command, because he believed that the torpedoes would be the proof that following the announcement concerning the capitulation of Germany, U 977 did engage in warfare. He acted differently than Lieutenant Otto Wermuth of U 530.

Schäffer managed to quell the mutiny before it began. He removed Reiser's side-arm and temporarily relieved him of his duties. He wanted to avoid further problems.

The ship continued the voyage in the tropical heat of the Mid-Atlantic. At that moment everything was the way it had been before. They dived during the day and came to the surface at night. Following accurate calculations, the commander of *U 977* decided that they would only dive if necessary, because it was a very wasteful procedure. He banned the use of the snorkel. He gave orders to proceed on the surface for 10 hours at a minimum speed on one diesel and for the remaining 14 hours on one electric motor. They could not afford to take account of any mishaps that might arise from traveling so slowly. According to optimistic calculations, they were to reach Argentina in mid-August. By then they should still have 5 tons of fuel in reserve. If the fuel reserves were not enough, the commander planned to sew the sails and, using favorable currents and winds of the South Atlantic, cross the remaining distance between them and the coast of Argentina. The alternative escape plan scenario was also temporarily considered – shortening the voyage and sailing to Brazil.

The mood of the crew had definitely improved. They passed numerous merchantmen along the way. Freighters were steaming with their position lights on as the war was over. One night a passenger steamer overtook the submarine, but nobody on her deck noticed the silhouette of the surfaced U-Boot.

U 977 did not intend to hide in the depths during daytime. They reached the point in the Atlantic, which was not closely guarded by the ships and aircraft of the former enemy. The men were a little less worried. They sailed on the surface of the ocean, listening to some music and news. For almost ten weeks they were isolated from any news from the world. The crew learned about the catastrophic situation in Germany. They were worried about the fate of their relatives and the loved ones. The vast majority of them had no news about them even before the ship had departed on the patrol.

In the evening of July 13, *U 977* arrived in vicinity of the Cabo Verde islands (present day Cape Verde), several hundred kilometers west of the western coast of Africa. The submariners had not seen the mainland for a long time. The U-Boot commander preferred to be careful before going ashore, although he did not expect to see any observation posts on the islands. The sight of a German submarine only a few weeks after the end of the war would have been a complete surprise for the local population. It was unlikely that any of the islanders would notice the water disturbance caused by the ship's propellers turning just beneath the surface. The Allies had no idea that a German submarine could be hiding among the islands of Cabo Verde, an island state in the Atlantic Ocean.

The ship remained on the surface for the following hours. She dived to the periscope depth at dawn. Then the hydraulic lifting mechanism of the combat periscope was activated, the only operational optical device for observation while the U-Boot was running submerged. They were passing by massive rocks with sharp edges emerging from the sea. Schäffer allowed the crew to look through the periscope. The ship was no more than 1,000 m from the shore. The place was perfect to stop for a few days before sailing south. Some of the islands were uninhabited. Schäffer steered the ship towards the Ilhéu Branco (16°39.60"N and 24°41.00"W). It took a few hours before the commanding officer gave the order to surface.

It was around noon on July 14, the submariners tried to make for the shore on anything that could float, but their attempts were thwarted by the breakers. People were swimming in the ocean, laughing and joking, sunbathing and singing sailors' songs on the weather deck of the ship, and even surfing on makeshift... water skis. The heat was unbearable, so they kept themselves cool by spraying water from the fire hose. They were fishing (also using hand grenades). Although the crewmen wanted to remain there for a longer while, to rest and regain some strength among the islands of the Cabo Verde archipelago, the commander decided that they would weigh the anchor and continue southward on one diesel on the same day, after a bath at 20.30 (following a four-hour stopover). Since then, the U-Boot was sailing on the surface as there was no need to hide underwater.

On July 15, at 20.30, lookouts in the conning tower spotted a vessel. The commander ordered to change the course of the submarine to avoid contact. Those on the watch (one officer and three lookouts) were responsible for spotting targets in the 90° sector of the horizon using the excellent Zeiss binoculars.

In the following days the situation repeated itself - the ships were spotted, but the U-Boot remained out of sight. In addition to regular lookouts, the mast was extended with a crow's nest for the observer installed on top of it. It had a disadvantage of being difficult to dismantle in case of emergency, like e.g. being spotted by an aircraft[146].

The canvas sheets, hung at the back of the conning tower, were used to create camouflage surfaces places in such a way as to make U 977's silhouette look like a small collier from afar. A funnel was rigged from tin cans with oil-soaked rags placed inside puffing clouds of smoke. From then on, the U-Boot did not doge any ships. They were well-camouflaged. If needed, dense clouds of smoke puffed skyward, scattering sparks did not arise any doubts.

On July 21, at 03.03, the lookout reported to the commander, who at that time was inside the ship in the control room, that a plane had been spotted. Undisturbed, the submarine continued her journey. On the following day, they passed the Saint Peter and Saint Paul Archipelago at a distance of about 25 nmi (46 km). U 977 approached the equator. It was hard to believe that only two weeks prior the majority of crewmen were desperate, living on the verge of mental breakdown, ready to fol-

---

[146] U 977 was probably illuminated and attacked by the Argentine destroyer *Mendoza* near the Bay of San Matias, off the shores of Argentina, at night of July 18, 1945. A declassified Argentine naval report states that an unidentified submarine was being tracked for an entire day using hydrophones. It appears that the event is not mentioned by other sources. See: H. Schäffer, *Geheimnis um U-977*, Buenos Aires 1950. Neither was the mystery solved by the search in the National Archives and Records Administration at College Park in Maryland, Record Group (RG) 59...., sign. 862.30/8-445 - 8-2145.

low the second in command and join the mutiny. The U-Boot resembled... a „water bus". There was a picnic atmosphere on the weather deck. Every sailor made a hat to protect his head and neck from the scorching sun. There was very little work to do on the ship. The quarters were cleaned up and glittered like new. The rust was gone. The tropical sun dried out the woodwork and the struggle with mold was finally won. Underwear had not been washed for a long time, it was tied to a line and towed astern. After an hour in the turbulent water it was thoroughly washed. The one who came up with that idea earned the respect of his colleagues.

On July 23, at 06.00, the U-Boot crossed the equator at about 30° meridian west and a traditional line-crossing ceremony was held on board. It was attended by 28 of the 32 submariners. Then, an airplane appeared in the sky. The crew, dressed up for the ceremony, took battle stations. However, there was no attack and the ritual was finished on the weather deck.

On July 24, unidentified planes were spotted three times by the lookouts of *U 977* – first, at 01.30, then at 02.30 and finally at 03.00 (it is possible that these were three different aircraft). On July 25, at 11.25, the next plane was spotted and then, a day later, another one.

On July 30, the crew of *U 977* learned from the wireless transmission that *U 530* arrived at the Argentine submarine base at Mar del Plata on July 10. The Argentineans handed the U-Boot over to the Americans. The people aboard *U 977* were in despair. They were terrified. Many wanted to scuttle the ship and secretly get to the Argentine shore. Schäffer decided not to scuttle the submarine before reaching the naval base at Mar del Plata. He suspected that such behavior could have seriously threaten their hopes for freedom. On the way, they saw the lights of Rio de Janeiro. The U-Boot continued down south. The weather changed and it got colder as *U 977* left the tropical zone.

As the U-Boot had been detailed for combat operations in the North Atlantic, they had no charts of the southern hemisphere. They navigated only by dead reckoning. The longitudes and latitudes of the cities along the east coast of South America were taken from commander's textbooks. They steered clear of the numerous rocks scattered off the coast of Brazil. They could have saved a few hours making shortcuts, but it was not worth the risk.

The news concerning the capture of the colleagues from *U 530* was a serious blow to the crew. Some submariners suggested that they should try to surrender in Brazil or Uruguay. Some hastened to sew makeshift backpacks and packed their modest belongings and tools to make a living as locksmiths or mechanics. However, the commander convinced the people that they should officially surrender the submarine in Argentina and try their luck there. The men regretted that none of them knew Spanish, because the radio broadcasts about the incredible escape of the *U 530* to Argentina were often in Spanish.

Two days after receiving the news of *U 530* internment and the 54 crew members being imprisoned, Lieutenant Schäffer performed a test dive to the depth of 40 m.

The U-Boot was watertight. On August 2, the lookouts spotted a large, unidentified ship. The U-Boot continued along the previously set course. Another freighter was observed on August 13.

Eventually, it was necessary to make a thoughtful decision - what should be done? The commander wanted to prevent the ship from being scuttled. The plan was simple - call at Mar del Plata. Buenos Aires was out of question, due to the lack of accurate charts, and even if they had had them, it would have been far too dangerous to risk the constantly changing shallows of a 100-mile river passage up to the capital of Argentina without a pilot. It was August 15 and according to recent calculations, they should be able to reach the Mar del Plata lighthouse within two days[147].

The commander did not want to make the decision concerning the fate of the ship on his own. Therefore, two hours before the termination of the voyage he called a meeting with the crew. He wanted to know his subordinates' opinions. People suggested various options for further escape. Scuttling of the U-Boot was not a difficult task. Submariners could have reached the shore using rubber dinghies. It was necessary to get rid of those dinghies, which unfortunately do not burn quickly or easily. Rising black smoke would have been visible from the coast and could easily betray their position. If need be, it was possible to bury the dinghies. Escaping deep inland in a large group was out of question. They would have been immediately detained and imprisoned. Schäffer was in a better position, as his family's friends lived in the capital of Argentina. The crew had no civilian clothes and they would have had to flee in uniforms. They had no money and without the knowledge of Spanish most of them would have soon fallen into the hands of the police. The Allies would have announced on the radio and in the press that there would be a substantial reward for capturing or indicating the hiding place of German submariners. After the publication of articles about German criminals who fled to South America in the Latin American press (the crew of *U 977* was unaware of that), a hunt would have began and it would have continued until every last one of them had been caught.

The optimal solution was to put into a port. The commander assured the men that their conscience was clear. Although they would be captured, they can expect a short prison sentence. If they decide to scuttle the ship and destroy the her equipment and documents, they would not be able to prove their innocence. The evidence would remain at the bottom of the sea.

One hour after the meeting, the second in command informed Schäffer that most people were in favor of putting into port and turning themselves in to the Argentine army. In the early morning of August 17, *U 977* was off the coast of Argentina. The entire crew was on deck. The Mar del Plata lighthouse came into view, but they were still far away from the shore. Since July 23, (the day they crossed the equator) until August 17, it took *U 977* twenty-five days to travel 5,200 km. They sailed on the

---

[147] H. Schäffer, *66 Tage unter Wasser. Die geheimnisumwobene U-Boot-Fernfahrt nach Argentinien*, München 1996, p. 61.

surface at the speed of approximately 4.7 knots. It was the 107th day of their voyage. They covered a total of 7,644 nmi (about 14,160 km)[148].

While still being outside the three-mile limit, the U-Boot, flashed the signal "German Submarine". The engines were stopped. Soon several fishing boats started to circle around the submarine. The fishermen looked with curiosity at the submariners sporting long beards.

The vessel of the Argentine Navy noticed the U-Boot from a distance of about 6 nmi (11 km) from the harbor of Mar del Plata[149]. It was 09.15 local time. The 450-ton Argentine minesweeper *Comodoro Py 10*, accompanied by two submarines *Salta* and *Santa-Fe*, came alongside *U 977*. The ships remained on patrol in their sectors off the coast of Argentina. Argentine officers were astonished to see that more than three months after the end of the war any enemy submarine was still „wandering" the ocean.

After some time, Lt. Rodolfo Saenz Valiente, the minesweeper's commander, accompanied by several sailors, boarded the submarine. The U-Boot crew stood in line on the deck. The ship looked good, it was freshly painted. Schäffer delivered his report in German. The Argentinean did not understand a word and therefore, at the request of the *U 977*'s commander, the conversation that followed was in French. The officer of the Argentine Navy and Lt. Schäffer went inside the conning tower.

Not long afterwards, a motor launch carrying a detachment of sailors (officers, petty officers and sailors) came alongside the U-Boot. They were supposed to bring the submarine into the harbor and, above all, prevent her from being scuttled or damaged. Commander of *U 977* managed to convince Lt. Valiente that he had no intention of destroying the U-Boot and that he himself would take the ship into the harbor. He made it clear, that the crew spoke only German and moreover, the unfamiliar personnel could hardly be able to handle the complex machinery. Lieutenant's word of honor was accepted and Schäffer commanded *U 977* for the last time. The U-Boot, assisted by tugboat, entered the harbor flying a black flag. The crew was given half an hour to leave the ship. The submariners kept their personal belongings and the ship's commander made a farewell speech:

Kameraden [....] we have put into an Argentine port. I am sure we have done right. None of us will ever regret this voyage. For most of us it will always remain the greatest experience of our lives, an achievement of which we can be proud. This is a hard parting for us after all we have been through together. Our very existences have been so closely interlocked that we have become almost a single being, but now each individual will be master of his fate and free to go his own way. But we must never forget that

---

[148] Report on the interrogation of prisoners from U-977 surrendered at Mar del Plata, 17 August 1945, NARA, Record Group (RG) 59 (U.S. Department of State Central Decimal Files), sign. 862.30/8-445 – 8-2145, typed, p. 1.

[149] Naval Attache, Buenos Aires, 24 August 1945; Alusna Baires Conf. Desp. 171500, 17125, 190315, of August 1945. Encl. (A) Crew List U-977, Official - personal knowledge, NARA, Record Group (RG) 59 (U.S. Department of State Central Decimal Files), sign. 862.30/8-445 – 8-2145, typed, p. 1.

we are German sailors, survivors of the most formidable arm of this whole war. That thought will be a bond between us in the years to come. I thank you for your trust and loyalty. I wish you each fulfilment of his hopes and the attainment of his desire[150].

The commanding officer shook hands with all his subordinates for the last time. Tears were running down their bearded weatherbeaten faces. It was difficult for the crew to master their emotions. After a while Lt. Heinz Schäffer gave the last order: „Three cheers for our loyal, our invincible *U 977*. Hip, hip, hurrah"! Argentine officers watched this small farewell ceremony with respect for the U-Boot crew.

On August 17, at 11.05, the intact U-Boot was handed over to representatives of the Argentine Navy[151]. The commander of *U 977* kept the ship's logbook, navigational data, nautical charts and other documents. There were about 5 tons of diesel oil left in the tanks. Unlike many other U-Bootwaffe submarines, *U 977* did not suffer any casualties. Minor mechanical defects were found aboard the ship, which were confirmed by an Argentine officer engineer. The damaged equipment included: the search periscope, Junkers air compressor (since the beginning of August), compressor (since June), oil pump pressure motor and the snorkel setting indicator[152].

She was the last U-Boot to lower the Kriegsmarine ensign[153]. The hand-over protocol stating that the submarine was surrendered to the Argentine Navy was made in four identical copies in German and Spanish. The same number of copies were made of the crew list. The content of this document is published below:

On August 17, 1945, at Mar del Plata, by this document and in the presence of the Commander of the Submarine Division of the Argentine Navy, Lt.Cdr. Julio C. Mallea, Lt. Heinz Shaffer [should be: Schäffer - M.B., P.W.] unconditionally surrenders the vessel under his command and the crew according to the list attached to this document.

The submarine U 977 was captured in the outer waters of Mar del Plata on August 17, 1945, at ten o'clock, by the minesweeper „PY" and was brought to the port under the command of Lieutenant of the Argentine Navy Rodolfo Saenz Valiente.

Lieutenant Heinz Schaffer testifies that the submarine U-997, after being disembarked by the entire crew, is in safe condition, that there is ammunition on board for the quick-firing guns [20 and 37 mm anti-aircraft guns – M.B., P.W.] and explosives, that of the ten torpedoes on board, five of which are located in the tubes, are equipped

---

[150] W. Schäffer, *U-Boat 977*, London 1953, p. 21.

[151] E.J. Lanigan, *Secret, A16-2*, NOB. Ser. No. 0040, 17 September 1945, NARA, Record Group (RG) 59 (U.S. Department of State Central Decimal Files), sign. 862.30/8-445 – 8-2145, typed, p. 1.

[152] First and only patrol of U-977, NARA, Record Group (RG) 59 (U.S. Department of State Central Decimal Files), sign. 862.30/8-445 – 8-2145, typed, p. 3.

[153] According to the official version, U 977 surfaced after 66 days of the first long-distance submarine voyage in history. The authors of memoirs, researchers and naval historians count the days of the German submarine voyage from May 2, until the night of July 6/7, 1945. According to documents, the U-Boot had already came to the surface on the eighth day of the patrol. In fact, U 977 was continuously running under water using the snorkel from the night of May 10/11, until the night of July 6/7, 1945. This gives 58 days of uninterrupted submerged voyage.

with fuses; that all these materials are located in the designated places and are secured accordingly; and expressly declares that there is no object or device on board which could sink or destroy the submarine in whole or in part.

The Spanish text is the only valid one (official). This document and the corresponding list are signed the two competent commanders of Argentina [Lt.Cdr. Julio C. Mallea - M.B., P.W.] and Germany [Lt. Heinz Schäffer - M.B., P.W.][154].

---

[154] Dokument der Ubergabe, NARA, Record Group (RG) 59 (U.S. Department of State Central Decimal Files), sygn. 862.30/8-445 - 8-2145, p. 1, typed.

CHAPTER VI

AMERICAN PRIZE

Truth is too naked.
It does not stimulate men.
Jean Cocteau

The crew of *U 977* was accommodated in crew quarters on board the depot ship, former armored cruiser *General Belgrano*, moored in the submarine base at Mar del Plata. Despite the fact that they were prisoners of war, they boarded the ship in accordance with maritime ceremonial. Crews of three Argentine submarines (*Salta*, *Santa Fe* and *Santiago del Estero*) were standing at attention in line. The band was playing a march, when thirty-two sailors from the U-Boot boarded the old depot ship, walking along the gangway. Good manners of the Argentineans took German submariners by surprise. Lt. Schäffer submitted a report to the duty officer and then they both marched along the line of sailors dressed in white uniforms. Then German submarines were fed and allowed to bathe and shave. Officers were accommodated in four-men cabins and they were separated from the rest of the crew.

On August 18, the U-Boot commander, asked by the Argentine commander of the Submarine Division, submitted a report concerning their over hundred-day long combat patrol. Schäffer also disclosed his (and his crew's) motives for doing so. Moreover, he revealed the reasons for not scuttling *U 977* at sea. One of the reason to take the flight to Mar del Plata, was the fact that there was never any hatred between Germany and Argentina[155]. He hoped his crew would be better-treated in captivity and later allowed to settle down in South America. They wanted to avoid being interned by the Soviets, since they feared they would not have been treated well, as they thought they would be considered "war criminals".

The interrogation had an unofficial character. Its proceedings are described by American investigator S. A. D. Hunter – the memo was written after receiving information from a representative of the Argentine navy:

---

[155] According to the testimony of the submariners, the crew of *U 977*, was not aware of the fact that in late March 1945, Argentina declared war on Germany. The country was considered both friendly and neutral.

[German submarine – M.M, P.W.] U 977 had surrendered to the Argentine Navy. The Commanding Officer of this boat was Lt. (jg) Heinz Schaeffer [Schäffer – M.B., P.W.] who is listed in the 1943 Rank List as a Lt. (jg) [...] There were 4 officers and 32 men aboard the U 977 when she surrendered, approximately 16 less than the normal complement of a boat of this type. Preliminary reports indicate that this ship left Kiel April 19 [actually on the 13ᵗʰ – M.B., P.W.] for Christiansand [should be Horten – M.B, P.W.] and a British official source reports it at sea 25 May [on May 2, she departed Kristiansand for patrol M.B., P.W.]. According to W.I.R. [military report – M.B., P.W.] 8 June 1945, 16 survivors from U 977 stated that their U-boat was wrecked on an island off Bremangen [Bremanger – M.B., P.W.], north of Bergen, on the night of 9/10 May while she was returning from a patrol with a damaged periscope.

On May 9 1945 the Admiralty reported that the U 874 had left Horten on 8 May after 16 members of the crew had been put ashore and the same number of notables from Oslo substituted. It took provisions for three months but later returned to port and surrendered. In a report from U.S.G.C.C. No. 7-S-45, 28 May 1945, the Naval Officer in Charge, Oslo, reported that the Commanding Officer of U 874, Lt. (jg) [Theodor – M.B., P.W.] Petersen, now P/W, stated that preparations were made to sail for Japan but the trip was not undertaken because one motor was unserviceable. There is no information as to the number of prisoners from the U 874[156].

It is apparent that the story told by the 16 men who claim to be survivors of the U 977 was not true and may have been told in an effort to give the U 977 time to make its escape. The dates of the departure of U 874 (8 May) from Horten and of the reported wrecking of U 977 (9/10 May) indicate that both U-boats were in Norwegian waters and a transfer of personnel from U 874 (the "notables" mentioned in Admty. message 9 May) to the U 977 could have been made, the U 977 continuing to Argentina and U 874 returning to port and surrendering. The further possibility presents itself that the 16 notables had been put ashore somewhere before the U 977 surrendered. The deficiency in the complement of the surrendered vessel of about 16 supports such a conclusion[157].

August 20, 1945, was the first day of the investigation. It was delayed by the fact that there was no interpreter. That task was given to a young Argentine sailor of German origin, who came from Buenos Aires. The interrogators were two intelligence officers of the Argentine navy. However, Allied naval investigators were also flown in.

The first to testify was the U-Boot's commander. Serious charges were brought against Lt. Schäffer: he was accused of war crimes. According to Argentinean in-

---

[156] At the end of May 1945, *U 874* was redeployed to the English base at Lisahally. On December 30, as part of Operation „Deadlight", the U-Boot left the base at Lisahally in tow of the British destroyer escort HMS *Mendip*. In the morning, on the next day, the tow snapped and the submarine was sunk with artillery fire of the British destroyer HMS *Offa*.

[157] Surrendered German Submarine, U 977 (500 t), NARA, Record Group (RG) 59 (U.S. Department of State Central Decimal Files), sign. 862.30/8-445 – 8-2145, p. 1, typed. [August 18, 1945 document – M.B., P.W.].

vestigators, *U 977* was responsible for sinking of the Brazilian light cruiser *Bahia*. The investigators made no mention, that initially Lt. Wermuth, commander of *U 530*, had been accused of sinking the ship and death of hundreds of her crewmen. Commander of *U 977* was not informed that the crew of *U 530* had been exonerated.

Schäffer was also accused of... embarking Hitler and other high-ranking Nazi officials, who fled from Germany. That fact was mentioned by Argentine press. Investigators were curious, what had happened to the legendary Nazi gold, which had supposedly been on board the U-Boot. To prove his innocence to the Argentine interrogators, commander of *U 977* presented the ship's log and navigation chart entries. He also revealed other documents. He confirmed that before departure for the combat patrol only 10 torpedoes had been loaded – six G7e T-III with Pi2a fuses and 4 G7es T-V with Pi4c fuses. During the tree-month-long journey they were not used once. He denied that had been responsible for sinking of *Bahia*. He presented the maps and revealed remaining navigation notes. Moreover, he gave a detailed account of the evacuation journey since May 9, 1945. He confirmed that near the coast of Norway, 16 crew members who had chosen to stay, were put ashore. In his testimony there is no mention that German Nazis were embarked in their place.

National Archives and Records Administration at College Park is in possession of an attachment to the Schäffer's statement:

I left Kristiansand S. on 2 May 1945, normally equipped, and under orders to proceed to the Channel (i.e. English Channel).

A few days later I picked up fragments of signals, which I suspected of being the work of enemy deception. When, however, these signals were not cancelled, I had to assume that the radio stations had fallen into enemy hands and that we had lost the war. The fact that uncoded signals signed "Allied Committee" were coming through, convinced me that the orders contained in these signals were illegitimate and not in agreement with the German High Command. When we began our patrol, an official slogan had been posted on all Naval establishments and ships which said: "The enemy shall find in Germany nothing but rats and mice. We will never capitulate. Better death than slavery".

It must be remembered that radio reception on board the U 977 was only sporadic since, for tactical reasons, we only occasionally came to Schnorchel depth. However, enough signals had been received so that I felt that I no longer had any superiors, and that I was relieved of my oath. In any case, I did not feel obligated without direct orders from my own government to accept enemy orders.

I no longer considered my ship as a man-of-war, but as a means of escape, and I tried to act for the best interest of all aboard. I respected the wishes of members of my own crew insofar as they did not imperil the ship or cause damage to it.

One of my main reasons in deciding to proceed to the Argentine was based on German propaganda, which claimed that the Americans and British newspapers advocated that at the end of war, all German men be enslaved and sterilized. Another con-

sideration was the bad treatment and long delay in return home suffered by German prisoners-of-war held in france at the end of World War I. Then again, of course, the hope of better living conditions in the Argentine.

It was absolutely my intention to deliver the boat undamaged into Allied hands, while doing the best I could for my crew. I felt that the ship's engines might be a valuable adjunct to the reconstruction of Europe. I carried out these intentions and delivered the boat in perfect condition[158].

On the day of *Bahia's* sinking *U 977* was 50 nmi (approximately 93 km) from the position where the Brazilian cruiser went down.

The U-Boot commander categorically denied the rumors concerning Hitler's participation in the voyage and that of other people who were then to be secretly put ashore in the south of South America. In addition, he answered numerous additional questions. He referred to the preserved ship's papers in order to prove his truthfulness, fighting to clear himself of the accusations thrown against him. He also said that he had needed such a long time to reach his destination (Argentina), because the ship was running at the slowest speed (about 3 knots), as the fuel was running out.

After hearing Kriegsmarine officer's explanations, the intelligence staff interrupted the investigation. The evidence was handed over to a team of experts for urgent translation. The fact that the ship's documentation was not destroyed spoke in favor of the U-Boot's crew. An additional advantage was that the undamaged *U 977* was handed over to the Allies.

Schäffer was isolated from the remaining colleagues and received a single cabin on the depot ship. Two guards were posted in front of the entrance to the officer's cabin. The rest of the crew was accommodated in spacious rooms on the ship and provisioned.

Answering questions of Argentine investigators, Lieutenant Dietrich Wiese said that in the present condition *U 977* required shipyard repairs. The U-Boot was unfit for combat deployment at sea. Her watch periscope was damaged and so was the compressor, the batteries were flat, the diesel clutches were worn out and so was the oil pump. The snorkel operating mechanism was damaged.

Argentine officers were interested in information concerning radar detection devices and new types of torpedoes, but that information was not within the chief engineer's competence.

Separate hearings of the remaining submariners confirmed all explanations provided by the commander of the U-Boot.

„Whoever believes that something can be kept secret on a submarine, should try to take part in such a cruise", Schäffer explained to the Argentine navy officers ques-

---

[158] Statement of Schäffer…, NARA, Record Group (RG) 59 (U.S. Department of State Central Decimal Files), sign. 862.30/8-445 – 8-2145, p. 1, typed.

tioning him on August 20. The U-Boot had no crates with valuable documents or Nazi gold.

CREWMEN OF *U 977* (- AGE), WHO SURRENDERED TO THE ARGENTINEANS AT MAR DEL PLATA ON AUGUST 17, 1945
Officers: Heinz Schäffer (commander) – 24, Karl Reiser (second-in-command – first watch) – 30, Albert Kahn (second watch) – 23, Dietrich Wiese (chief engineer) – 22; Chief non-commissioned officers: Hans Krebs – 26, Leo Klinger – 28, Erich Dudek – 23; Junior non-commissioned officers and seamen: Gerhard Meyer – 23, Karl Kullack – 21, Wilfried Husemann – 20, Heinrich Lehmann – 21, Rudi Schöneich – 21, Walter Maier – 19, Rudolf Weuwirther – 20, Hans Baumel – 21, Heinz Haupt – 21, Herman Risse – 21, Johannes Plontsch – 20, Heinz Blasius – 21, Alois Kraus – 20, Kurt Nittner – 21, Heinz Böttger – 20, Holdfried Wurker – 19, Heinz Waschk – 20, Kurt Nashan – 20, Gerhard Höfler – 19, Harry Hentschel – 19, Helmut Maros – 20, Alois Knoblich – 19, Heinz Franke – 21, Karl Komorek – 19, Adwin Baier - 19

On the first day of the hearings of the *U 977* crew, the second German submarine that called at Mar del Plata, the U.S. authorities prepared a memorandum, which was sent to the Argentine authorities through the local embassy in Buenos Aires:

Following a note from the Ministry of Foreign Affairs of July 17, 1945, the Argentine Government handed over the German submarine „U 530" with its crew and the results of an investigation conducted by the Argentine authorities into its possible actions to the governments of the United States and Great Britain. This investigation did not confirm any communication between the vessel and Argentine territory prior to its surrender.

The submitted information does not contain any confirmation of landing and in particular of the arrival of the submarine „U 977" (to the shore), which again raises the question, whether the crews of both ships had any contact with any person in Argentina or with any other contacts ashore. The Embassy has not doubts, that the Argentine authorities have taken this possibility into account when initiating the relevant investigations. We would be grateful, given the joint proposal of the governments of Argentina and the United States to eliminate the remains of fascist organizations in the world, for any information that the Argentine authorities may have at their disposal, such as the results of investigations. We would also like to inform the Government of Argentina that the military and naval authorities of the United States may (have the right) be interested in activities regarding submarines[159].

When the first members of the *U 977* crew were giving their testimonies, the Uruguayan newspaper „El Dia", published in Montevideo, printed an article, which undermined the credibility of the German sailors. The newspaper insisted that Adolf

---

[159] Memorandum. Embajada de Los Estados Unidos de America, Buenos Aires, 20 de Agosto de 1945.

Hitler was on board *U 977*, and that he later fled further to Antarctica through Argentina and Patagonia. This type of information was picked up by sensation-thirsty journalists in South America.

How did Latin American tabloids' journalists learn about the mysterious evacuation missions of German submarines to South America? Who was the „source" of these rumors? Where did the leak come from?

In the final months of the war there was a kind of hysteria concerning the widespread information related to the evacuation of Nazi criminals to Patagonia and other countries on the South American continent by sea. An unidentified submarine (bearing the resemblance of a U-Boot) was reported near the San Antonio lighthouse and in vicinity of the Mar del Plata area by the reconnaissance of the Argentine Navy and witnesses living on the coast. The latter even claimed to had seen people in a dinghy who had reached the shore.

That was not the only source of information that „leaked" into public opinion. The rumor about the Nazi U-Boots off the coast of South America originated in the United States embassy in Buenos Aires. Its author was the U.S. military attaché, General Lang, who in a casual conversation with high-ranking Argentine politicians did not hesitate to mention that in June 1945, German leaders fled to Argentina by submarine. Information about U-Boots off the coast of South America was immediately passed on to the President of the country, General Edelmirro Farell and the heads of the Argentine military intelligence service.

Meanwhile, on the basis of the collected evidence, the Argentine intelligence services determined that there were no indications that in July or August 1945 any persons were disembarked (or that the evacuated goods of particular importance were delivered), and in particular that *U 977* arrived at the shores of South America before calling at the naval base in Mar del Plata. The investigators were unable to prove that the *U 977* crew was in contact with any person in Argentina or made any other contact on the coast.

Copies of the testimonies given by German submariners during the investigation of August 20-23, 1945, as well as conclusions and comments written by Argentinian investigators, did not satisfy Americans who decided to question the entire *U 977* crew. All the more so, that the officers from *U 530* had been detained for some time at the POW camp near Washington. One of the documents, which summarizes the Argentine investigation, contains the following information:

The commander claims and the ship's logbook indicates that the average speed of a submarine during this journey was 3 knots.

The commander swears (for what it's worth) that no person entered or left the ship after 16 people disembarked from the submarine in Norway.

Officers and the remaining crew members are well looked after and better looking than the crew of „U 530". The people are in good health. They do not use Nazi salutes (at least for the moment).

The commander (Schäffer) said that he had spent a year in Ohio between 1937-38[160]. He speaks some English[161].

On September 5, 1945, at the El Palomar Air Base near Buenos Aires, Col. Ernesto Garcia Bates, representing the Government of Argentina, handed over thirty-two crew members of the German submarine *U 977* to the U.S. Naval Attaché, Lt.Cdr. W. W. Webb, in accordance with the instructions of the Navy Command and in compliance with decree No. 19160/45. Ten wooden boxes numbered from one to ten, three map boxes, one package containing personal belongings taken from *U 977*, two ship logbooks, two maps of the ship's route and one metal tube in which several additional naval charts[162] were stored were also handed over. Three days later, a large US Navy airplane with 32 submariners from *U 977* landed at Miami Airport in Florida.

On September 10, a complete set of confidential documents taken from *U 977* was sent to the Naval Intelligence Headquarters in Washington. According to Lt. Max Kaslo[163] (Reserve) of the United States Navy, who was the head of guards responsible for supervising the detained submariners (he received a Smith and Wesson cal. 38 revolver with a holster, a belt and 10 rounds of ammunition[164]), German prisoners of war cooperated all the time. There were no problems with them during their journey from Argentina to Miami, Florida[165].

A specially appointed team of U.S. investigators questioned Heinz Schäffer and the remaining three *U 977* officers for several weeks in a secret center at Fort Hunt (Rear Admiral Eberhard Godt, a close associate of Grand Admiral Karl Dönitz, was also there). The officers were separated from the rest of the crew. Senior non-commissioned officers, junior non-commissioned officers and seamen were sent to U.S. Army POW camps for German sailors in the USA.

---

[160] Owing to his father's financial generosity, seventeen-year-old Heinz Schäffer was sent to the United States by sea. The journey from Hamburg to New York, which was a great experience for the teenager, took place on the passenger liner *New York*. He travelled by train from New York to Cleveland, Ohio on Lake Erie. He attended one of the local schools for a few months, so he was able to improve his English.

[161] Confidential, NA. Series R-214-45, 24 August 1945, NARA, Record Group (RG) 59 (U.S. Department of State Central Decimal Files), sign. 862.30/8-445 – 8-2145, p. 1, typed.

[162] M. Kaslo, *German Prisoners of War – Transfer of.*, 11 September 1945, NARA, Record Group (RG) 59 (U.S. Department of State Central Decimal Files), sign. 862.30/8-445 – 8-2145, p. 1, typed.; Captain USN L. E. Kelly, Lieutenant USNR W. O. Mehrtens, German Naval Prisoners of War and Confidential Boxes – Receipt for., 10 September 1945, NARA, Record Group (RG) 59 (U.S. Department of State Central Decimal Files), sign. 862.30/8-445 – 8-2145, p. 1, typed.

[163] Since August 30, 1945, he has been temporarily assigned to the U.S. Naval Operations Base in Rio de Janeiro, Brazil. See: US Operating Base Navy, Number 153, P16-3/00 (1320), 30 August 1945. From: The Commandant, To: Lieutenant Max Kaslo…, [document signed by E. J. Lanigan], Record Group (RG) 59 (U.S. Department of State Central Decimal Files), sign. 862.30/8-445 – 8-2145, p. 1, typed.

[164] L.E. Kelly, *The District Intelligence Officer*, 7 ND, 10 September 1945, NARA, Record Group (RG) 59 (U.S. Department of State Central Decimal Files), sign. 862.30/8-445 – 8-2145, p. 1, typed.

[165] Secret, 17 September 1945; From: Commandant US. Navy Operating Base, Number 153, To: Commander in Chief US Fleets. [document signed by E. J. Lanigan], Record Group (RG) 59 (U.S. Department of State Central Decimal Files), NARA, p. 1, typed.

During the investigation, the recurring question asked to the U-Boot commander was „You have stowed Hitler away! Come on, where is he"? The Americans were
increasingly impatient, all the more so as the press on both sides of the Atlantic was
buzzing with unbelievable stories about the wartime adventures of *U 977*. For weeks
Schäffer tried to convince the American officers questioning him that their inquiries concerning the stay of the Führer of the Third Reich on board the U-Boot were
completely bogus and without any sense. The investigators told Schäffer, that from
their point of view, he was more valuable than Otto Skorzeny, who in September
1943, freed Benito Mussolini, the Italian dictator and the founder of Italian fascism.

The prisoner was subjected to various sophisticated investigative methods. They
ranged from getting him to cooperate, through solitary confinement, up to not providing him with water or food. During the interrogation by the Americans Schäffer
was never beaten or physically threatened.

American officers did not believe the testimonies made by Schäffer or the remaining *U 977* officers. Their conclusion, based on a meticulous investigation, during which they bombarded the prisoners of war with the huge amount of previously
collected information, differed from the results of the investigation carried out by
the Argentine investigators. They were mainly interested in obtaining confirmation
of specific details of the three-and-a-half-month-long voyage (e.g. it was not believed that the U-Boot had made such a long voyage submerged and without refu-
eling at sea) and to establish the circumstances under which Hitler, Bormann and
other high government officials and war criminals were smuggled out of Germany.

In his official statement to the Americans, Schäffer testified that he had decided to
flee by submarine from Norway to South America under the influence of the words
spread by Minister Joseph Goebbels, who, citing the findings of the Morgenthau
Plan[166], would announce that after the war Germany would be turned into a „goat
pasture" and that German men would become „slaves and sterilized". He had the
most sincere intention of handing over the intact ship into the hands of the Allies. It
seemed to him, that his ship's engines could become a valuable contribution to the
reconstruction of Europe!

It is difficult to judge whether these words were sincere, nor do we have any information, as to whether Schäffer knew about the Nazi crimes in Europe and if so,
exactly how much he knew.

---

[166] Henry Morgenthau, American Secretary of the Treasury, proposed a plan that would have shaped the future
of the post-war Germany. The Morgenthau Plan was presented on September 9, 1944 during the Second British-
-American Conference in Quebec (September 11-16, 1944) and received the support of Roosevelt and Churchill,
but was criticized by Secretary of State Cordell Hull and British Foreign Minister Anthony Eden. It was also
badly received by the American public opinion and business circles. Finally, in November 1944, it was rejected
by Roosevelt. The Morgenthau plan assumed: the division of Germany into South Germany and North Germany,
as well as international zones, total demilitarization, elimination of heavy industry, creation of an agro-pastoral
state, occupation of the created countries by the Allied forces, the northern part of East Prussia was to be annexed
to the Soviet Union. The southern part, Upper Silesia and a part of Lower Silesia would become part of Poland.
The area on the Rhine and Moselle would belong France.

German submariners were under constant surveillance. When they were at their quarters, their conversations were recorded and analyzed in order to obtain additional information. Apparently, that data turned out to be of little value. According to the preserved documents, it was not mentioned as a valuable source of information.

It is sufficient to mention that, after spending more than a year in the U.S. captivity, during which they were interrogated numerous times, the *U 530* and *U 977* submariners were released. By the end of 1946, as many as 86 of *U 530* and *U 977* crew members had returned to Argentina. At that time, the former Kriegsmarine POWs were not deported to Germany. The content of documents from the interrogation of German submarines by U.S. and British intelligence officers was kept secret for many years.

U.S. intelligence officers tried, at all cost, to obtain evidence that would allow them to accuse the commander of *U 977* of the sinking of the light cruiser *Bahia*. The Americans believed neither the navigation data recorded in the logbook, nor the fact that there were ten torpedoes on board. The investigators tried to prove that, similarly to other German submarines, 14 torpedoes had been loaded before *U 977* departed on combat patrol. Schäffer was accused of possibly falsifying all the war diary entries. In the end, however, the detailed entries in the logbook proved beneficial for the crews and led to an explanation. Together with the report concerning the sinking of *Bahia*, the Argentine Naval Ministry sent weather reports from the day and location of the accident, which were compared with the corresponding weather entries made on that day aboard *U 977*. Naturally, they did not match, as the ship was in a completely different location. It became clear to everyone, that the weather data could not have been falsified and the accusation fell. The investigation was sealed.

* * *

In September 1945, Lieutenants Otto Wermuth and Heinz Schäffer had an arranged meeting at the American investigation center near Washington. Their quarters were bugged. The officers did not know each other from submarine service in the Kriegsmarine. The Americans hoped that unsuspecting U-Bootwaffe officers, feeling casual in each other's company, would be more inclined to reveal unknown details concerning the alleged „ghost convoy", which was supposed to take Third Reich's leading individuals to South America. Their plan did not produce any results other than insignificant information about the wartime epic journeys of *U 530* and *U 977*. German officers suspected that hidden microphones were recording their every word and therefore avoided topics that could somehow incriminate them in the course of the investigations in progress.

In a report prepared by the U.S. naval intelligence officers on September 19, 1945, it was stated, that Lt. Heinz Schäffer had told the truth about his military

service in the Kriegsmarine and his maiden combat patrol aboard *U 977*. There
was no evidence to indicate that he had taken part in a special evacuation mission
to South America with Nazi dignitaries on board. There were also no gold bars
or secret plans of the Third Reich's wunderwaffe, as reported by South American
press. The document stated that such an event had never taken place. However,
the Americans have never revealed what was in the boxes that had been taken to
Washington.

As an „award" for cooperation and the transfer of two German submarines, the
U.S. Navy presented the Argentine Navy with... two G7es T-V electric acoustic torpedoes from *U 977*.

* * *

What do we know about the further fate of *U 977* after she was taken over by the
U.S. Navy? On August 28, 1945, the U-Boot was transferred to the United States.
It was manned by American sailors at the Rio Santiago base, where *U 530* was also
moored. On September 12, the tugboat USS *Cherokee* took both *U 530* and *U 977* to
the USA. *U 977* was towed to Boston on November 13, 1945, following a journey of
more than 6,000 nmi (11,112 km).

One of the temporary 34 members of the new U-Boot crew was Celestyn M. Ur-
baniak, who as a sailor on U.S. submarines, volunteered for that mission. His good
knowledge of German proved useful in operating the onboard equipment. According to that submariner, *U 977* was very dirty and in need of numerous repairs and
replacements of spare parts. The new crew needed a few weeks before the U-Boot
was more or less ready for her final voyage.

During the cruise, the diesel engines repeatedly failed and the arrival in Boston,
where the ship was sent to the naval shipyard, was only possible owing to the highly-
qualified and skillful American crew, who managed to cope with all the adversities.

After leaving the shipyard, the U-Boot was transferred to the U.S. Submarine
Base New London, Connecticut, where, together with the destroyer escort USS *Baker*, they were prepared for the so-called Victory Tour (as part of that particular propaganda event *U 530* visited seven harbors in Texas), which led through major cities
on the eastern coast of the USA. The Americans were able to become familiar with
one of the German Type VII C submarines, which so effectively harassed American
coasting trade in the first half of 1942. For three weeks the U-Boot, accompanied
by the destroyer, visited Albany, Poughkeepsie and Newburgh, New York, Wilming-
ton, as well as Lewes, Delaware, Richmond, Virginia and Washington. This unusual
„tour" lasted until December 8, 1945.

Then, *U 977* was sent to the U.S. Navy shipyard at Portsmouth, New Hampshire,
where she joined other U-Boots, which had surrendered to the USA at the end of
the war, already moored there.

In a document dated August 9, 1946, from the Chief of Naval Operations to the Bureau of Ships and the Bureau of Ordnance in the Department of the Navy in Washington, he writes about termination of the service of German submarines U 977 and U 1105 (Type VII C/41)[167]:

Chief of Naval Operations requests that the Bureau of Ships and the Bureau of Ordnance inform the Chief of Naval Operations when the exploitation of equipment, and cannibalization of equipment and spare parts of certain ex-German submarines was completed and these submarines ready for disposal.

At the request of the Bureau of Ships, the Portsmouth Naval Shipyard inspected the U-977 and U-1105, the only German submarines in Boston, and informed the Boston Naval Shipyard what material should be removed in view of possible use on the XXI submarines.

The Commander of the Boston Naval Shipyard reported that all the equipment and parts designated by the Portsmouth Naval Shipyard on the U-977 and U-1105 have been removed.

The Chief of Naval Operations is therefore advised that the Bureau of Ships has completed the exploitation and cannibalization of the U-977 and U-1105 and that as far as the Bureau of Ships is concerned these two vessels are ready for disposal[168].

On November 13, 1946, *U 977* was sunk in the North Atlantic, near Cape Cod (42°33'N i 69°43'W)[169], during a test, by a torpedo fired by the U.S. submarine USS *Atule*. It was a part of the implementation of a tripartite agreement between the Soviet Union, the United Kingdom and the United States.

* * *

At the end of 1946, Lt. Heinz Schäffer was transported to England (he was among 16 German officers who were transported by plane from the United States to Brussels), where he was subjected to the same investigatigation procedures.

---

[167] *U 1105* surrendered on May 10, 1945, after entering Loch Eriboll in Scotland. The U-Boot had previously made only one combat sortie (she left Kristiansand-Marviken, Norway on 12 April, 1945), operating against Allied shipping west of the North Canal. She was a British prize. On May 11, 1945, she sailed from Loch Eriboll to Loch Alsh. The next stage of her journey was the passage from Loch Alsh to Lisahally between May 13-14, 1945. Re-designated as the test ship HMS *N 16*, she was handed over to the United States for testing. She sailed from Portsmouth, UK to New Hampshire, USA between December 19, 1945 and January 2, 1946. She was struck from the US Navy list on February 11, 1946. She sank in Chesapeake Bay during tests with explosives. She was raised from the bottom in August 1949 during salvage tests. On September 19, 1949, she was sunk for the second time, during tests of the new MK 6 depth charges in the Potomac estuary, near the Piney Point Lighthouse. The position of her sinking was 38°08'N and 76°33,1'W.

[168] Ex-German Submarines U 977 and U 1105 – Completion of Exploitation, Report of 9 August 1946, NARA, Record Group (RG) 59 (U.S. Department of State Central Decimal Files), sign. 862.30/8-445 – 8-2145, p. 1, typed.

[169] A. Niestlé, *German U-Boat Losses...*, p. 93. See also: https://uboat.net/boats/u977.htm.

Among the prisoners of war, who were transported, was German general of para-troop forces, Herman Bernhard-Ramcke (1889-1968). He was captured in Brest, on September 20, 1944 and transported to the USA. He fled the POW camp twice and voluntarily returned to it twice and while being at large, he organized a cam-paign for better treatment of German prisoners of war. In December 1946, he was handed over to the French on charges of war crimes committed, among others, during the battle for Brest. On March 21, 1951, he was sentenced to five-and-a-half-year imprisonment (for kidnapping and murdering French civilians, for loot-ing private property and deliberate destruction and burning of civilian houses). He was released from prison on June 24, 1951 due to his previous imprisonment (57 months) and age.

As far as the investigation against Schäffer was concerned, it had started anew. It is known from rudimentary documentation that *U 977* commander had been ques-tioned several times by four British officers.

Schäffer learned that his submarine, as a war prize, had been destroyed by the Americans from a press release with a photograph of an exploding U-Boot pub-lished in the British newspaper „The Daily Telegraph".

The British were so impressed with the legend of *U 977*, that even after a fruitless investigation they decided to move Lt. Schäffer to a special camp for „hard cases", where he was treated as one of the most important high-ranking officials of the overthrown regime. He was detained for six months in a special intelligence center for German POWs, but there was no evidence (similarly to the Argentine and U.S. investigations) to convict him for „war crimes". The British found no confirmation that *U 977* was a part of a convoy of U-Bootwaffe submarines carrying gold and Nazi dignitaries.

During the lengthy investigation Schäffer was alternately treated either well or exceptionally badly. According to the minutes of the interrogation drawn up by the investigators, it was written that: „Schäffer is an ardent Nazi". Despite the fact that he was not found guilty, he was not released!

The commander of the *U 977* received the status of a political prisoner and was sent back to Germany. Then he was housed in a camp in Paderborn near Dortmund. He never found out why he was in a cell with political prisoners. He was quickly re-leased. He owed it to the recommendations of his influential friends (they received a secret letter from him smuggled out of prison), who did not abandon a former offi-cer of Kriegsmarine in need. In spring 1947, Heinz Schäffer left detention facility. He was a civilian and a free man. Still, the commander of *U 977* was very lucky, because he could have been imprisoned in a Soviet camp for 10 years, like other members of the U-Boot crews.

Twenty-six-year-old Schäffer traveled from his hometown Berlin to Düsseldorf on the Rhine and settled in a bachelor apartment, unsuccessfully looking for a job. The city was in ruin and the people were emaciated. At the same time, he read the sensational news in a newspaper, that Hitler was alive!

A German tabloid newspaper, citing agency reports from Buenos Aires, reported that Ladiszlav Szabó in his book "Hitler está vivo. El nuevo en El Berchtesgaden Antártido" („Hitler lives. New Berchtesgaden in Antarctica"), which had
just been published in Argentina (1947), wrote that *U 530* and *U 977* were the
only Nazi submarines that remained at large after the end of the war and reached
the coast of Argentina. The U-Boots were part of a „ghost convoy" that carried
Hitler and other Third Reich dignitaries to Argentina. Then, the Nazis made their
way to an Antarctic fortress, built at the end of the 1930s, near the Queen Maud's
Land. The fortress was named New Berchtesgaden. Apparently, artificial caves
and underground corridors had been built there, where food, fuel and weapons
supplies were stored. The article was accompanied by a map with a plan of the
mysterious cruise of the Kriegsmarine ships, taking into account the moment of
departure of both U-Boots from the „ghost convoy". It turned out that the myth of
the Antarctic Nazi lair was, on the one hand, fuelled by extreme leftists, who liked
to accuse the Peronist authorities in Argentina of cooperation with the Nazis, and
on the other hand, by the neo-Nazis, who wanted to prove that the Third Reich
had survived.

Based on an agency message from Argentina, the newspaper informed its readers, that the Hungarian journalist also stated that the submarine commanders, Lieutenants Otto Wermuth and Heinz Schäffer, were ready to confirm that the story was
genuine.

The author of the book was the same man who, in 1945, published an article in
the Argentine magazine "Critica", in which he claimed that Adolf Hitler had escaped
on board a U-Boot and remained alive. Schäffer's comment after reading the book
was short: „These are the conclusions of someone whose idea of U-Boots is like that
of an Eskimo about Central Africa".

In 1948, dissatisfied with his life in the ruined Germany, where he did not want
to just get by, Schäffer left for Argentina again. On the South American continent he
could count on the help of his relatives. He had more opportunities to get a permanent job and make a career in civilian life. He never revealed who and how helped
him to get to South America. Was there a secret organization behind it, which
helped to obtain funds for a trip to Argentina? That, we don't know. Upon his arrival
in Buenos Aires, Schäffer began to write down his memoirs.

In 1950, the „Prometheus" Publishing House in Argentina published a book
in German, written by Heinz Schaeffer (that is the name in the original publication), titled "Geheimnis um U-977". The story of the U-Boot commander was
published on the basis of his notes, which tell the story of the voyage of Type VII
C submarine, which lasted 107 days. When he started to write a book of memoirs,
he had a notebook (he kept notes) in which, on 66 pages, he published detailed
information on the course of his naval service in the Kriegsmarine and less important information about his participation in naval operations as the U-Boot
commander. In the book, there was no opinion about the Commander of the

Kriegsmarine, Grand Admiral Karl Dönitz or other U-Bootwaffe commanders. Not in a single word did the author mention Nazi crimes. He joined the Kriegsmarine as a volunteer and therefore, one can get the impression, that in that publication he defended his life choices. His memoirs were a tribute to the living *U 977* crew members, who had been able to overcome their weaknesses and their mental breakdown despite the harsh conditions on the ship. The patrol could have easily turned into a mutiny.

In 1950, the former commander of *U 977* married an Argentine of German ancestry, Ingeborg Schäffer. The wedding took place in the Evangelical church in Calle Esmeralda, Buenos Aires. The former commander of *U 977* was a recognizable and popular person with the local establishment. Local newspapers published reports on the occasion of the Schäffers' grand wedding ceremony in the stylish hotel „Alvear Palace", located in the fashionable district of La Recoleta, surrounded by vast parks, wide avenues and the architecture of luxurious, classical style buildings. Numerous respected people in Buenos Aires, who attended the ceremony, added splendor to the festive reception[170].

„He was the man who stowed Hitler away" – for many years that was the opinion circulating among the people living in the capital of Argentina. Schäffer was greatly surprised when he was mentioned as such. But the mysterious voyage *U 977* provoked further speculation and hypotheses among historians and those interested in the history of the Third Reich.

In 1955, Heinz Schäffer was the captain of one of the freighters which belonged to the Argentine shipping company „Elma", which cooperated with the German fleet during World War II. He lived in Argentina for over 30 years. For the rest of his life, he strongly denied that Hitler or other Nazis, who were supposedly evacuated to South America, were on board his submarine. He did not hide his regret concerning the fact that Germany lost the war.

In the final years of his life, he was seriously ill for a long period of time. He returned to Germany, where he died on January 15, 1979, at he age of 58. He was buried in Berlin. It is known that Heinz Schäffer's 70-year-old son is still alive, but he avoids contacts with the media and does not want to speak about the wartime epic voyage of *U 977*. He claims that his knowledge concerning his father's wartime fate, is not significantly better that the facts presented in the book.

In 2008 Lt. Schäffer's wife, asked if her husband had brought Hitler to Argentina, replied:

If he did not bring him, there were another two U-Boots that could have brought him, and [my husband] could have given them food and so forth, because the others went on to Puerto Madryn [a town in Argentina - M.B., P.W.][171].

---

[170] [N.N.], *Nichs mit Selbstmord zu tun*. Geister-Konvoi, „Der Spiegel", September 6, 1950, Issue 36.

[171] Quoted in S. Dunstan, G. Williams, *Grey Wolf...*, p. 223.

On August 17, 1945, Argentinian newspaper "Critica" informed its readers about the arrival of *U 977* at Mar del Plata.

Mariusz Borowiak, during his search for documents concerning *U 530* and *U 977* at The National Archives at Kew near London.

DECLASSIFIED & 928 SECRET

Op-16-FA-4
18 August 1945/af
SECRET

95 AUG 18
16
09

MEMORANDUM

From: Op-16-FA-4
To   : Op-16

Via :   (1) Op-16-FA
        (2) Op-16-F

Subj: Surrendered German Submarine, U-977 (500 ton)

1. On 17 August 1945 ALUSNA BUENOS AIRES informed CNO that the U-977 had surrendered to the Argentine Navy. The Commanding Officer of this boat was Lt. (jg) Heinz Schaeffer who is listed in the 1943 Rank List as a Lt. (jg) of the 1939 Class. There were 4 officers and 32 men aboard the U-977 when she surrendered, approximately 16 less than the normal complement of a boat of this type. Preliminary reports indicate that this U-boat left Kiel April 19 for Christiansand and a British official source reports it at sea 25 May. According to W.I.R. 8 June 1945, 16 survivors from the U-977 stated that their U-boat was wrecked on an island off Bremangen, north of Bergen, on the night of 9/10 May while she was returning from a patrol with a damaged periscope.

2. On 9 May 1945 the Admiralty reported that the U-874 had left Horten on 8 May after 16 members of the crew had been put ashore and the same number of notables from Oslo substituted. It took provisions for three months but later returned to port and surrendered. In a report from U.S.G.C.C. No. 7-5-45, 28 May 1945, the Naval Officer in Charge, Oslo, reported that the Commanding Officer of U-874, Lt. (jg) Petersen, now P/W, stated that preparations were made to sail for Japan but the trip was not undertaken because one motor was unserviceable. There is no information as to the number of prisoners from the U-874.

3. It is apparent that the story told by the 16 men who claimed to be survivors of the U-977 was not true and may have been told in an effort to give the U-977 time to make its escape. The dates of the departure of U-874 (8 May) from Horten and of the reported wrecking of U-977 (9/10 May) indicate that both U-boats were in Norwegian waters and a transfer of personnel from U-874 (the "notables" mentioned in Admty. message of 9 May) to the U-977 could have been made, the U-977 continuing to Argentina and U-874 returning to port and surrendering. The further possibility presents itself that the 16 notables had been put ashore somewhere before the U-977 surrendered. The deficiency in the complement of the surrendered vessel of about 16 supports such a conclusion.

S. L. D. Hunter

cc: Op-16-2
     Cominch (2)

SECRET 928

Secret, August 18, 1945 report concerning the surrender of German submarine *U 977* in Argentina.

EMBAJADA DE LOS ESTADOS UNIDOS DE AMÉRICA

MEMORANDUM

De conformidad con la atenta nota del Ministerio de Relaciones Exteriores, de fecha 17 de julio de 1945, el Gobierno argentino entregó a los Gobiernos de los Estados Unidos y de Gran Bretaña el submarino alemán U.530, junto con su tripulación y el resultado de las investigaciones practicadas por las autoridades argentinas acerca de sus posibles actividades. Las investigaciones mencionadas no dieron prueba positiva de alguna comunicación entre el submarino y el territorio argentino con anterioridad a su rendición.

Los subsiguientes informes completamente sin confirmación de desembarcos, y más particularmente la llegada del submarino U-977, hacen surgir nuevamente la cuestión de si las tripulaciones de ambos submarinos han tenido alguna comunicación con alguna persona en el territorio argentino o cualquier otro contacto con la costa. La Embajada no duda de que las autoridades argentinas han tenido en cuenta dicha posibilidad, iniciando aquellas investigaciones que consideren pertinentes. Mucho agradecería, dado el propósito común de los Gobiernos de la Argentina y de los Estados Unidos de eliminar los vestigios restantes de la organización nazi en el mundo, cualquier información que las autoridades argentinas quieran tener a bien comunicarle como resultado de sus investigaciones. Tendrá también el mayor agrado en obtener, a fin de ponerla en conocimiento del Gobierno Argentino, la información que las autoridades militares y navales de los Estados Unidos puedan poseer acerca de las actividades de los submarinos de referencia.

Buenos Aires, 20 de agosto de 1945.

ES COPIA.

ES COPIA FIE
DEL ORIGIN

...Argentinian, August 20, 1945 document concerning the transfer of two Nazi submarines *U 530* and *U 977*, which called at Mar del Plata, to the U.S. authorities.

(Op-16-Z)

REPORT ON THE INTERROGATION OF
PRISONERS FROM U-977 SURRENDERLD
AT MAR DEL PLATA, 17 AUGUST 1945.

I N T R O D U C T O R Y   R E M A R K S

The standard, type VII-C, 500 Ton U-977 surrendered in
the Argentine 17 August 1945 after 107 days at sea and after an
elapsed cruise of 7,644 sea miles. This German U-boat left on her
only war patrol from Kristiansand, Norway, on 2 May 1945, the day
after the German announcement of Hitler's death. The commanding
officer was Oberleutnant zur See (Lieutenant j.g.) Heinz SCHAEFFER.

According to the engineering officer U-977 left Kristiansand
with only 85 metric tons of fuel and arrived at Mar del Plata with
approximately 5 tons. The long cruise was possible only at extremely
slow average speed. The U-boat is said to have been turned over in
good working condition. Ten torpedoes (6 LUT's with pistols Pi-2a
and 4 T-5's with Pi-4C) were still intact. It was emphatically
denied that any attacks were made or any torpedoes fired.

E A R L Y   H I S T O R Y   O F   U - 9 7 7

Keel laid at Blohm and Voss, Hamburg, 24 July 1942.
Launched 31 March 1943. Commissioning 6 May 1943. During working
up exercises in the Baltic rammed at least 3 times, and damage to
pressure hull was considered serious enough to use U-977 only as
a schoolboat. Commanding officer during this period was Oberleutnant
zur See (Lieutenant j.g.) Hans LEILICH.

In mid-December 1944 command assumed by SCHAEFFER. Schoolboat exercises continued until late January 1945. Going by way of
Swinemünde, Kiel and Cuxhaven, arrived at Hamburg 20 February 1945.
In dock at Howaldt Yard from 26 February to 31 March for overhaul and
fitting of Schnorchel.

Fitted out and loaded in Kiel 1 April to 12 April 1945.
Departed 16 April and proceeded by way of Frederikshavn, Denmark,
to Horten, Norway. In crossing Skagerrak 4 dives made because of
aircraft. Lay on bottom in Oslo Fjord 6 hours. Arrived Horten
20 April and engaged in Schnorchel trials, moving on to Kristiansand
30 April 1945 at 0500.

- 1 -

? 02149

U 977 prisoners' Mar del Plata interrogation report, August 17, 1945.

(Op-16-Z)

F I R S T   A N D   O N L Y   P A T R O L   O F   U - 9 7 7

After loading provisions, celebrating May Day, and holding a flag ceremony for Hitler's reported death, U-977 left Kristiansand on her first and last war patrol 2 May 1945 at 2200. Using her Schnorchel 3 to 4 hours each night she proceeded submerged along the Norwegian coast. On 7 May the observation perisocpe was damaged due to its being left up while diving.

When the German surrender became official 8 May, there were long discussions on board U-977, then in the vicinity of Bergen. Those of the married crew members who so desired were given the choice of leaving the boat or continuing to Argentina. On 10 May between 0230 and 0330 three enlisted men and 13 petty officers accordingly took 3 of the large rubber boats, one of which was damaged and abandoned, and 16 of the one-man rubber boats and put ashore at the island of Holsenoy near Bergen. (O.N.I. Note: These men were subsequently taken into custody by the British and described themselves as "survivors" of the U-977.)

In the subsequent voyage the remaining 32 officers and men stood only their usual respective watches, 4 hours on and 8 off, however with less men on each watch. It was stated that the only one the remaining men regretted giving up was the pharmicist's mate.

U-977 made for the Iceland Passage on course 300°, diving once on sighting a plane and once on sighting a ship; she was also DF'd many times in late May. She passed Madeira about 100 miles to the west and made for the Cape Verde Islands on course 197°.

On 14 July 1945 the U-boat anchored for 4 hours, 1630 to 2030 on the SW side of Branco, in the Cape Verdes. The crew went swimming and also sang for a while on deck. The next day at 2030 a ship was sighted and avoided by changing course, and at 0303 on 21 July a plane was sighted. On 22 July St. Paul Rocks was passed 25 miles off the starboard beam.

At 0600 on 23 July they crossed the equator at approximately 30° W., and 28 of the 32 officers and men were given the customary Neptune ceremony. The next day at 0130, 0230, and 0300 a plane was sighted 3 times (or possibly 3 different planes). Another plane was sighted at 1125 on 26 July and a further one the next day.

It was on 30 July 1945 that SCHAEFFER learned that the U-boat preceding him in Argentina, the U-530, with her crew would be sent to North America, but this information caused no change in his plans. A test dive to 40 meters was made 1 August. A large ship was sighted the next day and another 13 August.

- 2 -

9 021

U.S. report concerning the first and final combat patrol of *U 977* in 1945.

When the U-977 was turned over to the Argentine authorities 17 August 1945, at 1105, she was said to be intact, including papers and documents. The following minor mechanical defects were mentioned by the engineering officer:

(1) One periscope damaged.
(2) Junkers air compressor damaged since early August.
(3) Supercharger damaged since June.
(4) Starboard diesel connection with supercharger stuck.
(5) Pressure oil-pump motor defective.
(6) Indicator for position of Schnorchel damaged.

The officers and crew of the U-boat had hoped by going to Argentina to avoid being turned over to the Russians and even possibly to be allowed to settle in South America.

S T A T E M E N T   O F   S C H A E F F E R, C. O.   O F   U - 9 7 7

"I left Kristiansand S. on 2 May 1945, normally equipped, and under orders to proceed to the Channel, (i.e. English Channel).

A few days later I picked up fragments of signals, which I suspected of being the work of enemy deception. When, however, these signals were not cancelled, I had to assume that the radio stations had fallen into enemy hands and that we had lost the war. The fact that uncoded signals signed "Allied Committee" were coming through, convinced me that the orders contained in these signals were illegitimate and not in agreement with the German High Command. When we began our patrol, an official slogan had been posted on all Naval establishments and ships which said: 'The enemy shall find in Germany nothing but rats and mice. We will never capitulate. Better death than slavery.'

It must be remembered that radio reception on board the U-977 was only sporadic since, for tactical reasons, we only occasionally came to Schnorchel depth. However, enough signals had been received so that I felt that I no longer had any superiors, and that I was relieved of my oath. In any case, I did not feel obligated without direct orders from my own government to accept enemy orders.

I no longer considered my ship as a man-of-war, but as a means of escape, and I tried to act for the best interests of all aboard. I respected the wishes of members of my crew insofar as they did not imperil the ship or cause damage to it.

CONFIDENTIAL

– 3 –

...another page of the same report held at the Archives and Records Administration at College Park near Washington.

DIO 7ND
(16-LEK-WOM-shp)
A16-2

10 September 1945

Subj: German Naval Prisoners of War and Confidential Boxes -
         Receipt for.

- -

2.   Receipt is also acknowledged of ten wooden boxes numbered 1 through 10
consecutively, three cloth chart cases and one metal tube (containing numerous charts) all being confidential documents taken from the U-977, for
shipment to the Division of Naval Intelligence, Washington, D. C.

3.   Receipt is also acknowledged of one package containing inventory of
personal effects removed from the U-977, two log books of the U-977, and
two grid track charts from the U-977.

L. E. KELLY
Captain USN
DIO 7ND

W. O. MEHRTENS
Lieutenant, USNR
By direction

ENCLOSURE 1

- 2 -

10 15

A document which confirms the transfer of German *U 977* prisoners and ten boxes with
mysterious content, a report of September 10, 1945.

In September 1945. *U 977* was taken over by U.S. Navy sailors (the photo shows some members of the American crew of the German submarine). On November 13, 1945, the U-Boot, after covering several thousand nautical miles, sailed from Argentina to Boston.

A unique photo of *U 147*, taken in 1945.

U.S. submarine USS *Atule* in a 1945 photograph.

U 977 with American crew, September 1945.

U 977 in Boston,
November 1945.

In November 1946, the
editorial office of the British
daily newspaper "The
Daily Telegraph" printed
information about the
destruction of the German
submarine *U 977* by the U.S.
submarine *Atule*.

The photo shows FuMB Fliege-Mücke radar
detector antenna. This type of radar detection
device was removed from *U 977* by the employees
of the Argentinian Navy in August 1945.
The Argentinians transferred Type VII C
submarine to the USA without the passive radar
detection devices.

Final moments of the German submarine *U 977*, taken over by Americans. The submarine is sinking in vicinity of Cape Cod, torn by the explosion of a torpedo fired by the U.S. submarine USS *Atule* on November 13, 1946.

...one more photograph of *U 977*'s final moments.

gerät reif zum Auswechseln und die zum Teil neue Besatzung nicht eingespielt . . . Soldatentum hat nichts mit Selbstmord zu tun."

Mit aufmontiertem Schnorchel marschierte U 977 im Verband zweier weiterer Boote zur Brennstoffübernahme in Richtung Norwegen. In einem dänischen Zwischenhafen wurden die pro vernünftigen Verpflegungslager - Intendanten Butterfässer, Schinken, Eier, Zigaretten usw. organisiert. Vorrat für ein halbes Jahr.

Am 2. Mai lief U 977 mit 48 Mann kriegsstarker Besatzung aus dem Stützpunkt Christiansund-Süd aus. Der Dönitz-Aufruf: „Wir kapitulieren nie! Lieber tot als Sklave!", befehlsgemäß auf allen Kriegsfahrzeugen auszuhängen, zierte U 977 nicht.

Obl. z. S. Schäffer hatte ohnedies eigene Gedanken über den Kriegsausgang. Er hatte 1938 in den Detroiter Fordwerken die Auto-Friedensproduktion von 5000 Stück täglich gesehen. Er hatte auch sonst noch eine Portion Auslandserfahrung. „Aber Krieg ist Krieg, und wenn schon, dann an der Seite des Vaterlandes."

Der Einsatzbefehl des OKM lautete, sich vor Southampton aufzuhalten und möglichst in den Hafen selbst einzulaufen. Das 600-t-Boot schnorchelte Kurs Süd.

Dem verschlüsselten Offiziersspruch: „Wir müssen kapitulieren. Ihr habt in Zukunft Befehle der Alliierten auszuführen . . .", schnitt die ins Wasser tauchende Antenne die Unterschriftsdurchgabe ab. Außerdem stand der Spruch in krassem Gegensatz zu Tags vorher übermittelten Befehlen.

Auch der alliierte Funkspruch: „U-Boote sofort auftauchen, telegrafisch Standort melden, Waffen vernichten und weiße oder blaue Flagge zeigen. Alliiertes Geleit wird sicher in englische oder amerikanische Häfen leiten!", wurde als fingiert angesehen. So handelte der Kommandant auf eigene Faust, als aus dem Aether nur noch das Wort „Kapitulation" ertönte.

Am 9. Mai hatte er sich zur Erkenntnis des verlorenen Krieges durchgerungen. Er klärte die Bootsbesatzung darüber auf. Weiter: „In geheimer, demokratischer Abstimmung ersuchte ich die 48 Mann, selbst über das Schicksal des Bootes zu entscheiden." 30 stimmten für Südamerika, zwei für Spanien, 16 verheiratete, fast ausschließlich technische Unteroffiziersdienstgrade für heim zu Muttern. Sie wurden an die norwegische Küste zurückgefahren.

In der dunklen, leicht-nebeligen Nacht vom 10. zum 11. Mai paddelten sie auf zwei Schlauchbooten mit Sack und Pack und Proviant für vier Wochen in einem schmalen Fjord in der Nähe Bergens an Land. Ehe die norwegischen Küstenbatterien sich eingeschossen hatten, manövrierte das mit dem Vorderschiff aufgelaufene Boot aus der Gefahrenzone.

U 977 schnorchelte mit beschädigtem Sehrohr blind unter Wasser, mit unausbleiblichen Maschinen- und Hauptkupplungsdefekten und 3 Seemeilen Unterwassergeschwindigkeit. Am 50. Tage stand das Boot immer noch zwischen England und Gibraltar.

Ausschlag und Furunkulose in der Besatzung, eine Exzem - Operation mit Schnapsbetäubung ohne Schiffsarzt, Rost- und Schimmelbildung im Schiffsinnern mußten ertragen werden. Die durch Salzwasser gezogene Wäsche trocknete nicht.

Fehlendes Tageslicht, mangelnde Frischluft, tropfendes Kondenswasser und Abwechslungslosigkeit machten selbst den Gesündesten apathisch und appetitlos. Die U-Boot-Bärte verfilzten, die Hustenfälle mehrten sich. Doch die im Radarwarngerät angezeigten Schiffs- und Flugzeugannäherungen zwangen weiter zur Tauchfahrt. 32 Mann wollten ihre Südamerikareise nicht abgebrochen wissen.

Nach 66 Tagen Unterwassertrip tauchte U 977 erstmalig in Gibraltarnähe wieder auf. 1800 zurückgelegte Seemeilen hatten 40 t Dieselöl gefressen. Für die noch fehlenden 5500 standen nur 40 t zur Verfügung. Aus Sparsamkeitsgründen waren die 120 t fassenden Tanks nicht voll gefüllt worden. Eine optimistische Berechnung ergab: „Bei größtmöglicher Sparfahrt kommen wir hin. Mit 5 t Ueberschuß".

Eine vorgesehene Landung auf dem unbewohnten kapverdischen Eiland Branca mußte wegen zu starker Brandung aufgegeben werden. Zur physischen Erholung herrschte nachts kriegsmäßiger Betrieb mit Brücken- und Radarwarngerät-Wachen und reinem Atlantikozon. Tagsüber wurde in Tauchfahrt geschlafen. Bei eventuellem Angriff alliierter Einheiten sollte die Besatzung zurückschießen. Schäffer: „Ich glaubte mich im Recht. Ein Angriff, sei er auch von der Siegerpartei, ist völker-

. . . der soll selbst fahren

Heinz Schäffer und Frau

rechtswidrig. Ich darf dann wohl genau so handeln."

Mit Leinwand, Segeltuch und Schornsteinimitation erhielt das Kriegsschiff eine friedliche Frachtersilhouette.

Da wurde die Funkmeldung aufgefangen: „U 530 im argentinischen Hafen Mar del Plata eingelaufen." Jetzt hatte Schäffer zwischen Selbstversenkung und Uebergabe zu wählen. Er entschied für Uebergabe.

U 977 fuhr am 17. August 1945 ohne gesetzte Nationalitätsflagge mit sämtlichen Schiffspapieren und allen zehn unverbrauchten Torpedos ein. „Wie zur Parade!" schrieb die Zeitung „La Razon". Die

folgenden militärischen Ehren rollten beim Marsch „Alte Kameraden" ab.

In Flugzeugen kamen sofort alliierte Marinesachverständige herbei. Bei den Verhören am dem argentinischen Kreuzer „Belgrano" konnte Oblt. z. S. Heinz Schäffer an Hand von Log-, Maschinen-, Kriegstagebüchern und Seekarten beweisen, daß U 977

- nicht den brasilianischen Kreuzer „Bahia" versenkte, der im Juli 1945 angeblich nach Torpedobeschuß durch ein U-Boot unbekannter Nationalität unterging;
- nicht den durch die Weltpresse entdeckten mysteriösen Geisterkonvoi, mit dem der Führer des Großdeutschen Reiches sich nebst Gefolge in Sicherheit gebracht haben sollte, geleitete;
- dafür aber die 16 Mann fehlende Besatzung auf eigenen Wunsch in Norwegen absetzte
- und die lange Fahrtzeit zum Zielhafen wegen Brennstoffmangels und somit geringster Geschwindigkeit brauchte.

Die Einzelverhöre der Besatzungsmitglieder bestätigten alle Punkte. „Wer glaubt, auf einem U-Boot etwas geheimhalten zu können, der soll selbst fahren!" erklärte Heinz Schäffer neugierigen Laien. Er hatte bewiesen, daß er auf jeden Fall Hitler nicht übers Meer entführte. Das alliierte Kriegsgericht sprach ihn frei.

In derselben Zeit allerdings behauptete „El Dia" in Montevideo, daß mit Hilfe von U 977 Hitler nach Argentinien Patagonien und in die Antarktis geflohen sei.

Zur besseren Durchleuchtung kam PW Heinz Schäffer ins Interrogation Camp für prominente Kriegsgefangene nach Washington, zu Admiral Goth und dem Chefingenieur des Heereswaffenamtes Pollert. Mannschaft und U-Boot folgten getrennt.

Das Kriegsgericht, das wieder den Fall „Bahia" verhandelte, sprach zum zweiten Male frei. Auch eine Konfrontierung in einer mit geheimen Mikrofonen gespickten Gefängniszelle mit dem Kommandanten von U 530, Otto Wermuth, brachte keine Ueberraschungen. Beide sahen sich zum ersten Male. U 530 und U 977 waren tatsächlich, unabhängig voneinander, dem gleichen Ziel zugesteuert.

U 977 wurde auf Befehl des amerikanischen Kriegsministeriums versenkt. Eigentlich hatte es Heinz Schäffer den Argentiniern zugedacht.

Im Sammeltransport zurückkehrender PWs war der einstige U-Boot-Ausbildungskommandant Schäffer unter den ersten 16. Zusammen mit den Handschellen tragenden und an einen jungen, weißhaarigen General gekoppelten Fallschirmjäger-General Ramcke. Nach der Uebergabe an die Engländer stellte Heinz Schäffer einen „Umschwung von ausnehmend guter in ausnehmend schlechte Behandlung" fest.

Das Protokoll über das Privatverhör durch vier englische Offiziere schloß: „Schäffer ist glühender Nazi." Daß Hitler an Bord des U 977 gewesen sei, konnten auch sie nicht feststellen.

Nach sechs Monaten Kriegsgefangenschaft folgte die übliche Entlassung aus der Wehrmacht. Dafür kam Schäffer als politischer Häftling ins Lager Paderborn. „Warum ich bei den Politischen saß, erfuhr ich niemals", stellt Schäffer fest.

Durch einen geschmuggelten Kassiber machte er einflußreiche Freunde mobil. Zwei Tage später fuhr der Zivilist Heinz Schäffer nach Düsseldorf und bereitete sich auf seine zweite Reise nach Argentinien vor. Wie er dahin kam, sagt er nicht.

Jetzt ist er glücklich mit einer Argentinierin deutscher Abstammung verheiratet. Die Hochzeitsreise soll ihn auch nach Deutschland führen: „Wenn bis dahin mein Buch-Dementi über den ‚Hitlerverstecker' Heinz Schäffer' im Manuskript fertig ist."

An excerpt from the article "Nichs mit Selbstmord zu tun" about the epic wartime journey of *U 977* under command of Lt. H. Schäffer, published by German magazine "Der Spiegel" on August 6, 1950.

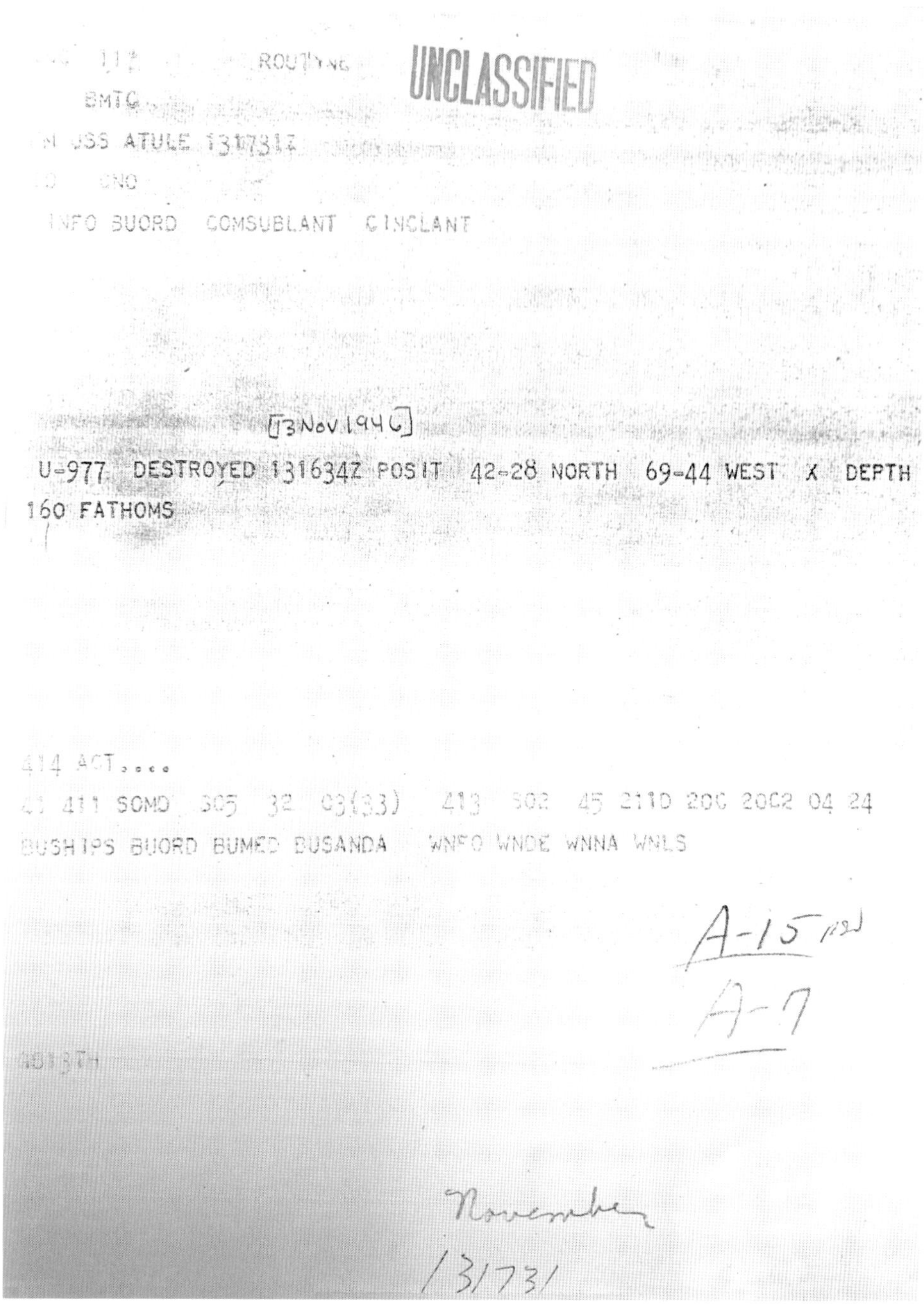

UNCLASSIFIED

ROUTING

BMTC

USS ATULE 131731Z

CNO

INFO BUORD COMSUBLANT CINCLANT

[13 Nov 1946]

U-977 DESTROYED 131634Z POSIT 42-28 NORTH 69-44 WEST X DEPTH 160 FATHOMS

414 ACT....

411 SOMO 305 32 03(33) 413 502 45 2110 200 20C2 04 24 BUSHIPS BUORD BUMED BUSANDA WNFO WNDE WNNA WNLS

A-15

A-7

November

131731

November 13, 1946 document informing about the destruction of *U 977*. It gives the coordinates and depth at which the U-boot went down.

U 234 fitted with a snorkel (Schnorchel in German).

Lt.Cdr. Joachim Heinrich Fehler, the first and last commander of U 234.

U 234 in a dry dock.

The German auxiliary cruiser Atlantis.

A photo of a POW, General Ulrich Kessler.

Cardboard boxes with documents concerning wartime careers of U 530 and U 977 kept by the Argentinian Navy. A photograph taken in January 2008.

The photograph shows Kapitänleutnant Johann Heinrich Fehler (on the right), the commander of U 234, accompanied by Fregattenkapitän Heinrich Lehmann-Willenbrock, commander of the 11. U-Flotille at Bergen, March 1945.

...second page of the aforementioned document held at the Archives and Records Administration at College Park, Maryland.

A unique document, ID card of prisoner of war, Lt.Cdr. Johann Heinrich Fehler...

Liste Der Tauchretter.

Lfd.Nr.	Dienstgrad	Name	Lfd.Nr.	Dienstgrad	Name.
1	Btsm.	Schölch	37	Ob. Gefr	Pagel
2	Ob.Btsmt.	Lühmann	38	"	Engelhardt
3	Btsmt.	Thies	39	"	Wintermeyer
4	Freg.Kapt.	Tomonaga +	40		Schramm
5	Ob. Fkmt.	Bachmann	41	2	Storkemeier
6	Mesch.Mt.	Huggele	42	Ob."Ltnt.	Hellendorn
7	Mtr.Ob.Gefr.	Spurk	43	Ob.Gefr.	Lehrmann
8	Freg.Kapt.	Schosi +	44	"	Obst
9	Mtr Ob.Gefr.	Schneiber	45	"	Steffen
10	"	Grünthaler	46	"	Winter
11	"	Mania	47	"	Willan
12	"	Schmidt	48	"	Hahn
13	"	Schreiber	49	"	Wiedenhöft
14	"	Möstl	50	"	Walter
15	"	Schilli	51	Dipl.Ing.	Bringenwald
16	Freg.Kapt.	Falk	52	Ob. Meist.	Ruf
17	Geschw.Richt.	Niesling	53	Ob.Ltn.	Menzel
18	Mtr.Ob.Gefr.	Fuchs	54	General	Kessler
19	Mesch "	Miehling	55	Oberst.	Sandrath
20	"	Meyer	56 57	Putzas	
21	"	Noll	57 ½ 58	Reserve	Köpp
22	"	Rathge	59	Kaptltn.	Fehler
23	San.Ob.Gefr.	Wiesmeier	60	" Ing.	Ernst P
24	Fk.Ob.Gefr.	Gebauer	61	Ob. Ltn.Ing	Pagenstecher
25	"	Huber	62	Kaptltn.	Bulla
26	"	Rauhe	63	Ltn.z.See	Pfaff
27	Ob,Masch.Mt.	Distler	64	Ob.Strm	Jasper
28	Masch.Mt.	Ziets	65	"	Rische
29	"	Rudolphy	66	Ob.Masch	Winkelmann
30	Korv.Kapt.	Schlicke	67	"	Sandmüller
31	Masch. Mt.	Quosdorf	68	Ob.Fkmstr.	Hirschfeld P
32	"	Richter	69	Mar.Stbs,Arzt.	Dr. Walter
33	"	Klatt			
34	"	Simon			
35	M.Hpt.Gefr.	Haase			
36	"	Meinelt			

U 234 crew list made in April 1945, held at the Archives and Records Administration at College Park, Maryland.

U 234's galley.

* * *

In 2009, at the request of the Argentine Minister of Defense, part of the Naval Archives documents (no. 35275/07) concerning *U 977* was declassified. The preserved archival photographs (they were in a file with other documents) clearly show the U-Boot's conning tower with three protruding antennas. Intelligence officers of the Armada de la República Argentina asked themselves why the crew of a German submarine from a training flotilla, which at the end of the war allegedly fled from Europe to Argentina in order to get a chance for a better life (as the commander of the U-Boot claimed), was equipped with such advanced radar detection devices? Let us recall, that the ship was equipped with the new, passive radar detection devices. She received the Naxos system FuMB Ant.24 „Fliege" antenna with additional FuMB Ant.25 „Mücke" horn antenna and the new FuMB 26 „Tunis" antenna. At the end of the war, such equipment was basically only used on board combat units, which took part in regular patrols in the Atlantic. Meanwhile, *U 977* was a training ship and had not previously participated in any combat patrols. The end of the war was near.

The report of Argentine intelligence officers is accompanied by a list of 32 crew members. The list includes the names of four submariners: radio operator Harry Hentschel and engineers Hans Krebs, Kurt Nittner and Gerhard Höfler, who completed additional specialist courses in electrical and engine mechanics. According to the Argentineans, that was not a necessary requirement on a training ship. Their theoretical knowledge and practical skills, which aroused the greatest interest among Argentine investigators, would have been put to better use on newer types of U-Boots. Why were they assigned to a training ship? There is no answer to that question.

It turned out, that the Americans „inherited" a U-Boot, which was deprived of the most important radio-technical devices. According to the documents, the Argentineans, removed everything that was possible and was of particular value in terms of technological progress in the naval war. That type of equipment was unknown to them. Therefore, the U.S. Navy received a disassembled German submarine.

* * *

What are the secrets of *U 977*'s voyage, which began in Kiel on April 13 and ended on October 17, 1945, at Mar del Plata? What do we not know about 107 days that the German submarine spent at sea on her way from Europe to South America?

We have no knowledge of what happened to the mysterious cargo that was loaded on board the U-Boot in the Danish base of Frederikshavn. It is obvious for proponents of conspiracy theories - the chests were full of gold and valuable Nazi documents. However, naval historians are convinced that they contained.... only the additional amount of provisions needed for the patrol. Submariners of *U 977* did not speak about the course of the voyage. The last witnesses took the truth to the grave.

* * *

What is the truth about the mysterious voyage of *U 977*, the ship's commander and its crew? It turns out that there is a number of historians, journalists and documentary filmmakers who in their theories have believed for years, that Lieutenant Schäffer and his subordinates outwitted the Allies. Although they invariably claim that *U 977* took part in a special mission, they do not have solid evidence to support their arguments. There are also no documents or witnesses' testimonies, that support the claim, that *U 977* belonged to a group of submarines that were a part of the „ghost convoy", which carried mysterious treasures of the Third Reich and secretly transported the German Nazis who escaped trial and punishment for the crimes they had committed.

It seems completely improbable that any high-ranking Nazi dignitary decided to flee aboard *U 977*. If any of the German dignitaries would have even taken that kind of risk, he would have certainly not chosen a shabby training ship with rough history and a young commander and inexperienced crew. They would have surely boarded one of Type IX D2 U-Boots or a modern Type XXI submarine. U-Boot-waffe had these types of ships at its disposal despite the war shortages. Admiral Dönitz was able to appoint an appropriate ship and a commander with extensive combat experience for a special mission, which would have met the expectations of the Nazis fleeing justice.

Before the mission, for the last time, Schäffer had been in the Atlantic in autumn 1943. Would his superiors have entrusted a secret mission to a lieutenant who had never in his life commanded a U-Boot during a combat patrol? The fall of Germany was only a matter of time. It should be remembered that the crew had no experience in using a snorkel, which had only been fitted shortly before the end of the war. According to Dietrich Wiese: „Personally, this voyage brought me a year in captivity and countless interrogations, because everyone was looking for Hitler".

CHAPTER VII

INTERRUPTED VOYAGE OF *U 234*

The truth, no matter how great it may be, becomes denial,
if imposed by violence.
Kazimierz Kozicki, "Księga mądrości"

Nearly ninety-meter-long German underwater minelayer *U 234* was commissioned on March 2, 1944. The ship was built by Germaniawerft shipyard in Kiel[172], in less than two and a half years since her keel had been laid. The construction dragged on a little, as on May 14, 1943, the ship was severely damaged during the air raid of American long-range Boeing B-17 Flying Fortress and Consolidated B-24 Liberator bombers on the Krupp-Germania shipyard, which significantly delayed her launching. It turned out that the entire forward section of the hull had been so badly damaged at that time, that it had to be replaced.

The ship was built in one of the three German shipyards (the others were: Blohm & Voss in Hamburg, which built 223 U-Boots and Deschimag A.G. Weser in Bremen, which built 163 submarines), which in the years 1935-1945 constructed the largest number of as many as 129 submarines for the U-Bootwaffe. Captain Johann-Heinrich Fehler (born on September 20, 1910 in Berlin-Charlottenburg), who was 34 at that time, was appointed the commander of the ocean-going underwater predator *U 234*. It was his very first submarine assignment.

Despite his lack of combat experience in the submarine warfare, Fehler took command of a modern ship. Moreover, he was to take part in a mission that was of great importance. However, it should be noted, that Fehler became the commander of the U-Boot when the war was coming to an end. At that time, Admiral Dönitz did not have many experienced officers capable of taking the ship all the way to Japan, carrying valuable cargo and several special passengers, who were ordered to perform an important task at the end of the war in Europe. On the other hand, those officers who were highly-qualified, i.e. those who took part in a few or more combat patrols,

---

[172] The remaining German Type X B submarine minelayers were: *U 116 – 119*, *U 219*, *U 220* and *U 233*.

were either needed to train young submarines or sent on „suicide missions" to the Atlantic. However, if the commander of U 234 was forced (for whatever reason) to abandon the voyage to Japan, the second variant of the plan, prepared by the Kriegsmarine high command, was to evacuate to Argentina (the choice of that country was known to a narrow group of officers who boarded the U-Boot).

Dönitz and Hitler did not want to accept the fact that Germany had actually lost the submarine war. The Allies have long since managed to eliminate one of the most important advantages the U-Boots had - the ability to operate on the surface at night. Since the Coastal Command had the sufficient number of planes and trained crews, and the Allies have significantly strengthened their anti-submarine surface forces, the situation of the U-Boots in the Atlantic was getting worse.

* * *

Recently promoted, Lt. Fehler[173], gained practical knowledge concerning the principles and possibilities of commerce raiding, between December 1939 and November 1941, when he served under the command of Cpt. Bernhard Rogge, an officer with extensive experience, on the first German auxiliary cruiser *Atlantis - Schiff 16*. She was an almost new, over 150-meter-long, ex freighter *Goldenfels* of 7,862 GRT, built at the Vulcan shipyard in Bremen. Following her two years of Hansa Line merchant marine service in Bremen, in autumn 1939, she was seized by the Kriegsmarine and rebuilt into a disguised raider. It turns out that Fehler had a lot of maritime experience, because at the end of the 1920s he began his service on merchant ships. Wolfgang Hirschfeld, a radio operator and non-commissioned officer of U 234 wrote more about that:

By his nineteenth birthday he (Fehler – M.B.) was too old for sail training and discovered that in order to sit his mate's certificate it would be necessary to serve fifty months at sea, of which at least twenty months had to be in sailing vessels. He signed on as deck boy with the small 140-ton oak-built galeasses which plied the ports of the Baltic until after twenty-seven months of this cold, harsh life he could finally become apprenticed aboard the motor ships and steamers of the great German shipping lines. Soon he was in the Far East aboard the 7,600-ton North German Lloyd motor ship "Havel".

On one of his infrequent returns to Germany in November, 1933, he was recruited into the Nazi Party during a membership drive, although no deep political conviction lay behind his decision.

On 2. April, 1936, Fehler entered the German Navy as an officer cadet and by the outbreak of war had command of the minesweeper "M -145" operating out of Wil-

---

[173] He was promoted to Lieutenant on October 1, 1939.

helmshaven. By the turn of the year [in December 1939 – M.B.] he had been drafted as Mines and Explosives Officer to the raider "Atlantis"[174].

As a crew member, Fehler took part in all combat operations of the German raider, which resulted in sinking of numerous merchantmen sailing under various flags. He survived the sinking of the auxiliary cruiser by the British heavy cruiser HMS *Devonshire* (under command of Cpt. Richard D. Oliver) in the South Atlantic on November 22, 1941[175]. For his service so far he was awarded the Iron Cross 2nd and 1st class. Fehler was also briefly in command of the Norwegian tanker *Ketty Brövig* (7,031 GRT), captured as a prize by *Atlantis* on February 2, 1941. However, that ship was soon sunk in the Indian Ocean.

Seven sailor were killed aboard *Atlantis* and 308 survived, abandoning the ship on 2 motorboats, 4 large metal cutters, 5 dinghies and several rafts made from parts of the wreck. The commander of the Royal Navy cruiser did not want to expose his ship to the danger of a possible submarine attack and left the area without taking any survivors. Soon, the ocean-going submarine *U 126* (Type IX C), under the command of Lt.Cdr. Ernst Bauer, came to help them. 55 survivors were taken inside: officers (Fehler was among them), specialists and the wounded. The remaining ones, wearing life vests, were taken on deck of the U-Boot, while the boats with over 200 people were taken in tow. Two days later, the submarine met with the refuelling ship *Python* (under command of Lt.Cdr. Gustav Lueders), which took the surviving *Atlantis* crew members on board, and then, in accordance with earlier orders, after supplying 4 U-Boots off the coast of South Africa, was to return to western France, where she would arrive in December 1941. Meanwhile, *Python* run out of luck. On December 1, she encountered the heavy cruiser HMS *Dorsetshire* (under command of Cpt. A. W. S. Agar), which, similarly to her sister ship *Devonshire*, operated from Freetown, Sierra Leone, with orders to intercept German surface units in the central Atlantic. The cruiser fired 2 shots and ordered the German supply ship to stop and her commander obeyed the order. The British did not continue to fire, as they assumed the presence of prisoners on board the ship. The supply ship's crew and the survivors from the auxiliary cruiser embarked on the boat (some of which were towed) and at 5.51 p.m. *Python* was blown up and after capsizing, sank 30 minutes later at position 27°50'S and 03°52'W. There was no casualties. The cruiser steamed southeast without rescuing the survivors, because Cpt. Agar was afraid of submarine attacks, the presence of which could be deduced from the sighted oil spills floating on the surface. The 414 survivors from *Python* and *Atlantis* were helped by the crews of four U-boats: *U 68*, *UA*, *U 129* and

---

[174] W. Hirschfeld, *Ostatni U-Boot*, Gdańsk 2007, pp.253-254.

[175] During her career as a raider, the auxiliary cruiser *Atlantis* was at sea for 622 days and covered over 102,000 nmi (188,904 km). She sank 16 and captured 6 (freighters and tankers) Allied merchant ships with a total tonnage of 145,697 GRT. She changed her appearance and ensigns ten times during her cruise. *Atlantis* was the third most effective German auxiliary cruiser of World War II.

U124 and four Italian submarines: *Tazzoli, Finzi, Calvi* and *Torelli*, which reached St. Nazaire on December 23-29.

* * *

Luckily surviving the ordeal, Fehler did not return to sea for a while and was not assigned to another surface raider. The Kriegsmarine command had different plans for a talented officer. On December 1, 1942, he was promoted to the rank of Lieutenant Commander of the navy and assigned to Marine Oberkommando Nord in Wilhelmshaven. In March 1942, following three months of staff work and sitting behind a desk, wishing to serve on a submarine, Fehler notified the High Command of his intention. It was decided to send the candidate as fit for service on board the U-Boots. The submariners belonged to a special group - „corps d'élite" - and were proud to belong to the elite clan of underwater hunters. Over 30-year-old Lieutenant Commander was sent to the Marineschule (Naval School) in Mürwik-Flensburg. More and more submarines of different types were being built in German shipyards. The U-Bootwaffe command needed well-trained officers. The U-Bootwaffe commanders, who were the backbone of the submarine fleet, were later selected from those on the basis of specific character traits. Warships taking part in fast, intensive actions, fighting against convoys, needed the leadership of young, energetic and aggressive people with quick sense of direction and full of optimism. There was a long way ahead of anyone who wanted to become a submarine commander.

Despite his general seamanship training, Fehler had to take part in one-year training (from March 1942 to March 1943) in navigation, tactics, gunnery and torpedo warfare and communications. At the beginning of his naval school training he was awarded the German Cross in Gold (23 April 1942). It was not until March to September 1943, that he took part in practical training in underwater weaponry. Then, from September to December 1943, he stayed in the training center of the 24. Unterssbootsflottille (U-Flottille) in Lithuania Klaipėda (then Memel). There, the training of future submarine commanders was carried out within the framework of Kommandantantenschiesslehrgang, i.e. KSL courses. Each of them lasted three months: during that time 10-12 officers were taught advanced fighting techniques and tactics. The course, among other things, provided for launching training torpedoes at real targets. When Fehler was undergoing the training - it was in the middle of the war - the main emphasis was on underwater detection and the use of that knowledge to avoid enemy attacks. The last stage of the training was a patrol organized as part of the Kommadantenschüler „Konfirmand" course. At the end of the training, the officers who participated were assigned to command a submarine, after obtaining required qualifications.

As a dynamic and aggressive officer, Fehler initially felt disappointed that his superiors entrusted him with the command of the submarine minelayer *U 234*. He wanted an attack submarine, but apparently the BdU (Befehlshaber der Untersee-boote) were of the opinion that since he had no previous combat experience on a U-Boot, it would be more sensible to entrust him with command of a Type X B submarine. The U-Boot was under construction. Since December 1943, the ship's commander and the rest of the crew (they had quarters near the shipyard) took part in all phases of the ship's construction in Kiel, in order to get to know her very well. The crew members had to be familiar with the ship's construction, literally see every rivet and nut, know the purpose of each of the thousands of pipes, wires, etc. The idea was that in extreme combat conditions, in danger, when there was darkness inside the ship, they would be able to locate every valve. That form of submariners' training was unprecedented and was not used in other navies. The system developed in the U-Bootwaffe allowed the crew to get to know the complex equipment and, in the event of a breakdown, to carry out repairs at sea, far away from the base.

GENERAL CHARACTERISTICS OF TYPE X B SUBMARINE MINELAYER U 234 [176]

Shipyard	Germaniawerf, Kiel
Ordered	December 7, 1940
Shipyard no.	664
Laid down	October 1, 1941
Launched	December 23, 1944
Commissioned	March 2, 1944
Lenght	89.8 m
Beam	9.2 m
Draft	4.71 m
Propulsion	two supercharged, 9-cylinder, four-stroke Germaniawerft F46 diesel engines (2 x 2,100 hp); two AEG GU720/8-287 electric motors (2 x 550 hp; 800 kW)
Fuel capacity	368 t
Displacement sufaced/submerged	1,763/2,177 t
Speed surfaced/submerged	17/7 kn
Range surfaced/submerged	18,450 nmi at 10 kn/93 nmi at 4 kn
Crush depth	200 m
Armament	2 stern torpedo tubes (15 torpedoes), 2 x 20 mm anti-aircraft guns, 1 x 37 mm gun, 66 SMA mines
Complement	5 officer, 47 non-commissioned officers and enlisted men

[176] E. Bagnasco, *Uboote im 2. Weltkrieg*, Stuttgart 1997, p. 80; R. Busch, H-J. Röll, *Der U-Boot-Krieg 1939-1945. Der U-Boot-Bau auf Deutschen Werften*, vol. 2, Hamburg-Berlin-Bonn 1997, pp. 146, 269; E. Möller, W. Brack, *The Encyclopedia of U-Boats. From 1904 to the Present*, London 2004, p. 105; E. Rössler, *The U-Boat. The evolution and technical history of German submarines*, London 2001, p. 110; K. Wynn, *U-Boat Operations of the Second World War*, vol. 1, London 2003, p. 170.

On March 2, 1944, *U 234* was officially commissioned as part of the 5. U-Flottille in Kiel. Then the crew spent almost 2 months on trials in the Baltic Sea. The training was postponed due to the mines dropped by the Allied air force. It was not until April 27, that the ship was redeployed to the harbor of Rønne on the Danish island of Bornholm, where it was also temporarily unable to continue the training due to the possibility of new minefields being laid at approaches. The men were subjected to simulated combat conditions, torpedo launching was being taught and so was laying minefield, and all elements of diving procedures were being practiced. Submariners had an opportunity to try out the operation of diving planes, trim and ballast tanks, they also learned about the strength of the hull. The permanent tasks performed during the demanding training included tests of diesel engines and electric motors, anti-aircraft armament, radio and echolocation equipment. It was also a time when people got to know each other, realizing that they were becoming a living part of the ship's organism. Practical exercises took place day and night and the training was intense. The commander required obedience and high level of training from the crew. All these skills would decide, if a U-Boot was able to complete its mission and safely return from a patrol.

On May 25, *U 234* arrived at Hel Peninsula in order to complete the training program, that would prepare the ship for combat operations. It was mainly about simulated emergency situations so the crew would get used to work under stress. The training lasted for four weeks.

For the following weeks, the U-Boot took part in tactical exercises with the submarine depot ship *Waldemar Kophamel*, near the Baltic settlement of Palmnicken (present day Yantarny, Kaliningrad Oblast), which ended on August 30, 1944 with the submarine entering the base in Kiel. When it seemed that the crew of *U 234* was prepared to go out on the first patrol.... the BdU decided to make repairs on the ship before she went into active service. *U 234* came close to not putting to sea at all. On the last day of August, the German liner *St. Louis* was heavily damaged during RAF bombers raid on Kiel. Shortly before the air raid, the U-Boot left the harbor basin and hid at a safe spot in the Heikendorf Bay. However, one of the aircraft dropped his load of bombs near the ship, but fortunately, there was no serious damage.

U 234 returned to Germaniawerft shipyard and was redesigned from an underwater minelayer into a transport. As a result, some of the armament was removed and the outer mine shafts on both sides were used for cargo holds. The slightly shortened on-board torpedo storage containers, adapted to carry cargo, were placed inside them. As per her previous function, *U 234* had six cargo containers in mine shafts located in the forward and midship sections. The six vertical containers were placed in the mine shafts on both sides and there were eight horizontal cylinders in each of the four cargo spaces. Four cargo containers, two on each side of the hull, above the deck, were the final elements of the ship's transport features. Following the completion of these modifications (dismantling of horizontal mine shafts), the technicians estimated that the ship could take about 260 tons of cargo and sufficient supplies to be able to remain at sea for 6 to 8 months. The vessel was additionally fitted with a snorkel. The snorkel mast and its lifting mechanism were in a special recess in the ship's deck.

On December 22, 1944, the ship left the shipyard and performed a trial cruise under the supervision of Kiel shipyard engineers. Soon the snorkel tests began, which took place in the Strander Bucht near Kiel, under the direction of WWI U-Boot-waffe ace, Captain-Junior Grade Max Valentiner. Quick familiarization of the crew (particularly the second-in-command and the chief engineer) with the operation and workings of this device, enabled the submerged ship, remaining at periscope depth, to release and intake air, simultaneously preventing the water from entering the vessel. That had an impact on the successful course of underwater navigation.

Lt.Cdr. Richard Bull, replaced Lt. Klingenberg, as the new Executive Officer. As a result, working relationship between the commander and the deputy commander improved, which significantly shortened the training time and raised the crew's level of training. Both officers knew each other well from their service aboard *Atlantis*.

At the end of 1944, Fehler was summoned to headquarters in Berlin. He was horrified by the tasks that the BdU ordered him to perform during the first combat mission - his ship, armed with 8 torpedoes (instead of 15) and without the 105 mm gun, was to be used as a transport unit and intended to carry passengers. She was to go on a voyage to Japan with a mysterious cargo and 26 passengers, including higher-ranking military personnel, scientists and two Japanese officers[177]. The commander categorically stated that taking on board such a number of passengers would be impossible. In his opinion, they would take place of 18 crew members. Moreover, they would be a nuisance and would endanger the mission. In the end, it was decided that 12 passengers would travel to Tokyo, and eight crew members would make space for them.

In January 1945, the preparations for the voyage gained momentum. A FuG 200 Hohentwiel radar, which was the invention of the Luftwaffe, was installed on the U-Boot. Its retractable antenna was placed in a vertical slot in the housing of the conning tower and operated with use of compressed air. This type of device, operating at low frequencies, was used to detect airborne targets with the help of radio waves. It gave the U-Boot the advantage of detecting an approaching aircraft before its own radar could get a fix on the boat. As it turned out, it was not without flaws - it became very hot, if left working too long.

In December 1944, the Marine Sonderdienst Aussland (Special Submarine Division) was created under the leadership of Dr. Becker, who was in charge of all the details, including communication with the Japanese. Captain Longbein was responsible for loading 240-ton cargo[178] and Leutnant zur See (Lieutnant-Junir Grade) Karl Ernst Pfaff, Second Watch Officer of *U 234*, was appointed to help him.

---

[177] G. Williamson, *Wolf Pack. The Story of the U-Boat in World War II*, Oxford 2005, p. 56.

[178] See: Records of the G-2 (Intelligence) Division – U 234, Record Group (RG) 165 (War Department General Staff), National Archives and Records Administration (NARA), College Park.

The cargo contained, among other things: 74 t of lead, 26 t of mercury (in 25 kg steel bottles), 465 kg of valuable medicine - Atabrine (synthetic alkaloid, used as antimalarial and antiparasitic drug), 106 kg of thallium, 12 t of stainless steel, 7 t of optical glass, 43 t of documents (including aircraft plans, e.g. the blueprints of Messerschmitt Me-163 and Me-262, as well as technical documentation concerning the construction of modern destroyers and submarines), onboard instruments, weapons and medical supplies, 5 tons of 20 mm and 37 mm ammunition, 6 tons of equipment for German submarine bases, 1 ton of mail, films and courier mail. In addition, a large number of prototypes of various devices, e.g. plano-convex lenses, vacuum tubes, detonators, recoilless gun ammunition, coils, elements for some kind of fire control system. On board the U-Boot there were also about 900 bottles of alcohol.... and probably 5 million U.S. dollars. The most important and secret cargo was loaded last - 560 kg of uranium oxide (stored in 10 metal cubes with about 22.9 cm-long sides). The valuable cargo was deposited in one of the vertical mine shafts in February 1945. The small cans had embossed inscription reading „U-235". Initially, the crew was convinced that they had mistakenly received a cargo for another ship, and only later they learned (on the grapevine), that the boxes contained highly radioactive uranium oxide ore, a key ingredient in the production of deadly weapon. It turned out that the amount of uranium oxide transported to Japan, would have yielded about 3.5 kg of ^{235}U, i.e. about one fifth of the amount needed to build an atomic bomb.

On March 25, 1945, *U 234* departed Kiel. At that time she was assigned to the 33. U-Flotille at Flesburg. Its core were the long-range units. The submarine transport was boarded by 11 passengers: two Japanese officers - Air Force Colonel Genzo Shosi (an aeronautical engineer) and Navy Captain Hideo Tomonaga (a submarine architect); three Luftwaffe officers - Colonel Fritz von Sandrath (former head of Bremen anti-aircraft defenses), Colonel Erich Menzel (technical aide to the Air Attaché and communications specialist) and Lt. Colonel Kai Nieschling (military judge); four Kriegsmarine officers - Lt.Cdr. Heinrich Hellendorn (specialist in naval anti-aircraft gunnery), Captain Heinz Schlicke (electronical engineer, radar, infra-red and direction finding scientist), Captain Gerhard Falk (specialist in shipbuilding and design) and Lt.Cdr. (according to some other sources he held the rank of Commander) Richard Bulla (specialist in air-sea cooperation) and two civilian Messerschmitt employees - August Bringewald (senior engineer, Me262, Me163 and rocketry specialist) and Franz Ruf (procurement specialist).

According to archival documents stored at NARA near Washington, Fehler had no illusions about the end and the outcome of the war. He was even able to interrupt his cruise to the Far East after the capitulation of Germany and on his way land on shore... using the weapons on board the ship for self-defense.

On March 27, a heavily loaded ship called at Horten. The stay in one of the three most important Kriegsmarine bases in Norway (the others were Trondheim and Bergen) was not a successful one. On March 29, during snorkel trials, she was rammed by *U 1301* (Type VII C/41). As a result, her diving tank No. 1 and the adjacent fuel tank were holed, which caused a leakage of about 16 tons of oil. Since the ship's commander could not find a suitable dry dock in Bergen, he sailed to a secluded fjord near Kristiansand. There, he submerged the bow, which raised the stern above the surface. That allowed the crew to make the necessary repairs. Steel plates were welded to cover the holes.

On Sunday, April 15, *U 234* left Kristiansand and set course for Japan. The final passenger to come on board was Luftwaffe General Ulrich Kessler (he was the higher-ranking officer who, if the mission failed, was to give the order to change the U-Boot course and escape to Argentina), a specialist in anti-aircraft and anti-ship missiles, who was appointed a new attaché in Tokyo. Kessler and his staff were to organize the air defense of the Japanese capital. Lawrence Petersen presented the personality of the Luftwaffe General in an interesting way (which was confirmed by extensive documentation from the interrogation of the would-be German diplomat in the Land of the Cherry Blossom):

Fehler took [...] on board the last passenger, an extravagant, rough-spoken Luftwaffe General Ulrich Kessler. [....] [on board the ship - M.B.] Kessler soon came into conflict with some of the more ardent national socialists – he was especially playing on Kai Nieschling's nerves with obscene jokes about high-ranking Nazis [he criticized Hitler and Göring - M.B.][179].

It is worthy of mention that General Kessler was a close friend of Admiral Wilhelm Canaris, the head of the military intelligence and counterintelligence Abwehr from 1935 to 1944. Moreover, he also cooperated with the famous spy, Dr. Horst Gustav Friedrich von Pflugk-Harttung (taken prisoner in the USA around 1944/1945).

Fehler did not believe in the success of the mission. Shortly after putting to sea, he informed the crew of the mission's objective, and was convinced that they would not be able to reach their destination. For sixteen days they continuously sailed submerged, using snorkel. *U 234* did not resurface until May 1. For the next few days, the U-Boot only surfaced for a few hours at night, to recharge the batteries and refresh the air. Upon receiving information about Hitler's death, the cessation of fighting by the decimated German army and the order of Grand Admiral Dönitz, the last Führer of the Third Reich, to surrender all U-Boots to the Allies, Japanese officers committed suicide. Before they intentionally took their own lives, they threw their secret documents overboard, said goodbye to the crew and lay down next to each other on adjacent cots, swallowing 12 Luminal sleeping tablets each. Their death was slow and their bodies, sewn into weighted hammocks, were committed to the deep.

The first report calling *U 234* to surrender was received when they were at 60°00' N and 20°00' W. An encrypted message from the commander of U-Boots FdU

---

[179] L. Paterson, *Szare Wilki Hitlera. U-Booty na Oceanie Indyjskim*, Gdańsk 2005, p. 240.

Group „West", Dr. Hans Rudolf Rösing, reached the ship, which read: "*U 234. Continue your voyage or return to Bergen*".

On May 8, when Germany surrendered, *U 234* was in the middle of the Atlantic. The closest harbor where they could surrender to the Allies was Halifax, Nova Scotia (Canada). Fehler deliberately misled Canadian warships, giving them a false position, because he suspected that the crew would be mistreated in a country fighting with Germany for so long. The commander decided to surrender to the Americans, mistakenly believing that they would go easy one them, whereas General Kessler and Colonel von Sandrath wanted to continue the journey. General Kessler failed to convince Fehler to sail to Argentina. During an interrogation on May 22, 1945, the former testified to the American investigators, that:

If the surrender had not occurred, he [Gen. Kessler - M.B.] planned to U-boat to land him in the Argentine. Here through his connections, he intended to approach the U.S. Embassy and offer to turn over the U-234 to the U.S. Naval Forces in exchange for safe haven for himself and his party in the Argentine[180].

Until the moment of receiving a radio message to abort the mission, the ship did not launch a torpedo attack or lay a minefield (she carried about 40 mines), nor was she attacked. As Captain Fehler testified during the interrogation in the second half of May 1945, all ciphers, ship's documents and blueprints containing technical data of modern weapons were thrown overboard. It happened at the order of the commanding officer of the BdU. On May 15, 1945, the crew got rid of the "Tunis" radar detector, the "Kurier" radio transmitter and the "Enigma" encryption machine. Then the ship resurfaced and the black flag was flown. The U-Boot's position was transmitted over the radio. *U 234* surrendered east of Flemish Cap to the destroyer USS *Sutton* (DE 771), which captured the ship and brought her to Portsmouth, New Hampshire on May 19. *U 234* anchored next to *U 805*, *U 873* and *U 1228* (which had previously surrendered). U.S. investigator, Lt. Hatton, arrived on board of the U-Boot.

The entire crew of *U 234* was transported for interrogation to the Portsmouth naval prison. The submarines were accompanied by the investigators, Lt. Maxell and Lt. J. H. Alberti. Some officers and important passengers were then transported to Fort Hunt POW camp, in the suburbs of Washington, and the non-commissioned officers were sent to the POW camp in Fort Edwards, Massachusetts, where they were repeatedly and quite brutally interrogated by the U.S. military services.

In the absence of the German crew, the ship went to the dry dock. During the unloading of supplies, it was suspected, that some of these secret devices were protected from unauthorized access by booby traps. It turned out that some of the cargo

---

[180] Memorandum of Capt. John L. Riheldaffer, US - Subject: Report on Events at Portsmouth Navy Yard in Connection with the Surrender of German Submarines U 234, U 805, U 873 and U 1228, 22 May 1945; sign. NND 813024, NARA College Park.

was hidden in closed, tube-shaped, steel containers, so the Americans had to use acetylene burners to open them. During the inspection of the ship, part of the cargo was opened on site and the rest was sent to Washington. For two years, the Americans were conducting a detailed search on the U-Boot, hoping to find secret documents and cargo!

The captain of *U 234* complained to investigators, that U.S. soldiers and sailors had plundered his and his crew's personal belongings. He said, that he was outraged the most by the attitude of the guards posted at the mine deck. If only he wanted to, he could pull the lever at any time and get rid of all the mines. The investigators took the captain's words seriously and immediately ordered chains and padlocks to protect the mine locks from being „accidentaly" released. In the evening of May 20, 1945, the chains with padlocks were put on the hydraulic mine release controllers. During the search, it was discovered, that there were five unsecured torpedo fuses inside the ship. Investigators suggested that the fuses should be removed in cooperation with *U 234* torpedo officer, who was on board the ship. The U.S. Navy command at Portsmouth refused to allow the fuses to be unloaded. There were still two armed torpedoes in the torpedo tubes.

U 234 was equipped with a modern type of snorkel. Lt.Cdr. Morgan of the U.S. Naval Intelligence expressed his willingness to dismantle it immediately in order to examine them it thoroughly. U.S. Navy officers assigned to the U-Boot were released from their daily duties. Several NCOs from *U 234*, who were temporarily not sent to the POW camp, were to take care of the U-Boot's technical condition.

It should be mentioned, that upon boarding *U 234*, USS *Sutton* crewmen, began looting the belongings of the crew. Evidence that could have potentially been of interest to the naval intelligence was irretrievably removed or destroyed. Most of the „souvenirs" fell into the hands of the Americans. The U-Boot's crew and their luggage were subjected to another search in the Portsmouth prison. The search was attended by guards in the presence of 5-6 U.S. Navy officers and at least two prison doctors. Practically all valuable items such as watches, pens, wedding rings, wallets, and even as personal ones as the photographs were stolen from the prisoners. There were cases, in which watches stolen from the submariners by prison guards were later transferred to their superiors, who considered them special spoils of war! Bad conduct of the officers had an enormously negative impact on the interrogated, who lost the will to cooperate in any way. It may be hard to believe, but the guards were even stealing the prisoners'.... combs and nail files. After being looted, *U 234* looked as if a cyclone had hit her. Cabinets doors were screaming with busted locks, their contents stolen, and pieces of clothing were all over the deck.

Colonel Rossell, the commander of the Portsmouth Naval Prison, was also involved in that procedure, as he did not even hide from the investigators, that he had several souvenirs that belonged to General Kessler. It soon turned out that on the day the Germans were arrested, officers and prison guards thoroughly searched the

General's luggage. The investigators did not manage to establish what exactly had been stolen. It was suspected that secret documents might have been among the stolen papers, which were later thrown away. The investigators called upon the guards and officers who took part in the search of Kessler's luggage. Following a consultation of Colonel Rossell with Admiral Withers, Commander of the U.S. Naval Base in Portsmouth, all those who had appropriated the German property were assured that disciplinary sanctions would not be taken against them until the interrogators determined what was of value for the intelligence and secured it properly. They were promised that they could keep any item irrelevant to the case. Among the souvenirs stolen, was General Kessler's wallet with 1,200 Swiss francs and several Norwegian crowns. One of the officers was in possession of the general's hat, while another one had a lot of shirts, sweatshirts, hats, medals (the Knight's Cross of the Iron Cross, among other things, was returned to the owner), watches, bladed weapons, etc. During the search, binoculars, a set of dental surgical instruments, a blood pressure measuring device, a Leica camera, general's war campaign ribbons (two sets) and other small items and personal belongings were recovered. During the investigators' conversations with the guards, it turned out that the papers, which had been in the general's wallet had been thrown into a dust bin by a person for whom they were of no value. During the interrogation, Kessler stated that he was involved in an assassination attempt on Hitler's life on July 20, 1944, and that he had managed to confuse the Gestapo.

The theft which took place, while *U 234* was dry-docked was committed on a large scale by both the people working there and the U.S. Navy guards. It is not possible to determine, also in this case, what and how much was stolen, especially since the ship was being looted... by two different groups, both workers and military personnel. That larcenous operation was put to an end, when the people, both civilian workers and military personnel up to the rank of lieutenant, were being checked upon leaving the deck of *U 234*. By the time the theft was stopped, plates, navigation devices, etc. had already disappeared from the ship. Therefore, it was obvious that security guards had also been involved.

Majority of the "special" passengers were involved in the special program, under Operation Paperclip, carried out by the U.S. special services at the end World War II and sfortly thereafter, and were recruited to help with the U.S. arms race. Captain Dr. Heinz Schlicke began work on modern acoustic technologies for submarines. Franz Ruf collaborated with the military aviation industry, passing on his extensive experience in the development of jet aircraft.

Under unexplained circumstances, a mysterious substance, i.e. 560 kg of uranium oxide, vanished into thin air. The US authorities have never admitted the theft. It is suspected that uranium ore was transported to the Manhattan Project's Oak Ridge diffusion plant, Tennessee, where, in the post-war years, it was probably converted into a raw material for production of nuclear weapons. Let us give Hirschfeld a chance to speak:

The ten specialist passengers were driven off to a secret destination. We located them all after the war with the exception of Captain Gerhard Falk. Possibly, like Peter Schölch, our Boatswain, and Lt. Pfaff, who loaded and unloaded the uranium cases, he accepted U.S. citizenship in exchange for his silence. But as Judge Nieschling said, Falk knew everything about the uranium oxide, and he probably knew too much for his own good. His eventual fate after he disappeared into the abyss on 19 May, 1945, remains a mystery[181].

It is no different as far as the seizure of Me 262 Schwalbe jet fighter components is concerned. For years, there was an opinion among the authors specializing in various conspiracy theories of World War II, that before the U-Boot's voyage, a dismantled jet fighter was crammed into the nooks and crannies of the ship. It turns out that the components of that aircraft are not mentioned in the unloading manifest. However, non-commissioned officer Hirschfeld was convinced that a dismantled Me 262 was in the holds of *U 234*. What is the truth? It turns out that at one time Japanese television produced a documentary about Dr. Hideo Tomonaga. It shows clips of U.S. archival footage, in which August Bringewald, *U 234* passenger and Messerschmitt engineer, watches a new jet plane at the Wright Field air base, California in May 1945. Where did the Americans take the plane from, if it had not been on board Type X B submarine transport?

* * *

On November 20, 1947, *U 234* was sunk by two torpedoes fired from USS *Greenfish* submarine (SS 351) during tests in the North Atlantic, 40 nmi north-east of Cape Cod (42°37'N and 69°33'W).

After staying in several POW camps in the USA, Captain Fehler and his crew returned to Europe. In April 1946, after eight months in Fort Edwards, Massachusetts, most of them were transported from there to New York, where they boarded the ship *Rushville Victory*. In Antwerp, they were handed over to the British authorities, who treated them as military and therefore, they were to remain in POW camps. First they were sent to a camp near Brussels, and then to another camp with designated 2228, located near Waterloo in Belgium, where the conditions were bad. The last of *U 234* submariners were released in Germany in 1947. Fehler died on May 15, 1993 at the age of 82. His nicknames were "Hein" and "Dynamite".

---

[181] W. Hirschfeld, *op. cit.*, p.281.

CHAPTER VIII

U-BOOTS' ESCAPES – THE UNWRITTEN CHAPTER

There are no lies, only crippled truths.
Baruch Spinoza

There has been much of either contradictory or fake information concerning secret U-Boot missions at the end of World War II. At the turn of winter and spring 1945, nine Type IX U-Boots: *U 518, U 530, U 546, U 548, U 805, U 858, U 873, U 880* and *U 1235*, which formed Attack Group "Seewolf", were to fight against Allied shipping in the waters off the East Coast of the United States, south of New York. Finally, the U-Boat high command deployed seven ships to carry out the objective (*U 530* and *U 548* received different orders). Naturally, Germans plans did not escape the American attention.

In order to avoid any possible losses in the U.S. waters and to prevent potential missile attack attempts against the territory of the United States, the intelligence section of the 10th Fleet and Admiral Jonas Ingram, the commander of the United States Atlantic Fleet, gathered a very strong force to annihilate the incoming German wolfpack. It comprised two groups, the First Barrier Force in the north, with two escort aircraft carriers *Mission Bay* and *Croatan*, accompanied by 20 escort units, and Second Barrier Force with escort aircraft carriers *Bogue* and *Core*, accompanied by 22 escort vessels in the south. The U-Boots not only had to pass through the "sieve" of surface units, they also had to avoid the additional air support the Allied had. However, it later turned out that extremely poor weather conditions significantly reduced the effectiveness of the air support, which failed to detect the majority of U-Boots slowly covering a long distance from northern Europe to the U.S. coast using snorkels. Successes in the fight against the U-Boots would primarily be scored by the surface units. Germans also lost the chance for greater success in the fight against shipping. After deciphering the German Enigma messages, the Americans diverted the convoys further south in advance to avoid the incoming wolfpack "Seewolf".

What was the fate of the Attack Group "Seewolf" submarines?

U 805 (IX C/40) under the command of Commander Richard Bernadelli, which departed from Bergen on March 17, 1945, turned out to be one of the lucky two submarines of the "Seewolf" group. She was not sunk and somehow penetrated the dense perimeter of U.S. ships. When the commander of *U 805* was informed about the capitulation of Germany, he and his crew followed the required procedure of surrendered to the Allied ships. Destroyer escorts *Otter* and *Varian*, arriving from Argentina, took the *U 805* to the Portsmouth Naval Shipyard, New Hampshire, where the U-Boot arrived on May 14.

Lt. Erich Krempl's *U 548* (IX C/40) was not so lucky. When the American tanker *Swiftscout* was sunk (April 18, 1945) and five days later the Norwegian tanker *Katy* was damaged (both fell victim to *U 857*), the anti-submarine group was dispatched to hunt the U-Boot. Its flagship was the veteran destroyer escort *Buckley* (Lt.Cdr. Reynolds Crutchfield), famous for its encounter and sinking of *U 66*. The chase was successful, although instead of the actual perpetrator responsible for the sinking, the group caught another U-Boot, Lt. Krempl's *U 548*. Following her detection, *Buckley* and the second escort destroyer USS *Reuben James II* sank her with fierce attacks at position 42°19'N and 61°45'W. The U-Boot's entire crew of 58 perished with the ship.

Following their departure from Horten on March 11, the crew of *U 858* (IX C/40), under command of Lt.Cdr. Thilo Bode, could consider themselves lucky. She also did not fall victim to the search conducted by numerous Allied anti-submarine groups in vicinity of the U.S. coast and managed to get through their defensive perimeter. However, just like *U 805*, she did not score any successes until the capitulation of Germany. Upon receiving orders to surrender, Lt.Cdr. Bode called the U.S. ships to the position of his submarine. Destroyer escorts *Carter* and *Muir*, which arrived at the scene, took her to Lewes, Delaware on May 14.

The other ships of the Attack Group "Seewolf" met tragic ends. Lt.Cdr. Gerhard Schötzau's *U 880* (IX C/40) left Bergen on March 14. Two U.S. destroyer escorts *Stanton* (Lt.Cdr. John C. Kiley) and *Frost* (Lt.Cdr. Andrew E. Ritchie), which were part of the First Barrier Force with the escort aircraft carrier USS *Croatan*, located *U 880* on April 16 (the day after sinking of *U 1235*). The 49 crew members did not stand a chance against their depth charge and Hedgehog attacks. They all perished with their submarine at position 47°18'N and 30°26'W. Lt.Cdr. Schötzau died just on his 28th birthday.

The aforementioned *U 1235* (IX C/40), under command of Lt.Cdr. Franz Barsch, left Bergen only on March 19, but was to be the first U-Boot detected and sunk by both previously mentioned U.S. destroyer escorts on April 15. She went down at position 47°54'N and 30°25'W. A total of 57 crewmen perished with the ship. During the sinking of both these U-Boots, the Americans recorded powerful underwater explosions at great depth. This made them suspect that their attacks caused the detonation of a „special cargo" transported by the Germans, which was allegedly a V-1 rocket. That was not true, but at that time it had not been known for certain.

U 546 (IX C/40), which departed Kiel on March 11, under the command of Lt.Cdr. Paul Just proved to be a tougher opponent for the Americans. Just reached the area patrolled by the escort aircraft carrier USS *Core*. On April 23, he attempted to attack her, but one of the patrolling Avengers (piloted by William W. South) spotted her in time, dropping three depth charges and initiating an additional alarm. The U-Boot escaped, diving deep, but the escort vessels approaching from all sides were hot on her heels and did not allow her to escape too far. In the morning of April 24, Just's submarine was the first detected by sonar of the U.S. destroyer escort *Frederick C. Davis* (1,200 t). Just was at periscope depth and fired a T-V acoustic torpedo, which found its mark. The explosion caused the destroyer to sink quickly with 113 crew members at positions 43°52'N and 40°15'W. Lt. James R. Crosby, her commander, went down with his ship. 82 men of her complement were rescued.

Just's single victory resulted in as many as eight other „hunters" bearing down on him. He stood no chance against such a superior force. U.S. destroyers *Flaherty*, *Neunzner*, *Chatelain*, *Varian*, *Hubbard*, *Janssen*, *Pillsbury* and *Keith* were tracking *U 546* down for 10 hours, dropping numerous depth charges and Hedgehog projectiles on him. The destroyer *Flaherty*, under command of Lt.Cdr. Howard C. Duff, was lucky. Her series of Hedgehog discharges reached Just's submarine, inflicting heavy damage and forcing the U-Boot to resurface immediately at 43°53'N and 40°07'W. The badly mauled *U 546* came under artillery fire of all the destroyers involved in the hunt. She went down quickly taking 26 men with her, there were 33 survivors, including Just. The survivors were taken to Argentia Naval Station, where they were questioned in order to extract information concerning the V-1 missiles allegedly carried by the submarines. Just recalled later, that during the interrogations the submariners were subjected to torture[182].

Lt. Hans-Werner Offermann's *U 518* (IX C) departed the base at Kristiansand on March 12. On April 22, despite the bad weather and rough seas, the U.S. destroyers *Carter* (Lt.Cdr. F.J.T. Baker) and *Neal A. Scott* (Lt. P. D. Holden), which were part of the escort force of the escort aircraft carrier USS *Croatan* and had already been heading for Argentia Naval Station, detected *U 518*. The U.S. attacks terminated the lengthy career of the German submarine at position 43°26'N and 38°23'W. *U 518* went down with all hands (56 men)[183].

---

[182] Although some American historians have tried to trivialize that case, everything seems to indicate that it actually happened. Moreover, other German submariners from the U-Boots which had surrendered were also mistreated upon their arrival in Portsmouth (they were being locked up at Charles Street Jail in Boston) by the prison staff composed of U.S. marines. The commander of *U 873* (former commander of *U 511*), Captain Friedrich Steinhoff, following a brutal treatment in that prison at the hands of Americans, committed suicide, perhaps fearing further torture. W. Hirschfeld, *Ostatni U-Boot*, Gdańsk 2007 pp. 280-284, wrote about the treatment he and his colleagues received at the same place, following the surrender of *U 234*. He mentioned being rather brutally treated by the guards and the fact that they robbed the U-Boot's crew of most of their personal belongings.

[183] C. Blair, *Hitlera wojna U-Bootów...*, vol. 2, p. 709; R. Busch, H-J. Röll, *Der U-Boot-Krieg 1939-1945. Deutsche U-Boot-Verluste von September 1939 bis Mai 1945*, vol. 4, Hamburg-Berlin-Bonn 1999, p. 343; P. Kemp, *Die deutschen und österreichischen U-Boot-Verluste in beiden Weltkriegen*, München 1998, p. 265; A. Niestlé, *German U-Boat Losses During World War II...*, p. 124; K. Wynn, *U-Boat Operations...*, vol. 2, p. 10.

U 873 (IX D2) left the base at Kristiansand on March 30, 1945. 35-year-old Lt.Cdr. Friedrich Steinhoff, who was in command of the ship, was most probably ordered to supply U-Boots in need with fuel or, if necessary, help the injured, because Dr. Carl Wilhelm Reinke was on board.

Upon receiving the news of Germany's capitulation a meeting was called on board *U 873*. Two options were being discussed, whether they should run with the ship to South America or surrender to the Americans. Since the majority of the crew was against the first option, modern T-V acoustic torpedoes, secret documents, „Tunis" radar detector and the "Kurier" transmitter were disposed of. After revealing the ship's position, the US destroyer escort *Vance* arrived at the designated place and on May 16, escorted the U-Boot to Portsmouth, New Hampshire. It is not known, whether the Americans discovered that Steinhoff had been involved in V-1 missile testing, when he was in command of *U 511* (December 1941 to December 1942). In any case, after the POWs had been taken to Charles Street Jail in Boston, the guards of the Marine Corps subjected them and Steinhoff in particular, to brutal treatment. He committed suicide by cutting his wrists with a piece of broken glass from a watch. He was apparently afraid of lengthy, violent interrogations, because even if it had not been immediately discovered that Steinhoff had previously been the commander of *U 511*, it was only a matter of time for the American intelligence service to find out.

There were attempts to assign *U 881*, under command of Lt. Dr. Karl-Henza Frischke, to the "Seewolf" Attack Group, however, the need to complete the refit meant that she departed with a considerable delay. It was not until April 7, that the submarine left Bergen, but she also did not escape her tragic end. She was tracked down and attacked on May 6, at position 43°18'N and 47°44'W, by the destroyer escort USS *Farquhar*. Americans attacks were accurate and *U 881* shared the fate of the majority of the "Seewolf" group U-Boots, which had previously been sunk. Her entire complement of 53 perished only two days before the end of the war.

That brief information concerning the bitter fate of the U-Boots, which were supposed to successfully prowl the United States waters at the end of the war, would not be surprising if it was not for the fact, that not so long ago there was information that one of these ocean-going, steel „sea wolves", namely *U 518*, arrived at the coast of Argentina on July 28, 1945, with... Adolf Hitler, Eva Braun and a valuable cargo (loaded in crates). According to official reports, that was more than four months after the U-Boot's departure from Bergen.

Simon Dunstan and Gerrard Williams wrote the following:

On July 28, 1945, three Admiral Graf Spee petty officers named Alfred Schultz, Walter Dettelmann, and Willi Brennecke were at the Estancia Moromar, equidistant between Necochea [in vicinity of Mar del Plata – M.B., P.W.] and Mar del Sur on the Argentine coast. With submachine guns slung from their shoulders, the sailors were or-ganizing eight trucks to drive to the beach. The vehicles all carried Lahusen markings;

five of them had been brought in by a potato farmer from his Lahusen-run property thirty-eight miles north of the Estancia Moromar, at Balcarce.

At 1:00 a.m. on July 28, 1945, SS Gen. Hermann Fegelein [? - M.B., P.W.][184], wrapped in a borrowed greatcoat to protect him from the Argentine winter's night, was waiting under a starlit sky on the beach at Necochea for his sister-in-law and his Führer. U-518 arrived off the coast an hour later.

Hans Offermann brought his submerged boat as close to the shore as he could, moving dead slow and with a tense hydrophone operator straining for the sounds of surface vessels; the commander had little detailed or recent information about the coastline he was approaching. Eventually he ordered the boat to periscope depth and cautiously raised the observation periscope; a careful 360-degree sweep satisfied him that no vessels or aircraft were nearby and that the light signals from shore coincided with those in his orders. Still taking no chances, he ordered his gun crews to prepare to man the 37 mm and 20 mm anti-aircraft cannons as soon as the boat surfaced [...]

Fegelein sent out a small motorboat [...] to meet the submarine. For the middle of the Southern Hemisphere winter, the water was surprisingly calm. As the launch approached the beach, lit by sailors' flashlights, Fegelein raised his arm in the classic Nazi salute. The Admiral Graf Spee men splashed into the small breakers on the beach and helped pull the craft up onto the sand, and Fegelein moved forward to help Eva Braun from the boat. Hitler was helped down by the boat crew, returned Fegelein's salute, and shook him by the hand.

The one-time ruler of the Thousand-Year Reich was almost unrecognizable. He was pasty-faced from the long voyage, the trademark moustache had been shaved off, and his hair was lank and uncut. Eva had made an effort to look good throughout the trip, but the prison-house pallor of her skin was highlighted by the lipstick and rouge she had applied before leaving the submarine. [...] No doubt Fegelein took the opportunity of the short drive to brief Hitler on the immediate arrangements. An avenue lined with tamarisk trees led to the main house of the Estancia Moromar, where they would spend the first night. Security at the ranch house was surprisingly light: the fewer people who knew about the visitors, the better.

The petty officers Shultz, Dettelmann, and Brennecke helped in the subsequent unloading of many heavy boxes, which were ferried ashore from the U-boat on repeated trips by the motorboat and the submarine's rubber boats. The boxes were loaded onto the farm trucks and driven to outbuildings on the Estancia Moromar; repacked in new boxes, the contents would be taken to Buenos Aires and deposited in Nazi-controlled banks. At the end of the unloading, most of the crew from U-518 came ashore in the rubber dinghies and marched in column in civilian clothes, their kitbags slung over

---

[184] At night of April 28-29, 1945, Major General Fegelein, Waffen-SS liaison officer at Hitler's Headquarters, was removed from his place of detention (he was detained in one of the apartments in Berlin, probably with the intention of escaping to neutral Switzerland; he was married to Eva Braun's sister Margarete) under the pretense of seeing Hitler and then shot in the back in the gardens of the Reich's chancellery by an RSD agent (Third Reich Security Service), who was escorting him.

their shoulders, to quarters on the Estancia. Meanwhile, an eight-man skeleton crew took U-518 out on its final voyage, to be scuttled further from shore. They would return in the motorboat, to join their shipmates for their first fresh meal in two months. They did not know that their operation had almost been compromised[185].

Although the authors have neatly described the event, not a single part of that story is true. Another part of that book is even more intriguing:

Don Luis Mariotti, the Police Commissioner at Necochea, had called his off-duty men in from their homes on the evening of the previous day, July 27, 1945, and ordered them to investigate unusual activity reported on the coast. The officers arrived at the beach to see an unidentified vessel offshore making Morse code signals, and they found and arrested a German who was signaling back. Interrogated through the night, he eventually admitted that the signaling vessel was a German submarine that wanted to put ashore at a safe place on the coast to unload.

The next morning a six-man police squad led by a senior corporal decided to comb several miles of beach north and south of the place where they had caught the signaler. After some hours, they found a stretch of sand bearing many signs of launches and dinghies being beached; heavy boxes had also been dragged toward the tire tracks of trucks. The police squad followed the tire tracks along the dirt road that led to the entrance of the Estancia Moromar. The corporal sent one of his men back to the station with his report, and then, without waiting for orders, he decided to enter the farm. The five police officers had walked a couple of miles in along the tree-lined drive when they came to some low hills, which hid the main buildings. Four Germans carrying submachine guns challenged them. The corporal had no search warrant and was seriously outgunned; he decided to withdraw and report back to his superior.

Commissioner Mariotti telephoned the chief of police at La Plata. The call was taken by the latter's secretary, who told him to do nothing and remain by the telephone. Two hours later Don Luis was ordered to forget the matter and release the arrested German. The following month an FBI message from Buenos Aires stated: "Local Press reports indicate provincial police department raided German colony located Villa Gesell … looking for individuals who possibly entered Argentina clandestinely via submarine and during search a short-wave … receiving and transmitting set found. Other premises along beach near same area searched by authorities but no arrests made[186].

But this is not the end of those sensational news! According to the statement given by Petty Officer Heinrich Bethe, who worked as a mechanic on board the battleship *Admiral Graf Spee*, which Dunstan and Williams refer to, the description of the area of the U-Boot's arrival, varies considerably. Bethe testified that the landing area

---

[185] S. Dunstan, G. Williams, *Grey Wolf…*, pp. 218-221.
[186] Ibidem., pp.221-222.

was "several hours" of driving over rough roads from the city of Puerto Madryn, which is much further south than Necochea. In the evening of July 28, he drove a truck to a determined area on the coast to load a large number of boxes that were delivered ashore on rubber dinghies from... two submarines. The trucks carried the boxes to two large warehouses where they were carefully unloaded. Later, about seventy (?) people disembarked from the U-Boot. In Bethe's opinion, the cargo was very valuable, and the people that arrived were not common sailors like himself, but presumably important German Nazis[187].

According to Dunstan and Williams, the two stories told by the crew members of the German battleship about the arrival of the U-Boots to South America concern two different events. So, there was a submarine with Hitler and his close associates, which arrive at Necochea, while a second U-Boot arrived further south, where the chests filled with money, which was to secure further peaceful existence of the Reich's leading representatives in South America, were unloaded.

Dunstan and Williams „discovered" that the second submarine was Type IX C/40 - *U 880*. That trail turned cold because, according to declassified U.S. Navy reports, that U-Boot was sunk with depth charges by two U.S. destroyer escorts *Stanto* and *Frost* in the North Atlantic (position 47°18'N and 30°26'W)[188] during her first patrol... on April 16, 1945. Her entire crew of 49 perished with the ship.

Years after the war, the Argentineans declassified part of the archives concerning evacuation voyages of German submarines to South America. According to these documents, at least one of the U-Boots (July 28, 1945), in that case either *U 235* or *U 236*, arrived near San Clemente del Tuyu, south of Mar del Plata. The police were aware of that fact (witnesses had given their testimonies), but did not demonstrate much commitment to confirm its authenticity. A report presenting that version of events disappeared (according to other witnesses it burned), probably at the beginning of the 1950s, which saved the then commandant trouble of answering many vexed questions. In general, the Argentine archives which held intelligence documents (including those concerning other countries) were affected by the plague of destruction between the years 1948 and 1967 (as a result they are almost nonexistent), caused by... water dripping from the pipes!

If a German warship arrived near the coast of San Clemente del Tuyu at the end of July 1945, it was none of the aforementioned U-Boots. On April 14, 1945, *U 235* (under command of Lt.Cdr. Friedrich Huisgen) was on the waters of the Skagerrak, when she found herself near the coastal convoy which comprised the ferry *Preussen*, the destroyer *Friedrich Inn* and the torpedo boat *T 17*. The latter mistook the U-Boot for a Soviet submarine, attacked with depth charges and sank her north of Skagens Horn at positions 58°09'N and 10°48'E. Her entire complement of 46 went down with the ship.

---

[187] Ibidem., p.223.

[188] C. Blair, *Hitlera wojna U-Bootów...*, vol. 2, p. 709; R. Busch, H-J. Röll, *Der U-Boot-Krieg* 1939-1945..., vol. 4, p. 341; P. Kemp, *Die deutschen und österreichischen U-Boot-Verluste in beiden Weltkriegens..*, pp. 263-264; A. Niestlé, *German U-Boat Losses During World War II...*, p. 132; K. Wynn, *U-Boat Operations...*, vol. 2, p. 182.

Lt. Herbert Mumm's *U 236* was attacked and damaged on May 4, 1945, west of Schlei-münde, by rockets and on-board weapons of the 9. USAAF (United States Army Air Force) and the 184. RAF Squadron aircraft. Despite the damage, Herbert Mumm's ship managed to dive and stay at the bottom until dusk. Upon resurfacing, *U 236* received a report concerning the current situation on the fronts. Soon afterwards, the watchmen reported to Mumm that they had noticed a serious fuel leakage, as one of the inner tanks had been perforated. Realizing that the ship was unfit for further service, the commander of *U 236*, in accordance with the orders of Operation Regenbogen, had his crew abandon the ship in an orderly fashion and go ashore. The operation lasted all day of May 5, and was completed just after midnight on May 6. The ship was scuttled by opening Kingston valves, west of Schleimünde, in positions 54°37'N and 10°03'E.

The fate of an unidentified submarine, which on July 18, 1945, was probably dam-aged (sunk, according to other sources) in the waters of San Matias Gulf, off the coast of Argentina, by depth charges of the Brazilian destroyer escort *Babitonga* (ex U.S. Cannon class ship) could not be established.

On July 19 1945, the "Critica" daily newspaper (published in Buenos Aires) an-nounced on its first page the news of another U-Boot which surrendered to the Argen-tine Navy ship, 30 miles off the coast, near Mar de Ajó, north of Mar del Plata. Nothing more was written about that event. It turns out that this laconic note, which had nothing to do with the truth, was years later used by Dunstan and Williams to present yet anoth-er hypothesis, that the mysterious U-Boot was one of the "Seewolf" wolfpack ships - *U 1235*[189]. However, that interpretation was also wrong, as it was already explained earlier.

Therefore, it is no wonder that when the crews of *U 530* and *U 977* were interned at Mar del Plata, every little rumor concerning German submarines, which probably operated along the entire eastern coast of South America, caused a lot of excitement among the Argentineans.

Two weeks after the end of the war in Europe, the Argentine Ministry of Foreign Affairs informed the navy of the potential presence of German submarines in the South Atlantic. These ships were supposedly trying to get through to Japan. On May 29, the Armada de la República Argentina conducted a naval operation against the U-Boots in the Strait of Magellan to seal it and prevent German submarines from escaping from the Atlantic into the Pacific. Naturally, there were no U-Boots.

On July 1, 1945, the Argentine Federal Police informed the Navy that two un-identified men disembarked from a German submarine near Puerto San Julián[190] and then sailed on a rubber dinghy towards a sailboat. According to the police, the

---

[189] S. Dunstan, G. Williams, *Grey Wolf....*, p. 227, wrote that the commander of *U 1235* survived the war and bought a farm in Cordoba, where he lived until 1952. It is completely absurd to say that the crews *U 518*, *U 880* and *U 1235* (152 people altogether).... dispersed among hundreds of German communities scattered all over Patagonia. According to Dunstan and Williams to many of them it was a better choice than to return to ruined, starved and occupied Germany.

[190] The two Nazis who disembarked from the U-Boot are also mentioned in a U.S. intelligence report of June 28, 1945.

U-Boot refueled from „barrels hidden along the coast". The report has never been verified and neither was the pennant number of the ship.

In early June 1945, the retired Colonel of the Argentine army, Rómulo Bustosa, who has been quoted here in connection with *U 530*, then being a young officer and commander of the anti-aircraft battery unit, was given the task of watching the wide stripe of coastline between Mar del Plata and the endorheic salt lake of Mar Chiquita (there are numerous small islands in the northern part of the lake). The watch was aimed at preventing any attempts to land or disembark people from German submarines. The orders of the superiors were clear: „every stranger who would disembark from a U-Boot should be arrested". Bustos' subordinates were to secure the area in vicinity of Mar Chiquita lagoon, a few miles north of the naval base. They had nine guns at their disposal and were ready to open fire. One dark night, close to the place where they were stationed, they saw a light signaling from sea to land. Bustos informed his superior. When the senior officer arrived at the indicated spot the light signals stopped, but before he left the position, the light from the sea appeared again. During the following nights there were no similar signals, so the entire operation was narrowed down to observation only. A report file annotated "secret" was sent to the commander of the Argentine Navy.

However, something was going on, because at the end of June 1945, one of the soldiers from Bustos' unit found a rectangular wide pit, at least 3 m deep. There were three wooden shelves - about 10-20 centimeters above the highest tide line. On the shelves there were about 5 x 20 cm cans without any marking... except for one letter. After opening a special tin container, there was bread inside. The next tin can contained chocolate bars, the remaining ones could have stored drinks or food. It was probably a place where the disembarked submariners or passengers who secretly arrived supplied themselves with food and water. Although the press was silent about the subject, „everyone in the area was talking about it".

Bustos had the opportunity to inspect *U 530* at the submarine base in Mar del Plata. The first thing that caught his attention, apart from the nasty smell of the submarine's interior, were metal cans identical to those found on the beach.

Further unidentified submarines in Argentine coastal waters, which emerged between July and August 1945, were mentioned in numerous police and military reports. The alleged U-Boots (or friendly submarines?) were reported by observers on board the Argentine surface vessels and pilots during routine patrol flights. The sight of the characteristic silhouette and the shape of the submarine's conning tower did not escape the attention of Argentineans.

On July 17, 1945, two months after the war, an officer of the Argentine Navy Staff, wrote the following:

1. The Head of the Ministry of War [Defense] notified at 14.10 that a report was received from the Buenos Aires Provincial Police that a submarine had been sighted in the San Clemente area.

2. Captain Rojas immediately sent the report to San Clemente, making contact with Mr. Longui, who had seen her [the submarine – M.B., P.W.]. He informed:

3. That at around 9 a.m. he saw a ship in vicinity of the San Antonio lighthouse, poorly recognizable due to the fog. Later, in the sunlight, he could see that she did not resemble an ordinary ship, and after comparing her with the published photographs of „U 530" he noticed a similarity to that submarine. It was, as if she was motionlessness at the distance of about 3000 m from the shore. Two cables protruded from what he considered to be the conning tower, one towards the bow, the other towards the stern. The ship had no funnels. When the plane was approaching, she submerged. Later, at ten o'clock, he, along with others who were a little further to the south, saw the ship heading towards Mar del Plata in the calm sea. Later she dived again and was not seen anymore[191].

The analysis of declassified documents (German, English, U.S. and Argentine ones) concerning the U-Boots in South America did not provide an answer to that question.

However, it cannot be entirely ruled out that *U 530* and *U 977*, acting in accordance with earlier orders of the Kriegsmarine High Command, served as cover for other U-Boots. The very decision to reveal the two submarines as scouts could have dulled the Argentineans vigilance, allowing other ships with Nazis and valuable cargo to land safely. Although more than 70 years have passed since the events described above, it is impossible to indicate who of the German Nazis managed to escape to South America aboard a U-Boot.

It is also not a secret, that numerous Germans (Third Reich supporters) had lands along the coast of Patagonia, where the harbors were deep enough to accommodate submarines. Everything is possible.... even the fact that other U-Boots were scuttled by their crews after reaching the coasts of Argentina, Uruguay or Chile.

According to Argentine fishermen, two German submarines were sunk in unexplained circumstances in the Bay of San Matias (South America), at the depth of 50 m (the place is called Caleta de los Loros), some 100 m apart, which may indicate that they travelled together. In November 1996, a team of divers from the Institute of Marine Biology in Almirante Brown, San Antonio, examined the alleged wreck's resting place. There was nothing in the area indicated by the witnesses.

In August 1997, the search for the sunken U-Boots was resumed (the operation was code-named „Calypso"). No trace of the wrecks was found at that time either. According to the representatives of the Argentine Navy, there are no U-Boots in Caleta de los Loros. One can safely reject another theory concerning German submarines transporting large amounts of documents.

It turns out that at the Laboe Naval Memorial and Museum near Kiel, there is a map of the world with marked locations of sunken U-Boots. The red cross marks the resting place of an unidentified U-Boot in San Matias Gulf.

However, it cannot be entirely ruled out that unmarked U-Boots reached the coast of Argentina with important Nazis in 1945.

---

[191] Information in: I. Witkowski, *Hitler in Argentina...*, p. 49; idem, *Supertajne Bronie Hitlera...*, pp. 50-52.

CHAPTER IX

SECRET GERMAN U-BOOT BASES

One may seek the truth for the sheer satisfaction of finding it.
Agatha Christie

One of the key questions concerning the fate of German submarines in World War II is that of the existence of secret bases in South America. Were there any locations where the U-Boots could have been safely repaired (where the emergency repairs could have been carried out, i.e. those which did not require the ship to be dry-docked) and the crews could find time to rest? Were warehouses with stores and provisions, ammunition and large fuel tanks kept in such a refuge, far from larger human settlements? Did the Kriegsmarine, in agreement with the highest political factors of selected countries in the southern hemisphere, consider such a project? Or were Dönitz's collaborators forward-looking enough to make sure that the U-Boot facilities, located in the unpopulated areas, had been prepared in advance?

Possession of hidden naval bases or U-Boot supply stations in South America was priceless for Hitler and Dönitz. These gave the ships the opportunity to operate in the area where not only the Allied supply routes leading from Asia around Africa and from South Africa and the Pacific around Cape Horn were interconnected, but they also greatly facilitated the operation of German vessels in the Indian Ocean.

At least three supply points are known to exist, which could have been used by the U-Boots:

Probably the most important one [supply point - M.B., P.W.] *was established near the port of Comodoro Rivadavia* [on San Jorge Gulf on the Atlantic coast - M.B., P.W.], *almost 1500 km south of Buenos Aires in a straight line. It was developed on the basis of the German flying club „Condor", founded in 1933 by the oil company Astra. It built, among other things, fuel tanks, which were disproportionately large in relation to the needs of a few aircraft it owned. [....] Astra was founded on the basis of German and Swiss capital, a fact, which in this context, is rather significant and suggests that it did not only supply the "base". According to Heinrich Jhontza, one of its former employees,*

[...], the base operated on typically military basis and, what is most important, in a completely undisturbed manner. Hitler salutes were the order of the day and it turned out that during the war a flag with a swastika was flown there. Jhontza worked there as a communications specialist and a pilot, but in all probability, he was also an agent of the German naval intelligence. Incidentally, airplanes owned by the flying club could also be used for reconnaissance purposes, e.g. observe shipping or check the vicinity of the base before the possible surfacing of a U-Boot. This case is a bizarre example of the peculiar inviolability of certain places in Argentina, which were of strategic importance from the German point of view. It clearly indicates that certain agreements had to be concluded at the interstate level. This case is all the more meaningful because formally all flying clubs were then subject to Argentine military aviation and it was completely unlikely that the authorities of that country never realized what was happening there, or were even unaware of the fact that the Nazi flag was flown there. It is clear that the Germans felt completely safe there, in the Patagonian wilderness[192].

The second base was probably established (or at least there were plans to do so) in the far south of Argentina, near the Strait of Magellan on Tierra del Fuego. It was located in a sparsely populated area on an island of almost 50,000 km². Presumably, the base was to be used as one of the transfer points in a secret operation code-named „Aktion Feuerland", i.e. preparations for the evacuation of strategic key Nazi personnel, huge amount of money and patents to South America. There has been so much exaggerated information concerning that story, therefore, it is hard to separate fact from fiction. According to foreign journalists, an extensive record of that operation is kept in Argentine archives.

The third base was allegedly located about 200 km southeast of Buenos Aires, in vicinity of Samborombón Bay. The knowledge concerning the possible location of that haven is sketchy at best, which is why it is extremely difficult to present more information. All the information we have comes from reports made by commanders of Argentine Navy warships, who reported "spotting" U-Boots in these waters during their patrols along the coast of Argentina.

According to the U.S. military intelligence services in South America, the beaches in Miramar, Buenos Aires province, were an ideal spot for disembarking important passengers from the U-Boots.

There are opinions among the researchers stating that similar U-Boot supply areas were also used in remote areas on the southern coast of Chile, where fjords made observation difficult. These were areas where over the distance of several hundred kilometers there was no human settlements (there were almost no roads at that time). The retreat was suitable for hiding submarines or for covert unloading (or loading) of cargo and personnel. Some of these fjords go over 100 km inland. Submarines could have felt safe there. Even weather conditions in that area were

---

[192] I. Witkowski, *Hitler w Argentynie...*, pp. 37-38

U 234 had six mine shafts in the forward section of her hull.

Major General of the Luftwaffe Ulrich Kessler aboard *U 234*.

German submarines, Type IX D *U 873* (from the left) or Type IX C/40 *U 805* with *U 234* in Portsmouth, a photograph taken in May 1945.

Destroyer escorts *Otter* and *Varian*, accompanying *U 805* to the Portsmouth Naval Shipyard, USA, where the U-Boot arrived on May 14, 1945.

From the left: *U 234* and *U 805* (probably) at the U.S. base at Portsmouth.

Naval engineer, Captain
Hideo Tomonaga.

German "trophies" from *U 234*.

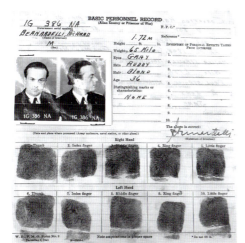

ID card of prisoner Commander Pichard
Bernadelli, commander of *U 805*.

Another photo of *U 234* and *U 805*
(probably) at Portsmouth,
May 1945.

German submarines in Portsmouth, a photograph taken in May 1945.

U-Boat Nemesis Here
Warship Captured General

The USS Sutton, destroyer escort here for Navy Day, was the ship which intercepted the German submarine U-234, which was running for Japan with a German general, uranium for use in atomic bomb experiments and members of a military mission after VE-Day.

The Sutton already had intercepted two other U-boats when ordered to bring in the U-234, according to her skipper, Lt. Com. Thomas W. Nazro, USNR, of Concord, N. H. "It sounded like just another sub to us," he said.

"We made contact with her and asked her size. We were pretty staggered when she signaled back 2,000 tons. That's a bit bigger than we are."

GENERAL ON BOARD

Lt. David K. Gottlieb, USNR, Davenport, Iowa, then gunnery officer and now executive officer, led a boarding party aboard the U-boat. He found the military mission, including Gen. Der Flieger Ulrich Kessler of the Luftwaffe complete with monocle. There had been two Japs aboard but the Germans declared at the word surrender, they had committed hara kiri. The bodies, they said, had been heaved over the side.

The general was taken aboard the Sutton. With him was a paperbound English version of Walter Lippman's "U. S. War Aims." Also aboard were a jet propulsion expert and plans for V-2 rocket bombs and jet propelled planes.

Gen. Kessler, stepping into the boat that was to transfer him to the destroyer escort, faced aft and saluted Judson W. Catlett, coxswain, of Kewanee, Miss. Catlett was too busy to return the salute, but said:

"That's okay, general, just carry on." Catlett has just left the ship for his Navy discharge.

LONG BUSY IN ATLANTIC

Five days later the Sutton brought the U-boat into Portsmouth, N. H., and turned her over to the Coast Guard.

The destroyer escort, now tied up at the Dumaine St. wharf, is (see Nemesis, Page 4, Col. 3)

Press note of one of the U.S. newspapers concerning the end of *U 234*'s wartime career.

República Argentina
Ministerio de Marina

INFORMATIVO

1º - Jefe Secretaría Guerra comunicó a 1410 horas que por conducto Policía Provincia Buenos Aires había recibido informe de que desde San Clemente se había avistado un submarino.

2º - Capitán Rojas requirió informe inmediatamente a San Clemente estableciendo contacto con el señor Longui que lo había visto. Este informa:

3º - Que a las 0900 horas aproximadamente vió una embarcación hacia el lado del faro San Antonio, poco identificable debido a la neblina - Que poco después con sol pudo constatar que era una embarcación que en nada se parecía a los buques comunes y que comparándola con las fotografías publicadas del U-530 la encontró parecida a ese submarino - Que estaba como parada a unos 3.000 metros de la costa - Que de lo que creía ser la torrecilla salían dos cables uno hacia proa y el otro hacia popa - Que no tenía chimeneas - Que al aproximarse un avión se sumergió - Que más tarde a eso de las 1000 horas lo vió él y otras personas un poco más al sud, como si se dirigiera hacia Mar del Plata - Mar calmo - Que luego se sumergió otra vez no viéndolo más.-

Buenos Aires, julio 17 de 1945.-

4º - Por el Estado Mayor General se hicieron dos despachos informativos a 15 horas para las Escuadras de Ríos y de Mar y se comunicó a la Prefectura Gral.Marítima.-

Argentinian July 17, 1945 report concerning an alleged submarine in vicinity of San Clemente.

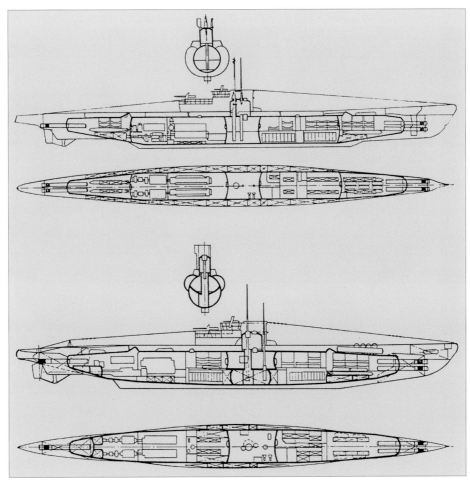

Cross-sections of Type VII C submarine *U 977* (bottom) and Type IX C/40 submarine *U 530*. Top and side view.

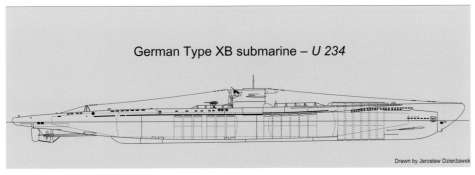

German Type XB submarine – *U 234*

Drawn by Jarosław Dzierżawsk

Type X submarine minelayer *U 234*. The lack of 105 mm deck gun, following the conversion to a cargo transport in May-June 1944, is apparent.

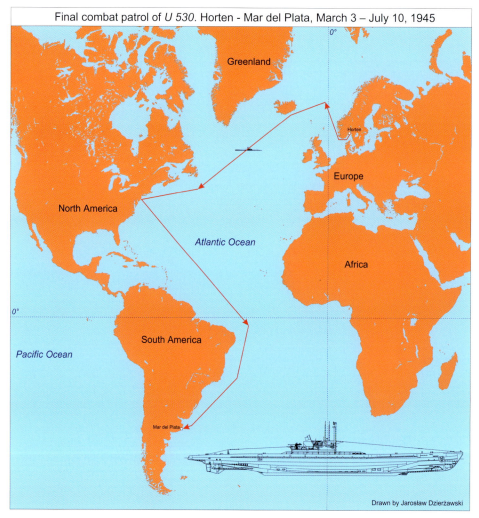

Final combat mission of *U 530*. From Horten to Mar del Plata, March 3 to July 10, 1945.

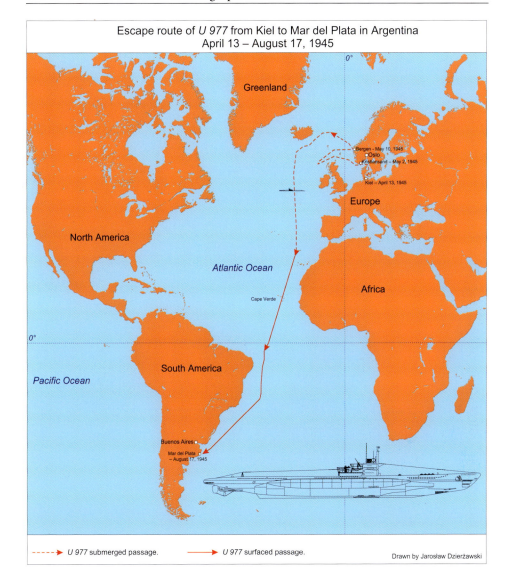

Escape route of *U 977* from Kiel to Mar del Plata in Argentina, April 13 to August 17, 1945.

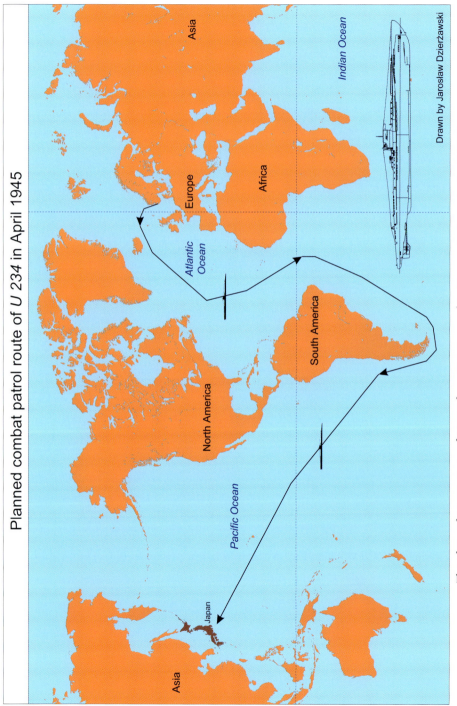

The planned secret route of *U 234* from Kristiansand in Norway to Japan in April 1945.

favorable for the U-Boots, as it rained regularly and there was a lot of clouds, which was an obstacle even for air reconnaissance.

Among the high vertical cliffs of Patagonia, also known as the Far South, on the Atlantic coast, far from human settlements, there are huge caves, which are ideal for submarine naval bases. According to local fishermen, there is a cave carved in the rock with some concrete elements, resembling a dry dock. The cave could have accommodated two U-Boots. The place is located in vicinity of Thetis Bay, several dozen kilometers from Tierra del Fuego. In fact, it is difficult to say, if this is not one of those tall tales told by seafarers.

ACKNOWLEDGEMENTS

The help of many people who supported the authors in writing of this book was invaluable. Thanks to their selfless kindness, we have been able to gather considerable amount of research material concerning the unknown fate of German submarines fleeing to Argentina in April and May 1945. We have managed to explain the fate of several other U-Boots, which have so far been credited with reaching South America in the final months of the war. Some materials, apart from the aforementioned document references from foreign archives in England and the United States, were received with the proviso that we would not disclose to the names of those who helped us as they wish to remain anonymous.

The following individuals deserve special thanks: Grzegorz Nowak, Jarosław Dzierżawski and Paweł Więcaszek from Poland, Łukasz Grześkowiak from England, Ryszard Leitner and Axel Niestlé from Germany, Regina Frąckowiak of the Library of Congress, Jacob A. Haywood, Sylvia Naylor and Paul B. Brown from National Archives at College Park and Robert K. Wilcox and Chris Kraska from the United States and Sergei Trubitcin from Russia.

The National Archives and Records Administration (NARA) in College Park, Maryland, USA, Library of Congress in Washington, D.C., Naval History and Heritage Command in Washington, The National Archives (British National Archive) in Kew, London, England, Deutsches U-Boot Museum in Cuxhaven, Germany and Fundacion Histarmar - Argentina were extremely helpful in compiling the research material for this book.

Owing to Polish and foreign historical websites, which provide information about the Kriegsmarine, we were able to compare our knowledge with the current state of research all over the world.

We are aware that we were not able to answer all the questions. Some of them have yet to be clarified. However, we have made every effort, having access to declassified documents concerning the crews of German submarines that evacuated to Argentina, to tell their story in an honest way and according to the current state of our knowledge. We believe that we have lifted a veil of secrecy, debunked myths and misinformation.

Having said that, we would like to stress that we, as the authors of the book, are solely responsible for any possible errors or mistakes. That is why we will be grateful for all comments and remarks. They can be sent to the following e-mail address: marboro1964@o2.pl.

Mariusz Borowiak, Peter Wytykowski
Cielimowo – Farmington Hills
June 2017 - June 2018 r.

BIBLIOGRAPHY

1. Archives

National Archives and Records Administration (NARA) w College Park, Maryland (USA)

Library of Congress w Waszyngtonie (USA)

Naval History and Heritage Command w Waszyngtonie (USA)

The National Archives w Kew, London (Anglia)

Deutsches U-Boot Museum w Cuxhaven (Niemcy)

Fundacion Histarmar - Argentina (Fundacja Histarmar w Argentynie)

Sharkhunters w Hernando, Floryda (USA)

2. Literature

Aharoni Z., Dietl W., *Operacja Eichmann. Jak było naprawdę*, Warszawa 1998.

Aarons M., Loftus J., *Akcja ocalenie. Watykańska przystań nazistów*, Warszawa 1994.

Bagnasco E., *Uboote im 2. Weltkrieg*, Stuttgart 1997.

Bahnsen U., O'Donnel J., *Katakumba. Ostatnie dni w bunkrze Hitlera*, Warszawa 1995.

Bar-Zohar M., Mishal N., *Mossad. Najważniejsze misje izraelskich tajnych służb*, Poznań 2012.

Bascomb N., *Wytropić Eichmanna. Pościg za największym zbrodniarzem w historii*, Kraków 2015.

Basti A., *Bariloche nazi*, Argentina 2004 (wyd. autora).

Basti A., *Dicen que El oro nazi ingreso en submarinos*, Manana del Sur, z 6 grudnia 1996 r.

Beeching P., Summerhayes C., *Hitler's Antarctic base: the myth and the reality*, "Polar Record", Cambridge 2007, nr 43 (224).

Beevor A., *Berlin 1945. Upadek*, Kraków 2009.

Belov v. N., *Byłem adiutantem Hitlera 1937-1945*, Warszawa 1990.

Bennett G., *Seeschlachten im II. Weltkrieg*, Augsburg 1989.

Bezimienski L., *Ostatnie notatki Marina Bormanna*, Warszawa 1976.

Bezimìenski L., *Śladami Martina Bormanna*, Warszawa 1967.

Bishop Ch., *U-Booty Kriegsmarine 1939-1945*, Warszawa 2008.

Blair C., *Hitlera wojna U-Bootów. Ścigani 1942-1945*, t. 2, Warszawa 1999.

Borowiak M., *Zabójcy U-Bootów. Bitwa o Atlantyk 1939-1945*, Warszawa 2013.

Borowiak M., *Żelazne rekiny Dönitza*, t. 2, Warszawa 2009.

Borowiak M., *Żelazne rekiny Dönitza. U-Booty typu VII*, Warszawa 2012.

Borowiak M., Kasperski T., *U-Booty typu IX. Oceanicza broń podwodna Hitlera*, Oświęcim 2018.

Botting D., *Die deutschen Unterseeboote im 1. und 2. Weltkrieg*, Bindlach 2001.

Boyd C., *The Japanese Submarine Force in World War II*, Annapolis - Maryland 2002.

Böddeker G., *Die Boote im Netz*, Augsburg 1999.

Breyer S., *Handbuch für UBootkommandanten. Die Ubootwaffe 1935-1945*, Podzun-Pallas, b.r.w.

Brézet F-E., *Karl Dönitz. Ostatni Führer*, Warszawa 2012.

Busch R., Röll H-J., *Der U-Boot-Krieg 1939-1945. Die Deutschen U-Boot-Kommandanten*, t. 1, Hamburg-Berlin-Bonn 1996.

Busch R., Röll H-J., *Der U-Boot-Krieg 1939-1945. Der U-Boot-Bau auf Deutschen Werften*, t. 2, Hamburg-Berlin-Bonn 1997.

Busch R., Röll H-J., *Der U-Boot-Krieg 1939-1945. Deutsche U-Boot-Erfloge von September 1939 bis Mai 1945*, t. 3, Hamburg-Berlin-Bonn 2001.

Busch R., Röll H-J., *Der U-Boot-Krieg 1939-1945. Deutsche U-Boot-Verluste von September 1939 bis Mai 1945*, t. 4, Hamburg-Berlin-Bonn 1999.

Carpenter D.B., Polmar N., *Submarines of the Imperial Japanese Navy 1904–1945*, London 1986.

Cooper H., *Hitler in Argentina. The documented truth of Hitler's escapade from Berlin*, Hernando, Florida 2016.

Cooper H., *More to U 530 skipper Wermuth*, KTB Nr 292 (The Official History Publication of the U-Bootwaffe), www.sharkhunters.com.

Cooper H., *Spook stuff from Pizzarro*, KTB Nr 292 (The Official History Publication of the U-Bootwaffe), www.sharkhunters.com.

Dönitz K., *10 lat i 20 dni. Wspomnienia 1939-1945*, Gdańsk 1997.

Dunstan S., Williams G, *Grey Wolf. The Escapade of Adolf Hilter*, New York 2011.

Federowicz P., *U-booty typu VII. Triumf i klęska*, Tarnowskie Góry 2007.

Felton M., *Polowanie na ostatnich nazistów*, Warszawa 2013.

Forsyth F., *Akta Odessy*, Poznań 1990.

Gajewski J., *Canaris*, Warszawa 1981.

Galland A., *Die Ersten Und die Letzten. Die Jagdflieger im Zweiten Weltkrieg*, München 1953.

Gama da S., *A tragedia do „Bahia"*, Historia Naval Brasileira, t. 5, cz. 2, Rio de Janeiro 1998.

Gaylor-Kelshall T.M., *U-Boot-Krieg in der Karibik*, Hamburg 1999.

Goñi U., *Prawdziwa Odessa. Jak Peron sprowadził hitlerowskich zbrodniarzy do Argentyny*, Zakrzewo 2016.

Gretton P., *Convoy Escort Commander*, London 1971.

Gröner E., *Die deutschen Kriegsschiffe 1815-1945*, t. 3, Koblenz 1985.

Grünberg K., *SS Gwardia Hitlera*, Warszawa 1994.

Hernández J., *Zagadki i tajemnice drugiej wojny światowej*, Warszawa 2009.

Heydecker J.J., Leeb J., *Proces Norymberski. Trzecia Rzesza przed sądem*, Warszawa 2016.

Herzog B., *Deutsche U-Boote 1906-1966*, Bonn 1993.

Hildebrand H.H., Röhr A., Steinmetz H.O., *Die deutschen Kriegsschiffe*, Herford 1978.

Hirschfeld W., *U 234. The Secret Diary of a U-Boat*, London 2000.

Hirschfeld W., *Ostatni U-Boot*, Gdańsk 2007.

Högel G., *Embleme, Wappen, Malings deutscher U-Boote 1939-1945*, Hamburg 2001.

Höhne H., *Zakon trupiej czaszki*, Warszawa 2006.

Irving D., *Norymberga. Ostatnia bitwa*, Warszawa 1999.

Ivinheim M., *The Secret Alliance. The Unknown Alliance between the Third Reich and Argentina*, Hernando, Florida 2011.

Kahn D., *Szpiedzy Hitlera. Niemiecki wywiad wojskowy w czasie II wojny światowej*, Warszawa 2004.

Kemp P., *Die deutschen und österreichischen U-Boot-Verluste in beiden Weltkriegen*, München 1998.

Kershaw I., *Hitler 1936-1945. Nemezis*, t. 2, Poznań 2002.

Kęciek K., *Tajemniczy rejs U-977*, „Przegląd" 2010, nr 36.

Kopp G., *Kampf und Untergang der deutschen U-Boot-Waffe*, Bonn 1998.

Kraft H.J., *Submarinos alemanes en Argentina*, 1998 [E-Book]; www.elsnorkel.com/2010/06/submarinos-en-argentina.

Lipiński J., *Druga wojna światowa na morzu*, Warszawa 1995.

Mader J., *Generałowie Abwehry zeznają*, Warszawa 1975.

Mallmann-Showell J.P., *Hitler's U-Boat Bases*, Gloucestershire 2002.

Mallmann-Showell J.P., *U-Boats under the Swastika*, Shepperton 2000.

Manning P., *Martin Bormann. Nazi in exile*, New York 1981.

Meding H., *Flucht vor Nürnberg? Deutsche und österreichische Einwanderung in Argentinien 1945-1955*, Köln 1992.

Mey-Martinez C., *La Base Antartica de Hitler: Mito y Realidad. Vistaron la Antartida los Submarinos U-530 y U-977*, www.histarmar.co.ar.

Miller D., *Submarines oft he World*, London 2002.

Morozow M., *Giermanskije podwodnyje łodki VII serii*, Moskwa 2005.

Morozow M., Nagirjak W., *Stalnyje akuły Gitlera. Seria VII*, Moskwa 2008.

Möller E., Brack W., *The Encyclopedia of U-boats. From 1904 to the Present Day*, London 2004.

[N.N.], *Nichts mit Selbstmord zu tun. Geister-Konvoi*, „Der Spiegel", 6 września 1950, nr 36.

Newton R.C., *The „Nazi Mence" in Argentina, 1931-1947*, Stanford 1992.

Niestlé A., *German U-Boat Losses During World War II. Details of destruction*, London 2014.

Omilianowicz A., *Dolina wilków*, Przekrój", z 17 i 24 kwietnia 1985.

Padfield P., *Dönitz. The Last Führer*, London 1993.

Padfield P., *War Beneath the Sea. Submarine conflict 1939-1945*, London 1998.

Paterson L., *Black Flag. The Surrender of Germany'sU-Boat Forces 1945*, Barnsley 2009.

Ramme A., *Służba Bezpieczeństwa SS*, Warszawa 1975.

Rohwer J., *Axis Submarine Successes of World War Two. German, Italian and Japanese Submarine Successes, 1939-1945*, London 1999.

Rössler E., *The U-Boat. The evolution and technical history of German submarines*, London 2001.

Rössler E., *U-Boottyp XXI*, Bonn 2002.

Salinas J., Nápoli de C., *Ultramar Sur. La última operacón secreta del Tercer*, Buenos Aires 2002.

Saverio Fabbri G., *L'ultimo U-Boot. La straordinaria avventura dell'U-977, il sommergibile Tedesco che raggiunse in Sud America: quale segreto a bodro?*; www.centrostuiintelligence.org/doc/6_103_112.pdf.

Scalia J.M., *Germany's Last Mission to Japan. The Failed Voyage of U-234*, Annapolis, Maryland 2000.

Schaeffer H., *Geheimnis um U-977*, Buenos Aires 1950.

Schäffer H., *66 Tage unter Wasser. Die geheimnisumwobene U-Boot-Fernfahrt nach Argentinien*, München 1996.

Schäffer H., *U-Boat 977*, London 1953.

Schlemm J., *Der U-Boot-Krieg 1939-1945 in der Literatur. Eine kommentiere Bibliographie*, Hamburg-Berlin 2000.

Sharpe P., *U-boat fact file*, Leicester 1997.

Schneppen H., *Odessa. Tajna organizacja esesmanów*, Warszawa 2009.

Schlicht A., Angolia J.R., *Die deutsche Wehrmacht Uniformierung und Ausrüstung*, t. 2 *Die Kriegsmarine*, Stuttgart 1995.

Steinacher G., *Zbiegli naziści. Jak hitlerowscy zbrodniarze uciekli przed sprawiedliwością*, Wołowiec 2015.

Stern R.C., *U-Boats in action*, Carrollton (Texas) 1977.

Stern R.C., *U-boats Type VII*, London 2002.

Stille M., Imperial Japanese Navy Submarines 1941-1945, Oxford 2007.

Tarrant V.E., *Das letzte Jahr der deutsche Kriegsmarine. Mai 1944 – Mai 1945*, Podzun-Pallas 1996.

Tarrant V.E., *Kurs West. Die deutschen U-Boot-Offensiven 1914-1945*, Stuttgart 1998.

Trevor-Roper H., *Ostatnie dni Hitlera*, Poznań 1966.

Toland J., *Hitler. Reportaż biograficzny*, Warszawa 2014.

White J.F., „*Mleczne Krowy". Podwodne zaopatrzeniowce atlantyckich wilczych stad 1941-1945*, Warszawa 2001.

Whiting Ch., *Skorzeny. Najbardziej niebezpieczny człowiek w Europie*, Gdańsk 1999.

Whitley M.J., *Cruisers of World War Two. An International Encyclopedia*, London 1999.

Whitley M.J., *Destroyers of World War Two. An International Encyclopedia*, London 2000.

Wilcox R.K., *Japan's Secret War. Japan's Race Against Time to Build Ist Own Atomic Bomb*, New York 1995.

Williamson G., *Wolf Pack. The Story of the U-Boat in World War II*, Oxford 2006.

Witkowski I., *Gestapo. Anatomia systemu*, Warszawa 2005.

Witkowski I., *Hitler w Argentynie i Czwarta Rzesza*, Warszawa 2009.

Witkowski I., *Supertajne bronie Hitlera. Tropem złota i ostatnich broni*, cz. 4, Warszawa 2000.

Worsfold R.M., *The U-234, U-530 and Martin Bormann. The Real Story*, New York 2011.

Wynn K., *U-Boat Operations of the Second World War*, t.1-2, London 2003.

Zwiagincew A., *Proces Norymberski. Nieznane fakty*, Warszawa 2014.

3. Internet

http://www.histarmar.com.ar/InfHistorica/Submarinos%20Nazis/ElU530.htm

http://www.historia.uwazamrze.pl/artykul/1146718/zagadka-u-977

http://myth.greyfalcon.us/gotter5.htm

http://www.spiegel.de/einestages/u-977-die-maer-von-hitlers-tauchgang-a-946576.html

http://dubm.de/die-letzte-fahrt/

http://www.paranoiamagazine.com/2013/01/dark-migration-nazis-in-south-america/

http://www.paperlessarchives.com/hitler.html

http://www.patagonia-argentina.com/en/nazi-submarines-in-caleta-de-los-loros/

https://worldtruth.tv/hitler-escaped-to-argentina-died-old-pictures-of-him-after-the-war-fbi-documents/

https://vault.fbi.gov/adolf-hitler/adolf-hitler-part-01-of-04/view

https://pl.scribd.com/document/212550269/209029872-the-Factual-List-of-Nazis-Protected-by-Spain-Doc

https://antoniocdelaserna.wordpress.com/2011/03/22/ngel-alczar-de-velasco-las-patraas-de-un-espa-de-opereta/

http://www.sharkhunters.com/Vet158%20Don%20Angel%20Alcazar%20de%20Velasco%20-%20Shark-hunters.htm

http://journals.openedition.org/diacronie/4762

https://www.history.navy.mil/research.html